STONES COOKBOOK

Vegetarian recipes from
Stones Restaurant

EBURY PRESS
LONDON

STONES AND THE MAGIC FEAST

Once upon a time, in the Kingdom of Culinary, there lived a huntsman who worked for the King and Queen. One day, whilst out in the vast forest chasing deer, he became lost amongst the dense trees. After riding around for hours searching for his path, he came upon a glittering stream, and decided to rest there a while. As he stooped to drink the fresh, clear water he noticed another reflection beside his own, and when he looked up, there before him on the bank was the most beautiful woman the huntsman had ever seen. She regarded him through saddened eyes.

'Why do you hunt my forest friends?' she asked.

'It is a necessity. We must hunt to eat. We must eat to live'.

'What of the fruits of the soil, the gifts of Mother Earth?'

'Are they alone enough to suffice?' the huntsman said cynically.

The lady's eyes brimmed with crystal tears, and the huntsman thought his heart might break if just one of those tears fell upon that lovely face.

'Forgive me, my lady. What must I do?' he begged.

'You must learn by what you eat. Come with me and I will show you'.

The huntsman followed the lady to an old stone and thatch dwelling near the faerie ring on the west side of the forest. Rich promises of good food filled the air and taunted his taste buds as he approached.

Inside, a large pot bubbled over the fire. The shelves were adorned with an array of jars and hessian sacks, and a neat row of rounded pebbles. People moved around, tasting from the pot, adding a sprinkle of this, a handful of that from the jars and sacks. A boy appeared clutching some fresh green herbs newly picked from outside the door. These also went into the pot. After some time the lady tasted it and nodded.

'It is ready now'.

She reached into the pot with a ladle, and filled up a deep earthenware bowl for the huntsman. He broke some of the warm bread from the platter on the table, and ate from the bowl. He was hungrier than he had ever been but he did not rush, for each mouthful of food was savoured as every delicate flavour touched his senses in unison.

When the bowl was empty, the huntsman looked up at the lady in wonderment. Yes, he had just eaten to live, but for the first time in his life he had eaten to enjoy. He felt full and satisfied, the taste of the meal still in his mind and heart like a cherished childhood memory.

'If only all men were so easily swayed', the lady said.

The huntsman tried to think of something he could give in return for this wonderful gift, and slowly a plan took shape in his head.

'Would you be able to prepare a feast? A feast fit for a King and Queen?' he asked the lady.

She looked around the kitchen.

Everyone had stopped at the huntsman's words, and was thinking of the possibilities. One by one they all nodded. The lady smiled at the huntsman, 'Very well. Two days from now at noon'.

The huntsman went home past the faerie ring. He had not been so far away from his path after all. The King and Queen listened to the huntsman's story with interest. Their palates had become jaded by the monotony of Royal Cuisine, and the prospect of something new was enticing.

Meanwhile, away in the forest the lady and her friends were busy. Each had a task to perform, whether it be collecting mushrooms from dew kissed fields, gathering vegetables from the tiny garden or milking the cows in the soft light of the setting sun.

The day of the feast dawned, and the kitchen awoke sleepily. Soon the smell of freshly baked bread spurred everyone on in their work. Ingredients were blended, sauces tasted, beans boiled furiously, and flour clouds hovered as pastry was rolled.

At noon, two days from when he had first visited, the huntsman returned to the dwelling beside the faerie ring, but this time he was not alone. The extensive royal entourage followed behind, dismounting some way off to tether their horses.

Outside the dwelling, trestled wooden tables decorated with garlands of fresh flowers groaned beneath the weight of the dishes they held. From inside, an aroma of which the King had never known the like drew him towards its source.

Hot food greeted him straight from the oven, the splashes of colour decorating his plate like an artist's palette. Everyone ate thoughtfully, trying different dishes and marvelling at the unique experience of each one.

The King, who had suddenly discovered he had an appetite after years of thinking it had disappeared when his hair turned grey, went into the kitchen for a second helping of soup from the big black pot over the fire. He dipped the ladle into the pot, and poured the contents into his bowl. As he scraped the bottom of the pot, the ladle picked up a small round stone. The lady was standing close by, and quickly retrieved the pebble. She washed it carefully and put it back on the shelf with the others.

'What is this, my lady. Faerie magic?' the King asked as he ate his soup.

'Perhaps', she said, smiling.

The King stood in the doorway, looking at the contented faces of his courtiers and the Queen.

'With your consent my lady, I will send some royal scribes to make a record of your knowledge and wisdom so that it may be shared with every mortal'.

The faerie smiled again. Many moons ago, a traveller had been given a pebble from the shelf in return for some rare spices from the East, and even now he was spreading the magic amongst humankind. Nevertheless, the book was an interesting thought.

And so it came to be.

Originally published 1995 under the title *Stones Spells for Magic Feasts.*
First published in this revised edition 1998.

1 3 5 7 9 10 8 6 4 2

© Digging Deeper 1998
Green St, Avebury, Marlborough, Wiltshire SN8 1RE

Hilary Howard has asserted her right
to be identified as the author of this work.

First published in the United Kingdom in 1998 by Ebury Press
Random House, 20 Vauxhall Bridge Road, London SW1V 2SA.

Random House Australia (Pty) Limited
20 Alfred Street, Milsons Point, Sydney, New South Wales 2061, Australia.

Random House New Zealand Limited
18 Poland Road, Glenfield, Auckland 10, New Zealand.

Random House South Africa (Pty) Limited
Endulini, 5a Jubilee Road, Parktown 2193, South Africa.

Random House UK Limited Reg no 954009.

A catalogue record for this book is available from the British Library.

ISBN 0 09 1865484

Design Stephen Nelson
Editor Michael Pitts
Story Lynda J. Murray
Printed and bound in Singapore by Star Standard Industries

CONTENTS

INTRODUCTION

Illustrations by Jerry Hoare

The chances are you will be asking yourself 'What is Stones Restaurant?' For many of us – 50 or so full and part time staff, regular customers running into thousands (many not even born when we first opened), our suppliers and gardeners, our potter Chris Lewis and the lady in the Australian outback who phoned for help with a recipe – it's necessary to be reminded that Stones is still new and relatively unknown.

Certainly in the context of our location we are upstarts: our building in the small Wiltshire village of Avebury, a Victorian stable block, stands against the largest and greatest stone circle anywhere, built over 4000 years ago. New, yes, but not, we hope, trendy. From our origin in 1984 we have been guided by some very simple principles. Few would argue with them, yet they are commonly not honoured by the food industries.

Good food is honest and fresh. Food that respects its location, its history and the seasons is the better for it. Avebury is a rural World Heritage Site, whose relics include the prehistoric enclosures on Windmill Hill, associated by archaeologists with some of the country's earliest farmers and growers. Avebury also has a modern spiritual dimension. Though the beliefs and rituals that inspired the great monuments are lost, the very existence of such powerful motivation so long ago brings its own force in the present. In such a place, how could we contemplate a restaurant that did no more than retail little pots of cheap frozen mush described in elaborate (and expensive) menus as

home-cooked food? (As an aside, we hope English Heritage feel the same when it comes to thinking about catering at the other half of 'our' World Heritage Site: Stonehenge.)

It started in a small way. We bought jam and cakes from our local Women's Institute, eggs by the dozen from anyone with free range hens, and stone ground flour from Rushall Farm, one of the longest established organic farms in this country. We even had a small garden, behind the village post office, where we grew rhubarb, herbs and spinach.

Hilary Howard and I had two things in common when it came to opening Stones: we were both archaeologists, and neither of us knew anything about running a restaurant. As the months passed, it seemed that our ignorance was a blessing. We didn't like UHT cream, so we didn't buy it. We didn't like portion packs, so we put bowls of sugar on our tables. And we didn't like multi-national corporations who pushed bland fizzy drinks in cans, so we didn't buy from them. On a government sponsored training course, Hilary was told she would have to use all these products or go out of business. Fortunately, our customers knew no more about catering than we did. We weren't even asked for chips.

Even by the end of the first year, we had come a long way. We had evolved the menu we still work to, of two hot lunches that change every day, a soup, five salads and a selection of cold savouries. We were baking all our own cakes and breads. We had found a large local free range poultry

farmer: we still buy eggs from Martin Pitt, just as we still use Rushall flour. And already, people were asking us for recipes.

We published our first book in 1989. *Cooking with Stones* (written by Hilary Howard with Julia Stapleton) was a compilation reflecting our early years. We sold over 12,000 copies in hardback: and could undoubtedly sell more were it still in print. But almost as soon as it was out, we wanted to do something new. Our food is always moving on, as we develop new ideas, find new supplies and acquire new skills. *Stones Spells for Magic Feasts* (by Hilary with Elizabeth Bullen, Simon Calley and Esther Smith) followed in 1995. This focuses especially on our 'megaliths', the main hot dishes. Every one of the nearly 60 hot dishes in *Stones Spells* was prepared for lunch in Avebury in the summer we wrote the book.

Stones Cookbook is a new venture in that we didn't publish it ourselves. Our hope is that the skills and resources at Ebury Press will take our ideas to a much wider public than we have been able to reach on our own. Owners of *Stones Spells* will recognise immediately the origin of the new book. The illustrations, design (by Stephen Nelson) and most of the recipes were prepared for this earlier title under my imprint, Digging Deeper. We have incorporated some new recipes to include cakes (prepared by Debbie Iles) and salads (Hilary again): to make way for these, many recipes from the original book have been dropped. We hope you find the result as inspiring to use as we did to create.

The enterprise reflected in this new book is very different from the Stones of 1984. Literally as I write, Lenny Blake, our head gardener, is opening up the turf of what will be our fourth vegetable plot in the village (our second actually inside the stone circle). We are now a small farm as well as a restaurant, and at the busiest times we feel like a large food producer. We also have a new cafe, seven miles down the road in Marlborough. There we are developing completely new food ideas and making an exciting range of espresso coffees. Mochas, lattes and cappuccinos are things we just cannot do in Avebury, where we face a thousand customers a day in an old stable.

Despite changes, we are still Stones and we still feel, in the true sense of the word, amateurs, lucky enough to work at what we like doing. Stones is about entertaining and enjoying good food in good company, and this book is for home entertaining with style. We have designed the recipes around a table of 8 people (as you use the book, you will learn to match this to suit yourself: light eaters may find our portions a little generous). Experiment, let us know what you think, and above all, have fun.

Michael Pitts

9

NOTES

Many recipes assume that you have a food processor.

Egg, vegetable and fruit sizes are medium unless otherwise stated.

The 'Spells In Store' chapter contains much information about ingredients, useful ideas and a few basic recipes, as well as a guide to compiling menus. You might like to read this through before planning a complex meal. Cross references to recipes are indicated with symbols (as «magic mash»).

Our crockery is still made for us by Chris Lewis. If you can't reach us or find what you want in Avebury, you may like to visit his workshop: he is at The Pottery, South Heighton near Newhaven in East Sussex.

Cooking temperatures (in Celsius) and times are for a convection oven. If you have a conventional oven, you will need to raise temperatures by 10-20°C and increase baking times a little.

TEMPERATURES FOR A STATIC OVEN

To convert, add 10-20° to temperatures given in recipes and read off the first column.

°C	°F	Gas Mark
110	225	¼
130	250	½
140	275	1
150	300	2
170	325	3
180	350	4
190	375	5
200	400	6
220	425	7
230	450	8
240	475	9
250	500	10

HOW TO SPELL IN AMERICAN

Most ingredients we use have their north American or other names bracketed in the Ingredient Index, which thus doubles as a dictionary. Here are a few more translations.

Cloisters cheese Substitute a soft cheese with a rich flavour (Cloisters is a revival of a cheese made by Gloucester monks in the thirteenth century).

Pencarreg A full-fat soft cheese like a Brie.

Red Leicester Can be bought west of the Atlantic, but sadly not at its best; a hard, deep red cheese.

Sage Derby A hard, full-cream cheese marbled green and flavoured with sage; a challenge to find in America!

Teifi A Gouda type cheese made in Wales that melts on pizza like mozzarella! Try Emmenthal, Gouda, Jarlsberg or Swiss.

Milk (full-fat) Homogenised milk.

Single cream Half & half or light cream.

Double cream Whipping or heavy cream.

Clotted cream Might look like whipped cream from a distance, but it's not: it's a very rich cream made from the skim of high fat milk, and we honestly can't think of a substitute. Come to Avebury!

Cider In Britain cider is by definition an alcoholic drink made from special apple varieties. Only to be found in the liquor store.

Bramley apples Our 1918 gardening encyclopaedia lists only 'the cream of the culinary Apples' – 32 of them! In Britain

4 tablespoons (60 ml)	¼ cup liquid
5 tablespoons (75 ml)	⅓ cup liquid
8 tablespoons (120 ml)	½ cup liquid
¼ pint (150 ml)	⅔ cup liquid
8½ fl oz (250 ml)	1 cup liquid
½ pint (300 ml)	1¼ cups liquid
1 pint (550 ml)	2¼ cups liquid
4 oz (110 gm)	1 cup flour
4 oz (110 gm)	1 cup grated cheese
8 oz (225 gm)	1 cup sugar
½ oz (15 gm)	1 tablespoon butter/margarine/vegetable suet
1 oz (30 gm)	2 tablespoons ditto
4 oz (110 gm)	1 stick ditto

today for most of us 'cooking apple' means just one of these: Bramley's Seedling. The fruit is greenish yellow, can be huge and flattened, and is too tart to eat raw. But it cooks in a way no dessert apple can. There doesn't seem to be anything like this in north America. The best available substitute is Granny Smith.

Runner beans It's unlikely you'll find the wonderful edible pods of scarlet runners in your store: they are grown for flowers! Substitute French or flat beans.

Plain or dark chocolate Bitter or semi-sweet chocolate.

Pancake Crêpe.

Frypan Skillet.

Grill; to grill Broiler; to broil.

SPELLS IN STORE

Illustrations by Louise Fairchild

Our store cupboard is our roof space (fortunately we occupy a long building). Here we keep a range of essential ingredients we use all the time. To take full advantage of this book, you will need a similar range in your store cupboard, so you don't have to run out shopping every time you want to make Stones magic.

As a general rule, always buy in small quantities to ensure maximum freshness. Don't bulk buy unless it's something you know you're going to use a lot and regularly. Once opened, decant everything into labelled airtight containers for storage, and keep in a cool, dark place, or in the fridge if indicated.

Keep everything in your store cupboard clean and tidy, and try to group similar ingredients together. This will save you lots of time when making things, and help with your 'stock control'. Never top up half empty containers. Wait until you've run out of something completely before buying more, then clean your jar or tin and refill.

In this guide to the Stones roof, we tell you all you need to know about our ingredients and any special storage requirements (though doubtless we will still get phone calls in the middle of Sunday lunch!). We have also brought together a few standard recipes, which should become part of your own store of wisdom if you use this book frequently. And don't miss the guide to planning a menu that begins on page 29.

Flours

ARROWROOT A very fine, white powder (ground from a dried tropical root) that makes a good thickening agent. Mix to a paste with a little cold water or other liquid and add to a simmering sauce. Continue to cook the sauce for at least 10 minutes until smooth and glossy. Undercooked arrowroot tastes pasty and gluey!

BUCKWHEAT FLOUR A dark, nutty, gluten-free flour used for pancakes and blinis.

CAROB FLOUR The secret ingredient in «magic bread», which we also use a lot in our sweet baking. Carob trees grow in southern Europe like old oaks, and produce pods not unlike a broad bean. The ground dried beans make a flour similar to cocoa but with a more robust flavour. Obtainable at any natural food store.

CORNMEAL, MAIZE-MEAL, POLENTA All mean yellow meal produced by grinding up maize. Use fine ground for our recipes here. Do not confuse with cornflour, which is a white powdery thickener.

GRAM OR CHICKPEA FLOUR Also gluten-free. Makes tasty yellow pancakes.

MALTHOUSE «Magic bread» needs a little malted flour with added whole grains. Malthouse is the name one of our local mills chose for their particular brand. It can be found in natural food stores and some supermarkets, but if you are unlucky, seek out another brand. Read the label to make sure it's not white flour coloured brown!

RUSHALL WHOLEWHEAT FLOUR This is the flour we use for virtually all our baking and cooking. We are lucky to have Rushall Farm on our doorstep (they have been fully organic for more than 10 years!). Experiment with all the 100% stoneground wholewheat flours you can find; decide which one suits you best, and stick to it.

STRONG WHITE Used infrequently for brioche dough and choux pastry. Buy unbleached strong white which has merely had the bran sifted out and not been further adulterated.

WHEATGERM OR WHEATGERM & BRAN This is what is taken from 100% wholewheat flour to turn it into strong white. Use for coating rissoles and croquettes, and sprinkling on baked tomatoes. Must be kept in the fridge, as it can quickly go rancid.

Sweeteners

APPLE JUICE CONCENTRATE We sometimes use this in savoury recipes. It also makes a change from sugar or honey in baking.

GOLDEN SYRUP A brand name alternative if you cannot eat honey, or afford maple syrup.

HONEY Use clear rather than set. There are lots to choose from.

MAPLE SYRUP Around St Patrick's day the Canadian maple tree sap starts to run, when it is tapped, then gently boiled to reduce it to a syrup. This is a sweetener for the gods! In addition to its role in our recipes, we suggest pouring a golden trickle over grapefruit halves; adding a soupçon to your morning cereal; warming gently with chopped walnuts and serving over ice cream; or mixing with butter and raisins and stuffing inside the hollowed core of a Bramley apple for baking. Keep in the fridge after opening.

SUGAR In the recipes, sugar means golden granulated, unless it says otherwise. Other sugars we use are demerara, which has a more caramelly flavour, and light muscovado, a finely ground sugar for baking.

Oils

The oils we use most of all are sunflower and olive. Sunflower oil is available in 1 l bottles in any supermarket. Use only extra virgin olive oil. Ours comes from Greece. It is intensely flavoured, and not prohibitively expensive. Much has been written on the subject of olive oil and there are many, many varieties on the market. Experiment and decide which you prefer: the most expensive are not necessarily the most exciting!

Both sunflower and extra virgin olive oil can be turned into flavoured oils. These can be used for sautéing and for salad dressings. Simply fill a clean jar with oil and add a few bruised garlic cloves, dried or fresh chillis, or fresh herbs. Choose strongly flavoured herbs such as rosemary or hyssop. Stand the jar, lidded, in a warm place for at least a week, and use sparingly!

In addition to these basic oils, we use a range of cold pressed nut and seed oils. Buy small bottles of groundnut (peanut) oil, walnut, hazelnut, grapeseed and almond oils. Toasted sesame oil is indispensable for oriental cooking. This dark sweet oil can be found in the ethnic section of your supermarket.

Ghee appears in several recipes. Clarified butter (usli ghee) is rarely used in Indian cooking: it's too expensive. In India, vanaspati ghee, a pure vegetable shortening, is the common cooking medium. It looks exactly like clarified butter, works in the same way but is dairy free. Vanaspati ghee (usually labelled 'vegetable') is widely available in health food shops and larger supermarkets.

Keep all oils tightly covered in a cool, dark place.

Butter & Margarine

You will need both salted and unsalted butter. Use salted unless unsalted is specified. Keep butter in current use in the fridge, and keep extra supplies in the freezer.

We use 2 types of whey-free (thus dairy-free) vegetable margarine. One is a soft variety, which is ideal for creaming. This is the one we use for most of our sautéing. The other is hard, and we keep it frozen for making pastry and savoury scones and cobbles. Just take it straight from the freezer, chop off what you need, and put the rest back.

Baking Needs

BAKING POWDER Buy in small quantities, as it can loose its oomph.

VEGETABLE SUET Use for dumplings and roly polys. Find this in 250 gm packets in a natural food store.

YEAST Buy active dried yeast available in 100 gm or 500 gm cans. Yeast is available in small packets (about a tablespoon each), but this is an expensive way to buy it. Keep yeast in its can, tightly closed in a cool, dry place.

Dried Fruit

If you bake, chances are you will have a good selection of dried fruit in your store cupboard already. If not, start out with sultanas or seedless raisins, currants and apricots. These feature in several of our recipes. As your imagination gets going, expand your range to include figs, dates, prunes and tropical fruits such as pineapple and papaya.

Nuts & Seeds

Buy in small quantities: nuts easily go rancid. You need a selection of almonds (whole, flaked and ground), brazils, cashews, hazels, peanuts, pecans, pistachios and walnuts. You also need pine nuts, which are not nuts at all, but the edible seeds of the stone pine tree. Most people who can't eat nuts can eat these with no problem. Keep pine nuts, ground almonds and brazils in the fridge.

Most nuts benefit from toasting before using. To toast nuts, preheat your oven to 200°. Scatter the nuts, not too thickly, on a lipped baking sheet. Put the

tray in the oven and set the timer for 7 minutes. If the nuts are not ready (time varies slightly according to variety) set the timer for another few minutes. WATCH VERY CAREFULLY. The most expensive (pine nuts, flaked almonds and cashews) are, of course, the easiest to burn!

Sunflower, sesame and pumpkin seeds are featured in our recipes. Like nuts, they are more flavoursome if toasted. Seeds can be oven toasted, but for small quantities it's easier and more controllable to

of blackeyeds, black and red kidneys, borlottis, butterbeans, cannellinis, chickpeas, flageolets, haricots and mungs. Red lentils and split peas are excellent for rissoles, croquettes and roasts. Always keep plenty of these in store. Green and brown lentils are for soups and sauces, and steely blue puy lentils make wonderful salads.

Dried beans can be divided into 2 groups, those which require soaking before cooking, and those which do not. The latter group either split and look horrible if soaked (butterbeans) or cook very quickly and turn to instant mush if not checked very frequently (mungs etc). For perfectly cooked beans, follow the instructions below. No times are given, as these will vary according to the quantity of beans you are cooking. Just munch on a bean every few minutes and you'll know the instant they are ready!

GROUP 1 Adukis, borlottis, cannellinis, chickpeas, flageolets (sometimes sold as fava), haricots, black and red kidneys, pintos, black turtles. Pick through the beans to remove any alien bodies, then rinse under a cold tap. Put in a large plastic pot and cover generously with cold water. Cover and keep in a cool place for several hours or overnight (preferably no more than about 12 hours, or they may start to bubble and this breaks the spell). Drain in a sieve or colander, rinse under the tap and cover with fresh cold water in a pan. Bring to the boil and boil hard for 10 minutes. Reduce the heat and simmer until tender but not mushy. Start testing for doneness after the first few minutes

simmering. Drain immediately they are perfectly tender, and refresh with copious cold water.

GROUP 2 Butterbeans, blackeyeds, lentils (red, green, brown, puy), mungs, split peas. Pick through the beans as for the first group; put straight into a deep pan and cover with cold water. Bring to a boil and turn the heat down immediately to low-medium. Simmer till tender and treat as for the first group. Butterbeans require a quick stir just after the heat has been reduced, to submerge the precocious ones.

SPROUTING Most whole beans (and seeds) can be sprouted, although we find chickpeas, mungs and lentils (green and brown together) to be the most successful. Put a handful of beans into a large, wide-mouthed glass jar. Secure a piece cut from a pair of tights over the mouth with a rubber band, half fill the jar with water and leave overnight. Next day strain out the water through the mesh. Rinse vigorously with clean water and strain again; keep doing this until the strain water is clean. Lay the jar on its side in a dark, warm cupboard. Rinse and strain twice a day for 3 to 5 days, until the sprouts are to your liking. Give them a final rinse and transfer to a plastic bag in the fridge.

For variety, sprout a small quantity of mustard or fenugreek seeds in a separate, smaller jar. These add a real zing to stir fries. Add your sprouts to salads, eat them in sandwiches or try mixing them into your favourite bread dough as you knead.

toast them in a heavy frying pan on medium heat till they smell toasty. Shake the pan occasionally. You will also need poppy seed for desserts and sprinkling on salads, rolls and some savoury dishes for garnish.

Beans & Pulses

These keep well, so can be bought in larger quantities (but bear in mind that they can get too old for successful sprouting: see below). Keep on hand a selection

Grains

Like beans, grains keep well, so they can be bought in bulk. Keep plenty of long grain brown rice in your store. Brown basmati rice is always useful to accompany Indian dishes; Camargue rice is colourful and has an unusual nutty flavour; a small quantity of wild rice stirred up with long grain adds a sumptuous touch. We also stock kasha (roasted buckwheat), whole grain barley (pot barley) and rye, millet, bulgur and quinoa. This Andean grain is now readily available in larger supermarkets.

Pasta & Noodles

It's fun to make your own pasta, but it requires lots of time and lots of space to dry it out. As we are not blessed with either, Stonesmade ravioli and tagliatelle are rare treats.

We rely almost exclusively on top quality, commercial pasta made from organically grown regular wheat and durum wheat. Keep a range of pasta shapes in your store. Buy strips or sheets (NOT 'no pre-cook') for lasagnes; penne or other tubular shapes to hold sauces; and spirals and shells for salads. Tricolore twists, naturally dyed in 3 colours are especially effective. Quick cooking tagliatelle (either wholewheat or verdi) is another important pasta variety. Although we never serve it at Stones, a little spaghetti tossed with any of our pasta sauces makes a quick and delicious supper.

We tend to avoid noodles for the same reason as we avoid spaghetti, namely they are nigh impossible to serve at speed with panache in full view of the waiting customer! However, there are times when only a noodle will do as an accompaniment. We therefore keep a stock of egg noodles (easily cooked by immersing in boiling water for a few minutes), ramen noodles made from buckwheat or wholewheat, and Japanese soba. These last 2 types require a quick simmer in broth or soup.

Fruit & Vegetables

Whatever the reasons (varieties grown is one), organic produce is usually far more exciting than the mass produced stuff – and your own grown is the best of all. Your produce store changes its shapes and colours with the seasons, but there are a few things you always need: onions (red and white), garlic, fresh ginger and parsley (flat leaved has more flavour) and lemons.

Dairy Products

With the exception of milk which you always have around anyhow, buy your

liquid dairy products only in the quantities you need. They have a very short refrigerated life, and it's heartbreaking to have to discard bad smelling expensive whipping cream. So decide on your menu and make a list! In addition to the familiar cream, soured cream, yogurt and cottage and cream cheeses, some of our recipes call for crème fraîche or fromage frais. These are both fresh cheeses, without milk solids and with negligible or low butterfat. As a rule of thumb they can be used interchangeably. Just check the fat percentage if it concerns you. Aside from their use in our recipes here, crème fraîche and fromage frais make wonderful toppings for cakes in place of the more usual sugary frostings. Remember, keep all dairy products refrigerated at all times.

CHEESE With 3 notable exceptions, all the cheese we use regularly at Stones comes from small farms in Wales and western England. Almost all are unpasteurised and all are made with non-animal rennet. The flavours of the grasses and clovers really come through! If you can't find one or other of the cheeses we suggest in these pages, ask your supplier to recommend a suitable alternative. Small, specialist cheese shops are your best bet here. Do experiment with cheeses local to you.

The first notable exception is feta. Buy this crumbly, salty goats' milk cheese from Greece in the imported cheese section of your supermarket. Alternatively try some of the excellent, increasingly available home-produced fetas. The second exception is Parmesan. There is no substitute for freshly grated Parmesan. We use Parmigiano-reggiano because, quite simply, it's the best. Mozzarella is the third imported cheese we could not do without. Real mozzarella is expensive compared to the more typical block form, but for special occasions look for little packets of fresh buffalo cheese. As with most cheese, there is an unfortunate but undeniable link between quality and price!

A word on keeping cheese. All soft cheeses should be refrigerated at all times, unless you are trying to encourage rapid ripening of, say, a Brie. Blue cheeses and crumbly cheeses should be wrapped and kept in the least cold part of the fridge close to the bottom. Hard cheeses such as Cheddar should also be kept in this lower part of the fridge, with their cut surfaces tightly cling-filmed. Try not to keep any of these cheeses for longer than a week once they have been cut.

Parmesan is, again, the exception. Parmesan and its hard, grating cousin pecorino, will keep for ages in the fridge with the cut surface tightly wrapped. Buy a lump and grate often! And don't forget, if you are serving cheese as a course, to remove it from the fridge in plenty of time to allow it to reach room temperature before eating.

Herbal hints

'Fresh is best' is the unswerving rule applying to all herbs and spices. Freshly picked herbs always have a better flavour than their dried counterparts, and in the case of some herbs, it's better to choose another recipe than use, for example, dried mint or parsley, both of which eat like sawdust.

Herbs are easy to grow. In fact, we have been virtually self-sufficient in herbs since the restaurant first opened in 1984, and then we had a very small garden! Once established, a few perennial herb plants (even a window box or patio tub full) will supply you with more than you can use in the course of a growing season. A single packet of annual herb seeds is just as prolific. Harvest your surplus and make «herb butters», or simply strip off the leaves and freeze them in bundles wrapped tightly in aluminium foil or freezer wrap.

If you buy fresh herbs, put immediately into a plastic bag or container. Sprinkle with a few drops of water. Cover tightly and refrigerate till needed. Buy dried herbs in small quantities, and keep airtight and out of the light. Throw away any you have not used after 6 weeks (and avoid buying any that look as if they have been sitting on the shelf for ever). We list opposite all the herbs we commonly use, indicating where dried should never be used, and where dried can be an acceptable, if not always perfect substitute for fresh. D means you can use dried if fresh is unavailable.

Basil
D

Annual, easy to grow from seed. Keep warm and well-watered. Holy basil is the authentic herb for Thai dishes.

Bay
D

Buy a bush from a garden centre. Slow growing. Dried is fine.

Chervil

Easily grown annual. Use for garnish and as an interesting change from parsley.

Coriander

Annual. Water well, or it will bolt. Used extensively in Thai and central American dishes. Careful! Can be an acquired taste.

Dill
D

Annual: water well. Adds a north European accent.

Fennel

Annual from seed. Aniseed flavour. Use fronds for summer Mediterranean dishes. Use bulbs as a vegetable from late August.

Hyssop

Perennial. Grow from seed. Cut continuously for new growth. Strong flavour. Use sparingly in salads. Make hyssop butter.

Lovage

A wonderful celery-flavoured herb. Grow this perennial from seed. Only a few plants needed.

Marjoram
D

Sweet marjoram grown as annual, with useful flowers late summer, and finer flavour than pot marjoram – a valuable tough perennial. Small leaves can alternate for thyme. Same Mediterranean genus (*Origanum*) as stronger flavoured oregano.

Mint

Invasive perennial: confine area of planting. Lots of lovely varieties, including apple, pineapple and spearmint. Start a collection!

Oregano
D

Perennial. Keep cutting! Indispensable Italian flavouring.

Parsley

Grow both curly and more flavoursome flat leaf every year. Start seed in warmth, and transplant. Plant lots: you never have enough! Can be cut till July the year after planting.

Rosemary
D

Buy a few plants and cut often to make a bush. Once this perennial is established in a tub or border, you'll never need to use dried again!

Sage
D

Perennial best grown from seed. Northern European flavour, especially when used with thyme. Strong when dried, so be careful.

Sorrel

Perennial. Looks and cooks like spinach. Sharp, lemony flavour. Grow from seed and keep cutting for lots of leaves. Don't allow to flower.

Summer savory

Annual. Fresh northern European herb for salads, butters and casseroles.

Tarragon
D

Use and grow only French tarragon: Russian is flavourless. Not easy to grow, as it needs lots of protection. Buy a plant and pray! Quality dried is fine.

Thyme
D

Easy perennial to grow from seed. One packet makes a hedge! Widely used throughout Europe and the Mediterranean. Match with sage and lemon.

Watercress

Buy this one! Peppery flavour. Use in salads as well as a flavour for casseroles and baked dishes. Choose only very fresh, crisp leaves.

21

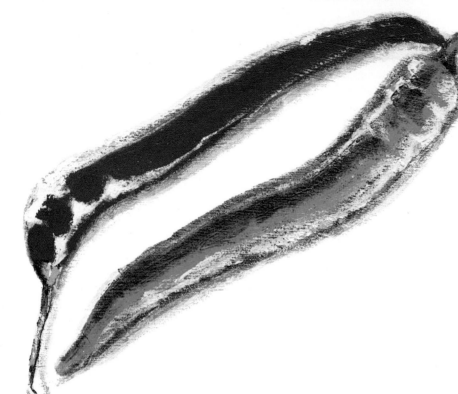

Spicy spells

Freshly ground spices are far superior to their powdered descendants, because as soon as a spice berry or seed is cracked it starts to lose its flavour. You want that first burst of flavour to occur in your food, not in a packet. There are, however, a few spices that are virtually impossible to grind yourself. Buy these only in very small amounts, store in opaque airtight containers and, like herbs, discard any unused after 6 weeks. Some spices exude their flavour better if toasted before grinding. Do this by shaking them in a heavy based frying pan over medium heat until they begin to colour and smell roasty. The easiest way to grind all spices is in a domestic electric coffee mill. They cost only a few pounds, and are tough enough even for our constant use!

Here we list our most important spices, and note which should always be freshly ground (F); which are best toasted before grinding (T); which (for one reason or another) are generally bought ready ground (R); and which can be used whole (W) for flavouring curries and spicy casseroles.

Allspice F W	A single 'berry' combining flavour of cloves and nutmeg.
Caraway W	For breads and baking (especially with rye flour), potatoes, salads and cabbage.
Cardamom F T W	Used extensively in Far Eastern cooking. Green pods are easy to buy but try pungent black cardamom seeds if you can find them.
Cayenne R	Can only be obtained in ground form. Use sparingly to bring out flavours of lots of dishes. Put a pinch in savoury pastry!
Celery seed W	Good for potato salads (with caraway and cumin).
Chillis F W	Grow your own in a greenhouse and dry those you don't use fresh, or buy whole dried chillis and grind. If you use whole, remember to remove from dish before you serve!
Cinnamon R	Too tricky for grinding at home. Use for both sweet and savoury cooking. Perfect with apples.

Cloves
R W

You might like to try grinding, but we found cloves bent our mill blades! Important to simmer with milk to take the 'cloying' taste from cream based sauces. An essential seasoning for many savoury and sweet dishes.

Coriander seed
F W

Used in dishes all over the world. Coriander was created for carrots! Can be toasted before grinding.

Cumin
F T W

Use the seeds whole, or grind, toasting first for better flavour.

Curry powder

Forget this bland, confused substitute for freshly ground spice mixtures!

Dill seed
W

Dry your own or buy in small quantities for an east European accent.

Fennel seed
F T W

Similar flavour to aniseed, but sweeter. Use in Greek and Italian dishes.

Fenugreek
F W

Mainly used whole for Asian inspired dishes. Sprouts well.

Ginger
R

Too hard for a little mill to grind. Do not interchange with fresh ginger root: the characters are completely different.

Juniper
F W

Use crushed (too soft to grind) or whole for northern European dishes. Excellent with cabbage.

Mace
F R

Expensive but intense. Perfect with spinach. The fibrous outer shell of the nutmeg, difficult to find whole.

Mustard seed
F T (R) W

Black and yellow seeds used in eastern cooking; yellow more generally. Ready ground yellow mustard is used in some salad dressings and for baking, where a fine powder is called for.

Nutmeg
F

Must be hand grated. Prepare just what you need and store the rest of the meg in an airtight container.

Paprika
R

Only Hungarian paprika will do! Spanish etc are tasteless.

Peppercorns
F W

Usually black, for grinding. Use green pepper whole. Ground white pepper complements Far Eastern dishes.

Saffron

Buy only threads, usually sold in 1 gm packets (never buy powder, it isn't real saffron). Steep threads in a little boiling water or cooking liquid to use.

Turmeric
R

Used in Indian and eastern cooking. An interesting, yellow coloured spice for rice salads.

23

There are occasions when you will want to add just a touch of Indian, Oriental or fiery Cajun magic to a cooked dish or salad. Here it is often impractical to roast and grind a whole range of spices. We make a wide variety of spice blends ourselves (on quiet days!), but also keep on hand small quantities of the following three proprietary mixtures. All are available in health food shops, delicatessens and some supermarkets. Recipes vary, but might typically include the following spices:

Chinese 5 spice	Star anise, cloves, cinnamon, fennel and Szechuan peppercorns.
Garam masala	Cardamom, cinnamon, cloves, coriander, cumin, fennel, nutmeg and peppercorns.
Rhogan josh	Coriander, turmeric, cumin, fenugreek, peppercorns, chillis, ginger and paprika.

Stock bases & flavourings

For the majority of our stock requirements, we simply boil up a big panful of 'nice' vegetable trimmings (easy on the cabbage and other brassicas!) and blend the strained liquid with vegetable stock concentrate. There are several brands on the market in cube, paste or powder form. Follow the instructions on the box or can for regular stock, and decrease the proportion of concentrate to liquid for light stock. If you have no vegetable cooking liquid to hand, simply blend the concentrate with plain water.

TABASCO We often use a dash of this hot pepper sauce to spike up a dish that just needs that extra 'something'.

TAHINI A paste made from toasted, hulled sesame seeds; widely used in middle eastern cooking. Both light and dark tahini are available. We prefer the light, but it's up to you!

TAMARI, SOYA SAUCE, LIGHT SOYA SAUCE & MISO These are all sauces and pastes derived from the soya bean. We favour tamari over soya sauce for most purposes because of its fuller flavour. Tamari is also wheat free, an important consideration for gluten intolerant folk.

Miso is a fermented soya bean paste with added barley, rice or wheat. It makes an unusual alternative to vegetable concentrate for soups, casseroles and gravies, particularly those with an Oriental theme. Available in ethnic food departments and health food stores, miso must be kept refrigerated after opening.

VINEGARS Always keep on hand red and white wine vinegars and cider vinegar. All are indispensable for salads, dressings and sauces. Flavoured vinegars are readily available, but are very easy to make at home. To make herb vinegar, loosely pack a wide mouthed glass jar or ceramic crock with the herb of your choice. Fill the jar with white wine vinegar, cover and leave in a cool dark place for a month or 2 (check the flavour to see when it's strong enough). Strain the infusion through cheesecloth and pour through a funnel into clean bottles. Cap or cork the tops. For fruit vinegars (we use lots of raspberry!) proceed in the same way, half filling your jar with soft fruit and top up with white wine vinegar. Leave 2 to 3 weeks until you like the flavour, then strain, bottle and seal. Try simmering strong raspberry vinegar with sugar and serving over Yorkshire pudding (an invention of Hilary's granny!). Garlic and hot chilli vinegars can be made in the same way.

Balsamic vinegar, aged for years in wooden vats, and hence very expensive, is important for special salads and sauces. It's strong, so a little goes a long way. Keep tightly corked in a dark place after opening.

Oriental rice wine vinegar and mirin (not really a vinegar but a cooking wine made from sake) appear in some of our recipes. You should find these in the ethnic section of large supermarkets. Try rice wine vinegar with sunflower oil and a little light soya sauce over oriental salad leaves.

Alcohol

The quality of any alcohol you use in cooking does make a difference. Cheap and nasty alcohol is unworthy of your efforts. After all, you have chosen your other ingredients with great care, so why skimp on the alcohol? You don't need that much of it anyway, and it keeps if properly sealed.

BRANDY/COGNAC Really cheap brandy is horrible, and won't do justice to your cooking. Invest in the best you can possibly afford and keep tightly sealed. Remember, you only need a little at a time.

CIDER Go for a good quality medium dry.

SHERRY A very important flavouring agent in many recipes here. Use a reasonable quality medium dry sherry, and keep

your bottle tightly sealed in a dark place.
WINE We use a palatable dry French white and French red table wine for all our cooking needs, and we use quite a lot of it. Don't panic! The alcohol vapourises in the cooking process. You are left with the subtle, indispensable afterglow. Buy in boxes (will keep up to 3 months) if you

cook a lot, or buy in bottles and seal or drink any remaining. White wine will keep only a few days in the fridge. Red is less temperamental and keeps in a cool spot for up to 2 weeks before the flavour noticeably deteriorates. Fruit and flower wines can only be bought by the bottle. It is unlikely you will have any left over!

OTHER LIQUORS Cointreau, Tequila, Pernod, Drambuie etc. Initially expensive, but will keep forever if tightly sealed and in the dark. If in doubt, buy a miniature!

Tofu & Tempeh

Tofu, a fresh soybean curd usually sold pressed into cakes, has little flavour of its own, but is quick to absorb flavours of other ingredients. It is a very versatile commodity, and can be simmered, marinated, sautéed, baked or grilled. It is an excellent source of protein and thus answers many prayers of those aiming for a dairy free diet.

Most of our recipes specify firm tofu. This should be pressed before using. To press, put your cake(s) of tofu on a board covered with a folded clean teatowel or several sheets of paper towel. Cover with another towel or a similar thickness of paper. Put another board on top and weight down with bricks, canned tomatoes etc. Leave for several hours then peel away the soggy wrappings. Extra firm tofu (if you can find it!) requires no pressing.

Delicious smoked tofu is an invaluable ingredient. There is scarcely a day when it is not to be found lurking in one of our salads. Some of the recipes here require smoked tofu, so if your natural food store does not stock it, get them to order it for you. If you've never tried it, it's a revelation.

Tempeh, a staple food in Indonesia, is made from fermented whole soya beans, again compacted to form a cake. It has a chewy texture and is great for barbecues served with an oriental or tangy tomato sauce.

Cans, Jars & Preparations

There are certain culinary elements which are impractical to make in the kitchen, or which can only be bought ready prepared. It is a good idea to keep a small stock of the following on hand.

AGAR AGAR Available in flakes or powder (easier to use), this is a seaweed preparation for making jelly.

JAR OF CAPERS Tangy Mediterranean buds bottled in brine with many uses in sauces, spreads and salads.

CREAMED COCONUT Buy in 200 gm blocks from natural food or ethnic shops, and cream and dilute according to package instructions.

FILO PASTRY This is normally sold frozen. Always try to keep a spare packet in the freezer in case of the unexpected. It can be thawed in about 3 hours at room temperature, or overnight in the fridge. As you work with filo, keep all sheets awaiting your attention covered with a damp cloth. This will stop the pastry

drying out and cracking, and thus prevent much frustration!

FRUIT JELLIES These are rewarding to make in large batches when the fruits are in season, but we just haven't the room for long term straining processes. Try to find for your store cupboard apple jelly, apple with thyme or sage, mint and red-currant. Any delicatessen should stock all these. Good sources of unusual home-made jellies are summer fêtes, bazaars and local produce stalls at weekly markets. At a recent bazaar, for example, we picked up greengage, damson, hot pepper, and pear and ginger jellies, and Paradise Island Jelly which is a delicious mixture of quince, cranberries and crab apples!

STEM GINGER IN SYRUP Again a good keeper. Use in both sweet and savoury recipes. Try adding a little finely chopped to your fruit salad. Lifts banana milk shakes to the ambrosial strata.

JARS OF HORSERADISH & CREAMED HORSERADISH For adding a zip to casseroles and salad dressings.

JARS OF OLIVES Black pitted, green pitted, stuffed.

JAR OF CONCENTRATED MINT SAUCE Buy the jellied formula for emergency use with new potatoes. For 2 lb/1 kg new potatoes simply melt 2 oz/55 gm of butter or margarine with 2 tablespoons of mint concentrate and 3 tablespoons of white wine vinegar. Stir well and toss with the hot, steamed potatoes.

MUSTARDS Keep a range of coarse grained and mild mustards in your larder. We have more than a dozen different varieties including beer, tarragon, lime, cider and garlic-chive. When you spot a new one, buy it and try it! Mustards keep well.

PEANUT BUTTER Look for unsweetened chunky.

SEAWEEDS We use reconstituted dried weeds in many of our salads. Arame, hiziki, kombu and nori (laver) can also be added to stock when making oriental dishes. Kombu (kelp) is especially flavoursome, and can be bought in dried strips from oriental food suppliers or some wholefood shops.

SUN DRIED TOMATOES Keep on hand at all times. Buy packed in oil for (expensive) convenience, or buy plain dried and reconstitute in boiling water. You can then pack the drained tomatoes in a jar and cover with olive oil to use as required.

TINNED TOMATOES Only buy those canned in juice. Tomatoes canned in water taste just that.

CARTON OR TIN OF TOMATO JUICE

SMALL CANS OF TOMATO PASTE Decant any unused purée into a non-metal container and store, covered, in the fridge.

VINE LEAVES Available in little packets at delicatessens, wholefood shops and some supermarkets.

CANS OF WATER CHESTNUTS Good for stir fries and for adding a surprise crunch to salads.

CONJURING UP A FEAST

Being able to compile a good menu is an essential part of being a good cook. Whether entertaining guests or planning family menus, first think practically. Do I have all day to prepare this meal? Must the meal be on the table as soon as possible after we return tired and hungry from a day at the beach or in the hills? Do I have only a couple of hours between returning from work and the arrival of the first guests? The complexity of your menu will depend on how much time you have and

how much you can get done beforehand. Don't be too ambitious.

Next think: what's in season? What is plentiful and of superb quality in the market? What is there lots of in the garden? Write down your ideas. Next, consider any food hates, allergies or dietary requirements of your guests. If you don't know, ask when you invite them and keep a note for future reference. This is the best way to avoid embarrassment on both sides!

Now, choose a main dish in celebration of seasonal produce. Your decision will lead you both to a general ethnic style (eg Mediterranean or Indian) and to dominating ingredients such as nuts, chillis or mushrooms. This is your fixed point. Bearing in mind the nature of your main dish, you can then go on to decide on accompaniments, appetizer and dessert. Think: BALANCE, FLAVOUR, TEXTURE, COLOUR.

Draw a picture of the main dish as you plan to serve it on the plate, leaving room for accompaniments. Now colour your picture and label the main parts.

Make notes on what you see and how you imagine the flavours and textures. For example: rich runny sauce (no dairy), filling, rich dough but light and not

27

starchy, lots of mushrooms, quite soft texture throughout.

Now, consider your picture and notes to plan your accompaniments. In this example, accompaniments should be lightly dressed (a little dairy dressing is OK) to complement the rich sauce, crisp and firm textured, and brightly coloured. Draw and colour in your chosen accompaniments and any garnishes and make notes.

When you are satisfied that your main course is perfect, turn your attention to the appetizer and dessert. For a dinner party, it's a good idea to serve a soup or cold appetizer and a cold dessert. This way you can do most of the work in advance, allowing time to concentrate on the final cooking of the main course, and have time to talk with your guests, which is, after all, why you invited them. Also you are less likely to panic if you know your appetizer is plated and your dessert components all ready to assemble.

Your appetizer should be just that, a lead into the main course. Keep appetizers light, and go for ingredients, textures, flavours and colours which balance the coming meal. Draw pictures to help you with presentation.

Choose your dessert carefully. No one can eat lots of rich dessert after a rich meal, but rich desserts are fun to linger over on a warm evening following a light, summery meal. Cold desserts can be made in advance and assembled quickly once the main course is cleared. Whatever sauces or coulis you are using, and whatever garnishes you choose (leaves, berries,

fruit segments, flowers, chopped nuts etc), again draw a picture so that you will have a precise idea of presentation at serving time.

Now make a shopping list (checking your store cupboard to make sure you're not going to run out of any staples) and a work schedule. Write down things you can prepare in advance, when you are going to prepare them and where you are going to put them. List things to be done on the day and last minute preparation. Decide on crockery, cutlery, napkins, flowers, drinks (are you or your guests providing?). Lay the table well in advance

of your first arrivals. Relax, and have a great party!

Finally, keep a file with all your dated drawings, notes, lists and schedules. Keep a diary with the date of your party, the names of your guests, any food hates or allergies, and reactions to the meal. This way you will be sure not to repeat the same meal for the same guests, and retain valuable information as to their preferences and size of appetites!

Using the principles above, here are 4 examples of magic feasts. Draw them out with garnishes and make notes for practice in menu planning!

A MEDITERRANEAN INSPIRED SUMMER DINNER PARTY

Green aïoli with crudités

Herbed polenta with eggs florentine
Or
Sorrel & lovage frittata

Courgette & roast aubergine tian with Pernod

Salad of mixed leaves with walnut oil & lemon dressing
Olive-garlic bread

Fruit en papillote
Or
Honey brulé

A HINT OF THE ORIENT

Pumpkin & coconut soup
Or
Salad of papaya & melon on oriental leaves with Eastern Magic dressing

Oriental spring rolls with lime-ginger sauce

Pineapple-cashew rice in pineapple boats
Sesame broccoli
Stir fried red pepper and carrot strips

Iced mango soufflé
Or
Tangerine & lychee ice cream

A MENU FOR A WINTER CELEBRATION

Roast sweet potato, celery & apple soup
Or
Chicory, grapefruit & walnut salad

Mushroom tourtière

Cranberry-onion gravy
Parsnip pyramids with nutmeg and saffron infused cream
Marjoram braised baby carrots
Lightly steamed, buttered broccoli
Garlic-rosemary roast potatoes

Port poached pears

A CENTRAL AMERICAN FIESTA

Chilled leek & avocado soup with lime

Torta Mexicana

Soured cream
Fresh tomato salsa
Cheesy zapallo
Succotash

Poppy seed parfait

STANDARD PASTRY

This pastry making method is foolproof. Everyone working in the restaurant has got it right on the first attempt. The spell won't work unless you use frozen margarine.

> 14 oz (400 gm) Rushall wholewheat flour
> ½ tablespoon salt
> 9 oz (250 gm) hard vegetable margarine (frozen), chopped small
> 2 tablespoons lemon juice
> 4-5 fl oz (100-150 ml) ice cold water

Mix the flour and salt in a bowl. Stir in the margarine slivers with a wooden spoon just to coat. Now stir in the lemon juice and mix with enough cold water to make a slightly sticky dough.

Turn onto a floured board, and knead lightly just to gather together. Don't worry about the bits of margarine you can still see. Wrap in cling film and refrigerate for at least 1 hour before using. To use, knead lightly again until smooth.

SAVOURY CHOUX PASTRY

Use for profiteroles, gougères or shoo pies!

> ¾ pint (425 ml) water
> 6 oz (170 gm) butter
> 4½ oz (125 gm) wholewheat flour
> 4½ oz (125 gm) strong white flour
> 1 teaspoon salt
> ½ teaspoon cayenne pepper
> 1½ teaspoons baking powder
>
> 6 eggs
> 5 oz (140 gm) Cheddar, grated

Bring water and butter gently to the boil in a saucepan. When the butter is melted, immediately add all the dry ingredients and stir quickly until a ball begins to form. Remove from the heat and leave to cool.

Beat in the eggs, one at a time, till the mix is smooth and glossy. Then stir in the cheese. Drop by dessertspoonfuls onto a baking sheet for profiteroles, or into a ring mould for a gougère. Bake at 225° for the first 15 minutes, then turn down to 150° for a further 25 minutes.

31

SWEET PASTRY

Perfect for sweet fruit flans or dessert tartlets. This pastry is better made by hand. Do not use a processor or the texture will be all wrong. Instead of all wholewheat, you can use half wholewheat flour and half unbleached white.

12 oz (340 gm) wholewheat flour
1 teaspoon salt
1 teaspoon golden granulated sugar
6 oz (170 gm) frozen butter, cut into very little bits
2 large egg yolks
2-3 tablespoons chilled orange juice

Put the flour, salt and sugar in a large bowl. Stir in the butter to coat all surfaces. Add the egg yolks and orange juice and mix with your hands just enough to amalgamate everything. If it seems dry, add a little more orange juice. Don't try to rub the butter in. Now knead lightly till you have a smoothish, silky feeling ball. Wrap in cling film and chill 30 minutes, or until you are ready to use. Knead lightly again before rolling.

STANDARD PANCAKES

Pancake batters feature in several of our recipes (eg crêpes, galettes, tortas and blinis). The quantity of liquid required will vary according to the type of flour used. Always add your liquid gradually and stop when the consistency is just right (think rich double cream). It's much easier to thin a thick batter than thicken a thin one!

4½ oz (125 gm) Rushall wholewheat flour
1 teaspoon salt
2 eggs, beaten
5 fl oz (150 ml) milk
3½ fl oz (100 ml) water (or use all water)
sunflower oil for frying

Combine the flour and salt. Mix in the eggs, then slowly beat in the milk and water until the batter is very smooth. Stand in the fridge for at least half an hour. Beat again and add a little more liquid if necessary to make a double cream-like consistency.

The best way we have found to fry pancakes is to set out your stall like this (adjusting your kitchen fan if it's a hot day). Pour some sunflower oil into a small bowl and put this on a flat surface by your stove. Put a ball of kitchen paper (2 crumpled sheets) beside the bowl. Put an upside down plate ready for the pancakes within easy reach. Put your pancake mix with a 3-4 tablespoon ladle in it, as close to the stove as possible. Have your frying slice handy.

Now heat your pan (8 or 10 inch/20 or 25 cm) on a high setting. Dip one side of the paper towel ball in the oil and quickly wipe over the pan. Replace the paper beside (not in!) the bowl. When the oil begins to smoke, quickly swirl in about 3 tablespoons pancake mix, tilting the pan to coat evenly. Cook for 20-30 seconds each side, loosening and turning with your frying slice. Slide immediately onto your upturned plate. Repeat until all the batter is used up.

BUCKWHEAT PANCAKES
Use 3 oz (85 gm) buckwheat flour and 1½ oz (40 gm) wholewheat.

GRAM PANCAKES
Use 4½ oz (125 gm) gram flour instead of wholewheat, and use all water for the liquid.

CORNMEAL PANCAKES
Use 2½ oz (70 gm) corn or maize meal and 2 oz (55 gm) wholewheat flour. Use all water for the liquid.

MAYONNAISE

As the owner of a processor or blender, it's crazy not to make your own mayonnaise. Using vinegar and oils superior in quality to those listed on the labels of shop bought products, it still costs a fraction of the price. Also, it takes less than 30 seconds to make a whole litre. Magic!

Mayonnaise is a truly versatile kitchen staple. Use alone, or with yogurt or soured cream for dressing potato or crunchy vegetable salads, or use it in place of butter and milk when mashing potatoes. Made with lemon juice and warmed gently in a bowl over hot water, it makes a simple alternative to béarnaise sauce for serving with steamed asparagus.

---

1 egg
5 tablespoons white or
red wine vinegar/lemon juice
1 teaspoon salt
1 teaspoon pepper
1 tablespoon coarse grained mustard of
your choice
1 tablespoon golden granulated sugar

1 l bottle sunflower oil, olive oil or
combination

Put the first 6 ingredients into your processor bowl or blender, and process till creamy. With the motor still running, slowly pour in the oil till it's all used up.

MORE MAYONNAISE

To make garlic mayonnaise, process 2 or 3 cloves of garlic before adding the first group of ingredients. For herb mayonnaise, add lots of your choice of chopped fresh herbs after all the oil has been used up, and give the processor a quick whizz to mix them in evenly.

DRESSINGS, RELISHES & SAUCES

Illustrations by Sally Gaden

HERB BUTTERS

In the summer when fresh garden herbs are plentiful, we make lots of herb butters and freeze them in small packages for the winter. Herb butters will keep up to one week refrigerated, and up to 6 months in the freezer. We use herb butters to top crostini, to make garlic-herb bread and for topping freshly steamed vegetables (and see «vegetable medley in herb butter»). Bread cubes pan- or oven-fried in herb butter, make wonderful croûtons for serving with soup or as an unusual topping for baked savoury dishes, perhaps mixed with a distinctively flavoured grated cheese?

BASIC RECIPE

¼ lb (110 gm) salted butter/vegetable margarine
3-4 tablespoons finely chopped herbs
¼-½ teaspoon freshly ground black pepper

Soften the butter until creamy, and thoroughly mix in the herbs and pepper. What could be simpler! Store in an airtight container in the fridge till ready to use, or form into a log shape, wrap tightly in 2 or 3 layers of freezer quality film, label and freeze.

HORSERADISH & DILL BUTTER

Make this towards the end of the season, when dill is beginning to seed.

¼ lb (110 gm) butter
2 tablespoons finely chopped dill feathers
1 tablespoon dill seed
1 tablespoon prepared horseradish & dill
zest and juice of 1 large lemon

TARRAGON-TARRAGON

This butter accents mildly flavoured vegetables and is especially good with asparagus. Do not substitute Russian for French tarragon.

¼ lb (110 gm) butter
3 tablespoons finely chopped French tarragon
1 tablespoon tarragon vinegar
1 tablespoon tarragon mustard

MINT BUTTER

We celebrate the arrival of our first new potatoes from the garden (this year first dug were Belle de Fontenay, followed by Charlotte and la Ratte) by serving them simply steamed with this flavour enhancing butter. Any variety of mint can be used, but it is better not to mix them. Apple mint was invented for la Ratte potatoes!

¼ lb (110 gm) butter
4 tablespoons finely chopped mint
zest and juice 1 large lemon
1 teaspoon salt
½ teaspoon freshly ground black pepper

MEDITERRANEAN BUTTER

Great stirred into pasta and for superb garlic bread. Vegans can use margarine and omit the Parmesan.

¼ lb (110 gm) butter
3 large cloves garlic, crushed
2 tablespoons finely chopped basil
2 tablespoons finely chopped oregano or golden marjoram
3 tablespoons freshly grated Parmesan

LOVAGE BUTTER

Strongly flavoured and excellent with new potatoes or braised celery.

¼ lb (110 gm) butter
3 tablespoons finely chopped lovage
1 tablespoon snipped chives
zest and juice 1 lemon
1 teaspoon celery seed

APPLE SAUCE

If you intend to make apple sauce often, or if like me (Hilary) you are an apple sauce addict, it's a good idea to invest in a 'mouli' grater. These are available at good kitchenware shops and cost only a few pounds. Aside from making apple sauce, they are ideal for puréing cooked vegetables for baby food. Putting the finished sauce through the machine leaves just the tough skin, and no precious apple behind. Eat apple sauce with «Glamorgan sausages», cakes, rissoles and patties. Also wonderful with fried eggs, fried potatoes or spread on French toast! The butter can be omitted if you're vegan, but it makes the sauce really nice!

> 1½ lb (700 gm) Bramley apples, weighed after quartering and coring
> ½ oz (15 gm) butter
> 3 fl oz (75 ml) lemon juice
> 1½ oz (40 gm) demerara sugar

Roughly chop the apples and put in a pan with the butter and lemon juice. Cover and cook on very low heat until the apples 'fall' (disintegrate). This will take 15-20 minutes. Put the cooked apple through the mouli and discard the skins (or just mash with a potato masher or back of a wooden spoon). Beat in the sugar. Serve hot or cold.

BRANDIED APPLE SAUCE

Serve warm with celebratory roasts, or cold with American style pancakes for a very special brunch! Avoid butter and honey for a vegan sauce.

> 1½ lb (700 gm) Bramley apples
> ½ oz (15 gm) butter
> 4 tablespoons lemon juice
> 2 tablespoons clear honey, golden syrup or maple syrup
> 2 teaspoons cinnamon
> 4 tablespoons brandy

When the apples 'fall', put through the mouli or mash and beat in the honey, cinnamon and brandy. This way, the brandy won't evaporate and the full potency will be preserved.

APPLE & CIDER SAUCE

This goes beautifully with «Glamorgan sausages» or any cheesy pie. Serve hot or cold.

> 1½ lb (700 gm) Bramley apples
> 2 oz (55 gm) butter
> 4 tablespoons lemon juice
> zest of 1 lemon
> 1½-2 oz (40-55 gm) demerara sugar
> 5 fl oz (150 ml) dry cider
> 1 teaspoon freshly grated nutmeg

Cook the apples with the butter and juice and lemon zest. When apples 'fall', beat in the sugar, cider and nutmeg. Return to heat and cook gently, uncovered, until the sauce is medium thick and smooth.

CRANBERRY & APPLE SAUCE

A sweetish sauce with a strong cranberry 'bite' to serve with roasts or rissoles. If you prefer a tarter flavour, substitute 2 Bramleys for 4 of the dessert apples.

8 dessert apples
½ pint (300 ml) water
4 oz (110 gm) cranberries
1 teaspoon cinnamon
2 oz (55 gm) sugar

Core and chop the apples. Put everything into a pan, and cook on a low heat until the apples form a pulp. For a smoother sauce, push the cooked pulp though a fine sieve. If you prefer a chunkier texture, simply mash the pulp roughly with the back of a wooden spoon or a potato masher.

CRANBERRY-ONION GRAVY

Serve with «mushroom tourtière», roasts and rissoles. Cranberries vary in sweetness, so you may need to add a little extra sugar at the end of the cooking time.

1 large onion, sliced into thin rings
1 oz (30 gm) margarine
2 tablespoons sugar
6 oz (170 gm) cranberries
1 oz (30 gm) wholewheat flour
1½ pints (850 ml) miso stock
4 tablespoons brandy
tamari
black pepper

Sauté onion rings in the margarine with the sugar on low heat until the onion is very soft and golden brown. Add the cranberries and cook, stirring occasionally until the berries are also soft. Crush the cranberries with a potato masher. Sprinkle in the flour and stir until absorbed. Gradually add the hot stock and brandy and stir to make a thick sauce. Season to taste with tamari and pepper and adjust the sugar.

Parmesan can be used here, but fresh is best.

3 cloves garlic, peeled
3 oz (85 gm) toasted pine nuts
2-3 handfuls fresh basil leaves
1 oz (30 gm) freshly grated Parmesan cheese
3 fl oz (85ml) olive oil
1 tablespoon lemon juice
salt and freshly ground pepper

Grind the garlic in the processor, then the toasted pine nuts. Add all the remaining ingredients and process everything to a smooth paste. Season.

RED PESTO

1 quantity «pesto»
1 large ripe red pepper
2 tablespoons tomato paste
Tabasco

Process the red pepper and add to the pesto. Then stir in the tomato paste with the rest of the ingredients. A dash of Tabasco gives an extra bit of zest!

PESTO

Pestos are perfect with pasta. Simply cook your chosen variety of pasta al dente, then drain and toss with pesto and a little extra olive oil. Sprinkle with more freshly grated Parmesan to serve. Mash potatoes with pesto instead of the more usual butter and cream, or add to soups for an instant summery zing! This is a highly flavoured creation, so a little goes a long way. Just 4-5 tablespoons is ample to dress pasta for 8 people.

Pesto keeps for up to 2 weeks refrigerated (drizzle the surface with a little extra olive oil to prevent discolouring) or when herbs are plentiful, make lots and freeze in small quantities for use in the winter months. Pre-grated

SORT OF PESTO

You can make lost of different 'pestos' simply by varying the herbs and/or nuts and oil. Try spinach, coriander, parsley, dill or tarragon (or combinations) instead of basil. Try almonds, hazelnuts or pecans instead of pine nuts. Try walnut, grape seed or hazelnut oil instead of olive oil. Omit the Parmesan for a herby vegan 'pesto'.

DARK MUSHROOM & COGNAC SAUCE

This sauce should be made with full flavoured Paris mushrooms, also known as marrons or chestnut mushrooms. Substitute, if you like, a few fresh shiitakes for some of the Paris, but do not use button mushrooms: the magic would not work. This is wonderful with winter roasts.

3 tablespoons butter/margarine
2 large cloves garlic, crushed
8 oz (225 gm) Paris mushrooms, thinly sliced
1 pint (550 ml) water
2 teaspoons paprika
2 fl oz (50 ml) tamari
2 tablespoons arrowroot
3 tablespoons cold water
6 tablespoons cognac
salt and pepper

Melt the butter and sauté the garlic on gentle heat. When the garlic is beginning to brown, add the mushrooms and stir for one minute. Add the water, paprika and tamari, and simmer gently until the mushrooms are very tender. Take off the heat and allow to cool for at least one hour, or better refrigerate overnight, for the flavours to mingle.

Reheat the mushroom mixture. Meanwhile mix the arrowroot with the water and brandy to a smooth cream. As soon as the mushrooms return to simmering point, slowly beat in the arrowroot cream. Stir vigorously until you have a smooth sauce. Remove immediately from the heat and adjust the seasoning.

ROAST PEPPER RELISH

Use only red and/or yellow peppers for this recipe. Green ones are the devil to peel! Makes about 1 pint (550 ml) and keeps up to 5 days refrigerated.

3 red and 3 yellow peppers (or use 6 red if you can't find yellow)
1 teaspoon (1 gm) saffron strands
3 fl oz (80 ml) olive oil
3 tablespoons balsamic vinegar
1 clove garlic, crushed (optional)
1 tablespoon dried oregano
1 teaspoon salt

Sear the peppers under a very hot grill, turning often till their skins are blackening and blistered all over. Quickly drop them into a clean tub with a tight fitting lid (a 4 l ice cream tub is ideal for this) or into a strong paper bag. Seal them up and leave to cool. The steam inside the container helps to loosen the skins.

Meanwhile warm the saffron in the olive oil with the vinegar, optional garlic and oregano. When the peppers are cool enough to handle (5-10 minutes), put them onto a cutting board and remove and discard the stems and seeds. Peel off the charred skins, and reserving the neatest pepper, roughly chop the rest and add to the saffron infusion. Cool the mixture slightly then process or blend to a smooth purée with the salt. Chop the reserved pepper into neat squares and stir into the purée. Refrigerate and serve cold.

GOLDEN TOMATO SAUCE

For the last 2 years we have grown Golden Boy, a medium sized, succulent yellow tomato, in one of our greenhouses. When you have access to a plentiful supply of well-flavoured yellow tomatoes, make this simple sauce for a refreshing change.

1 onion, finely chopped
2 cloves garlic, crushed
1 tablespoon olive oil
1 lb 12 oz (800 gm) golden tomatoes
2 tablespoons dry white wine
2 tablespoons chopped fresh dill, or
1 tablespoon dried
salt and pepper

Sauté onion with garlic in the oil. Puré tomatoes and add to onion. Pour in the wine, add the dill and cook for 10 minutes. Season to taste with salt and lots of freshly ground black pepper.

SPICED TOMATO SAUCE

A versatile tomato sauce that requires no cooking! The quantity of spice can be increased or decreased according to taste. Add to mayonnaise to make a delicious dressing or a dip for crackers or crudités. Halve hard boiled eggs, mash the yolks with a little of the sauce (together with some chopped fresh herbs) and pile back into the white 'shells'. Use instead of commercial ketchup on French fries! Keeps, covered and refrigerated, up to 5 days. Makes 1⅓ pints (¾ l).

6 fat cloves garlic
14 oz (400 gm) tomato paste
8½ fl oz (250 ml) cider vinegar
2 teaspoons salt
1 tablespoon dried oregano
1 teaspoon ground cumin
1 teaspoon ground mace
1 teaspoon ground black pepper
1 teaspoon whole grain mustard
1 tablespoon demerara sugar
8½ fl oz (250 ml) water

Crush the garlic and place in a large bowl. Add all the other ingredients and beat to combine thoroughly. Can also be made in a processor, processing the garlic as the first step.

GUACAMOLE

The definitive accompaniment for fiery chillis or any Mexican dish. Guacamole can also be served as a dip for crudités in place of «green aïoli», or mix a few tablespoons with mayonnaise or yogurt to make a dressing for potato, pasta or crunchy vegetable salads. For a uniquely Mexican flavour, add a little finely chopped fresh coriander.

3 cloves garlic, peeled
3 large ripe avocados, stoned, peeled and roughly chopped
4 tablespoons lemon juice
3 heaped tablespoons soured cream
½ teaspoon cayenne pepper
½ teaspoon salt
fresh coriander, finely chopped (optional)

To make in a processor, first process the garlic then add the avocado and process again. Now add all the rest of the ingredients and process to form a thick, creamy purée. Adjust the seasoning to taste.

To make by hand, first crush the garlic into a bowl. Add the avocado and mash, making sure no lumps remain. Now beat in the rest of the ingredients. Adjust seasoning and stir in the chopped coriander if using.

HERBED CRÈME FRAÎCHE

This is a nice alternative to guacamole if you are already using avocado in your main dish, or if you are not a great avocado fan. It can also be gently warmed and served as a sauce with rissoles or croquettes. Excellent spooned over falafel (hot spicy chickpea balls) in pitta bread. You can substitute soured cream for the yogurt, but only if you're using fromage frais.

½ pint (300 ml) crème fraîche or fromage frais
¼ pint (150 ml) yogurt
¼ pint (150 ml) single cream
pinch salt
2 large handfuls fresh mixed herbs, eg dill, parsley, chives or coriander
2 tablespoons lemon juice

Beat everything together except the lemon juice. Add this a few drops at a time to prevent curdling, beating after every addition. Serve chilled, or gently warmed.

AVOCADO RELISH

Cool, clean and fresh, this relish is the perfect foil for a hot chilli. It also goes well with spicy croquettes and rissoles. Vegans can make this whenever guacamole is called for. You can omit the coriander, but only if you really don't like it.

3 cloves garlic, peeled
1 small onion or 3 spring onions, roughly chopped
1 red pepper, seeded and roughly chopped
3 avocados, stoned, peeled and roughly chopped
4 tablespoons olive oil
2 tablespoons lemon juice
salt and pepper
Tabasco (optional)
2 tablespoons freshly chopped coriander

First process the garlic then add all the ingredients except the seasonings and coriander to the processor bowl. Process to a rough textured relish. Season to taste with salt and pepper and optional Tabasco, and stir in the coriander saving a little for garnish.

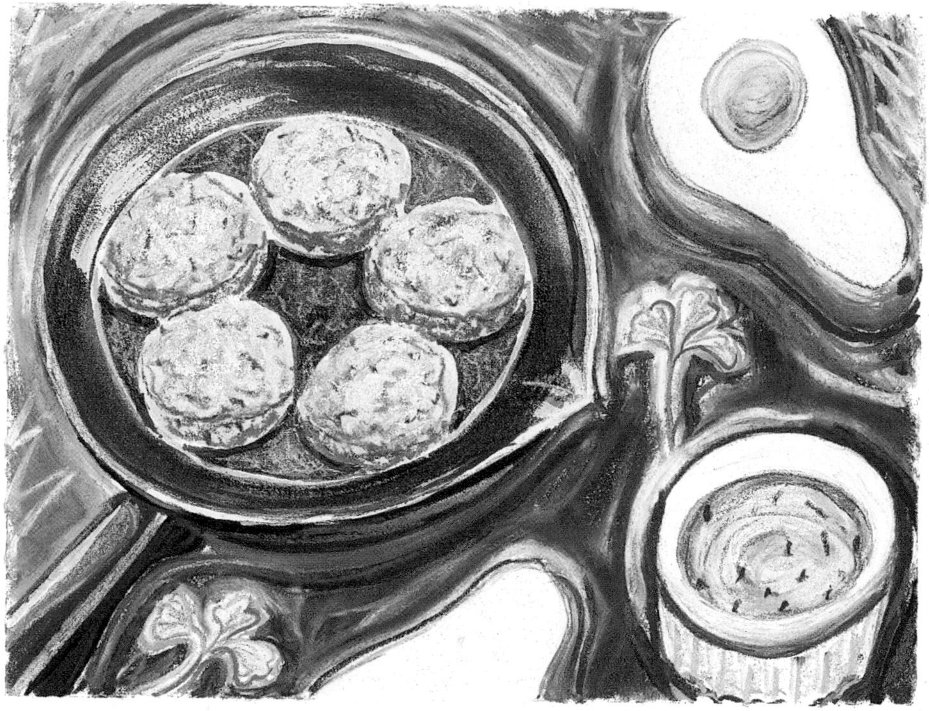

RED PEPPER-ALMOND SAUCE

The toasted almonds act as a thickener and add a toasty nutty element to the flavour of this sharp-sweet sauce.

4 large red peppers
1 red onion, roughly chopped
5 garlic cloves, peeled
2 tablespoons olive oil
6 tomatoes
4 tablespoons red wine vinegar
2 oz (55 gm) ground almonds, toasted
1 tablespoon sugar
salt and pepper
stock to thin (optional)

Follow the method for roasting and peeling the peppers in «roast pepper relish».

Process the onion and garlic, and cook gently in the oil for 1-2 minutes, just to remove the sharpness. Take the pan off the heat.

Process the tomatoes with the roast pepper flesh and add to the onion-garlic mix. Stir in the vinegar, almonds and sugar. Season to taste. Heat gently to serve, thinning with a little stock if required.

SAMBALS

These are relishes designed to complement far eastern or Indian inspired dishes. Whenever we feature kormas, curries, shuktas or spicy Thai creations we generally serve a selection of 3 of these relishes in individual small bowls. The flavours are distinctive so a little goes a long way. Think carefully about the ingredients in your curry, and what all the colours, textures and flavours will be like when you plan your sambals. As a rule of thumb, choose either 2 sambals with fruit and one without, or one with fruit and 2 without.

Choose from the following, then think up your own combinations.

Tiny cubes of cucumber folded into set natural yogurt with chopped fresh mint and lemon zest.

Melon balls stirred with finely chopped stem ginger and grated fresh ginger root.

Finely chopped red onion and green or red tomato with a dressing of mango chutney thinned with lemon juice. Sprinkle with cinnamon and sliced spring onions or chives.

Sliced banana with lemon juice, ground ginger and toasted desiccated coconut.

Peanuts fried till 'roasty' in toasted sesame oil. Garnish with freshly chopped coriander and sesame seeds.

Mango chutney with toasted pine nuts, lemon juice and chopped parsley.

Tiny courgette cubes, blanched for 1 minute, with equal measures of fresh lime juice (zest the limes first) and sunflower oil. Sprinkle with lime zest, salt and pepper and chopped fresh basil.

Grated mooli with orange zest, a little rice vinegar and light soya sauce.

fruit is tender. Add sugar and raisins. Turn down heat and stir constantly until chutney is thick. Cool.

BANANA & COCONUT RAITA

Another slightly more complex but excellent mix (also very interesting spooned over muesli or granola for breakfast!).

2 tablespoons lemon juice
2 bananas, sliced
4 oz (110 gm) creamed coconut
¼ pint (150 ml) yogurt
pinch salt

Put the bananas in a serving dish, and sprinkle lemon juice over. Soften coconut in a warm place, and blend with the yogurt with a pinch of salt until smooth and creamy. Pour over the bananas and mix carefully.

FRESH PINEAPPLE & RAISIN CHUTNEY

This delicious, if slightly more complex sambal, keeps for 3 or 4 days covered and refrigerated. Especially good with «golden temple curry».

1 ripe pineapple
3 tablespoons vegetable ghee or sunflower oil
1 whole dried chilli, finely chopped

½ tablespoon cumin seed
½ tablespoon coriander seed
¼ teaspoon ground cardamom
½ teaspoon garam masala
3 oz (85 gm) brown sugar
3 oz (85 gm) raisins

Peel the pineapple and chop into small cubes. Heat ghee or oil in pan. When hot, add chilli and seeds and toast till they darken slightly. Add pineapple, cardamom and garam masala. Cook until

MANGO CHUTNEY

We are including this recipe just in case you ever have access to a mango mountain. Ask your produce supplier to keep an eye out at the wholesale market and let you know if there's ever a glut of cheap mangos. Because ... this is simply the best mango chutney we have ever tasted. The recipe was devised by Hilary with Diana Brown on Kapa Island in Tonga during the annual January mango season. For just 2 short weeks, it literally rained mangos. We cooked our chutney over an open fire (warding off inquisitive pigs, dogs and chicken) as there was no propane on the islands at the time. The recipe fills 15-20 assorted sized jars, or about 25 lb (10 kg). Can be eaten immediately.

18 lb (8 kg) green mangos weighed whole before peeling
7 lb (3 kg) onions
8 lb (3½ kg) light muscovado sugar
6½ pints (3 ¾ l) cider vinegar
16 tablespoons finely chopped fresh ginger, peeled first if necessary
2 large heads garlic, peeled and crushed (use your processor)
10 tablespoons salt
16 fresh red chillis, seeded and finely chopped (wear rubber gloves!)
zest of 8 large lemons
1½ lb (750 gm) raisins

Peel, stone and chop mangos and put in 1 or 2 large glass or ceramic bowls. Add the vinegar and sugar and stir. Cover loosely with teatowels and let stand in a cool place overnight. The next day, tip the mango mix into a very large saucepan. Add the rest of the ingredients except the raisins. Bring to boil and simmer on very low heat, stirring occasionally until the mangos are almost tender. Add the raisins and continue to simmer until the mangos can be pierced easily with a fork, are transparent and the syrup is thick. Cool slightly then pour into sterilised jars and seal.

CELERY & STILTON SAUCE

This is a splendid sauce to serve with hollowed vegetables filled with a mildly flavoured stuffing of beans or nuts. Magical with simply steamed root vegetables. Indispensable with potato and vegetable pies (see for example «cauliflower, broccoli & potato pies»).

---

1 oz (30 gm) butter
4 spring onions, finely sliced
3 sticks celery, finely sliced
1 tablespoon celery seed
1 oz (30 gm) wholewheat flour
½ pint (300 ml) milk, warmed with 2 teaspoons tamari
¼ pint (150 ml) single cream
2 fl oz (50 ml) dry sherry
4 oz (110 gm) blue Stilton, grated
salt and pepper
extra tamari for seasoning if needed

Melt the butter and sauté the spring onion and celery with the celery seed. When the celery is soft, stir in the flour and cook over low heat for a couple of minutes before gradually stirring in the milk. When all the milk has been added, you should be stirring a thick, smooth paste.

Now slowly mix in the cream and sherry, stirring continuously (still over a low heat), until the sauce is rich and creamy-smooth. Stir in the Stilton, and when it has melted, remove from the heat. Season and serve.

TOMATO GARLIC SAUCE

Adding raw crushed garlic right at the end of the initial cooking makes this sauce really garlicky! Cook the vegetables slowly in a pan with a tight fitting lid and shake the pan occasionally rather than stir. This way everything cooks in the steam trapped in the pan and no extra liquid is needed. Best made the day before required and gently reheated to serve. Freezes well.

---

4 medium red onions, finely chopped
4 cloves garlic, crushed
3 tablespoons olive oil
½ loosely packed teacup roughly chopped fresh basil
1 teaspoon dried thyme
2 teaspoons dried tarragon
2 lb (1 kg) very ripe tomatoes, quartered
3 fl oz (75 ml) red wine
3 tablespoons red wine vinegar

---

1 tablespoon sugar
2 teaspoons salt
1 teaspoon pepper
1-4 cloves garlic, crushed (add as you dare!)

Sauté the onion and first 4 garlic cloves in the olive oil until the onion softens. Add everything else except the final wicked garlic. Cover the pan and simmer on very low heat, shaking occasionally, for 45 minutes.

Remove from the heat and allow to stand, still covered, for a final 15 minutes. Take off the lid, mash lightly with potato masher and stir in the crushed garlic cloves. Cool and refrigerate, covered, for several hours or overnight. Reheat gently to simmering point to serve.

CREAMY GARLIC SAUCE

For a creamy sauce, stir in 4 fl oz (100 ml) double cream, crème fraîche or fromage frais when the sauce has been reheated.

STANDARD CHEESE SAUCE

Whenever a cheese sauce is called for in a recipe, use this basic formula, varying the cheese to suit the other ingredients. The sauce can be thinned with extra milk or stock as required.

1 pint (550 ml) milk
large pinch ground cloves
a few bay leaves
1½ oz (40 gm) margarine
1½ oz (40 gm) wholewheat flour
½ teaspoon mustard powder
dash tamari
pinch cayenne pepper
12 oz (350 gm) cheese of your choice, grated
salt and pepper

Warm milk with cloves and bay leaves.

Melt margarine in another pan on gentle heat and stir in the flour. Cook for 1 minute, stirring. Gradually add the warmed milk (remove the bay leaves), stirring all the time, and simmer, still stirring, until a smooth, thick sauce is achieved.

Stir in mustard, tamari, cayenne and cheese. Season to taste.

SPICED PLUM SAUCE

The spices should not be ground for this sauce, but instead crushed with a pestle and mortar, or with a clean heavy stone on a solid board. This is delicious with «mushroom & potato kebabs» or with «oriental spring rolls».

1 onion, chopped
2 tablespoons sunflower oil
15-20 allspice berries
6 whole cloves
6 cardamom pods
1 teaspoon pickling spice
12 flavoursome plums, stoned
4 tablespoons red wine vinegar
4 tablespoons water
1-2 teaspoons sugar
1-2 teaspoons salt

Sauté the onion gently in the oil until softening. Meanwhile, lightly crush all the spices. Add spices to the onion and stir fry 1 minute.

Add the plums, vinegar and water. Cover the pan, and simmer on the lowest possible heat setting for about 35-40 minutes, or until the plums are very soft. Lift the lid once or twice during cooking and mash the fruit with a wooden spoon. Push everything through a fine sieve, extracting as much liquid as possible. Discard the solid residue. Stir sugar and salt into the purée to taste. Serve warm.

FRESH TOMATO SALSA

The ultimate chunky salsa for all things Mexican. The addition of horseradish (available in jars at your delicatessen) makes this relish extra special. Use a dash of ground dried chilli or Tabasco if you can't find horseradish.

1 tablespoon peanut or sunflower oil
1 onion, diced small
1 large green pepper, seeded and diced small

6 large tomatoes with most of the seeds scooped out, diced
2 teaspoons sugar
1 teaspoon salt
2 tablespoons red wine vinegar
1 tablespoon tomato paste
1-2 teaspoons preserved grated horseradish
1 tablespoon finely chopped coriander or parsley

Heat the oil and sauté the onion and pepper for 2 minutes. Stir in the tomatoes and simmer on low heat until the onion is almost tender. Stir in everything else, except the chopped herbs, adding horse-radish to taste. Simmer until the vegetables are tender but not mushy, and the sauce is slightly thickened. Cool and stir in the coriander or parsley. Adjust the seasoning to taste. Refrigerate covered several hours before serving.

SIMPLE NO-COOK SALSA

If you're short of time, simply rough chop the vegetables and puré all the ingredients together in your processor. Check the seasoning and chill. The texture will not be so interesting but it will still taste good!

ORANGE-WINE SAUCE

This is an unusual sauce, wonderful with «potato cakes». It can also be used in place of «cranberrry-onion gravy» as an exciting if un-authentic accompaniment for «mushroom tourtière». It's a good idea to zest all your 8 oranges before juicing, and save half the zest for another use. Cointreau, tamari and Tabasco are optional – but don't miss the liqueur!

zest of 4 oranges
juice of 8 oranges
1½ teaspoons vegetable stock concentrate
1 small onion, very finely chopped
4 fl oz (100 ml) dry white wine

4 tablespoons arrowroot
3 tablespoons cold water
3 tablespoons Cointreau
½ teaspoon salt
1 teaspoon freshly ground cardamom
(black if possible)
salt and pepper
tamari
Tabasco

Put the zest in a pan which has a tight fitting lid. Blend or process the orange juice with the vegetable concentrate. Add this blend to the pan together with the onion and wine. Put the lid on and bring to simmering point. Simmer very gently for 20 minutes. Uncover and simmer a further 5-10 minutes to reduce the liquid by about a third.

Meanwhile, mix the arrowroot with the water until you have a smooth paste. Stir in the Cointreau, salt and cardamom. Stir until really smooth, then add gradually to the simmering orange mixture, stirring all the time. Continue to simmer and stir until the sauce is smooth and glossy but still pourable. Season to taste with salt and pepper and a dash of tamari and Tabasco if you think it needs it!

RICH TOMATO SAUCE

This is a thick, bright red, fresh tasting sauce to serve with gnocchi or pasta, or any dish needing a tomatoey dressing. Excellent with spinach and cheese filled pancakes.

4 cloves garlic, crushed
1 large onion, finely chopped
4 tablespoons olive oil
1 large red pepper, thinly sliced
16 ripe tomatoes
handful chopped fresh basil
3 tablespoons tomato paste
½ pint (300 ml) red wine
salt and pepper

Sauté the garlic and onion in oil until soft. Add pepper strips and cook until soft. Cut each of 6 tomatoes into 8, and puré the rest. Add all the tomato, basil, tomato paste and wine. Season and continue to simmer for a few minutes till it just begins to thicken.

ITALIAN DRESSING

Try this spooned over piping hot, lightly steamed vegetables – it's magic with asparagus!

4 large cloves garlic
2 tomatoes, roughly chopped
3 fl oz (75 ml) red wine vinegar
8½ fl oz (250 ml) olive oil
8½ fl oz (250 ml) natural yogurt
1 tablespoon lemon juice
1 tablespoon tomato paste
2 tablespoons fresh oregano, or
1 tablespoon dried
1 teaspoon salt
½ teaspoon freshly ground black pepper
2 teaspoons celery seed
½ teacup finely chopped parsley

First process the garlic, then add tomatoes and process to a coarse purée. Add the next 5 ingredients and process until everything is well blended and smooth.

Add the oregano and the seasonings and whizz briefly. Add parsley last of all and process until evenly distributed.

SALADS

Illustrations by Jessica Jenkins

CURRIED LENTIL, WILD RICE AND BARLEY SALAD

This spicy salad is an unusual combination of a pulse with two different types of grain. Serve as an accompaniment to an Indian inspired meal or as part of a salad selection.

8 tablespoons currants
8 tablespoons dry sherry

8½ fl oz (250 ml) pot barley
7 fl oz (200 ml) wild rice
8½ fl oz (250 ml) green lentils
1 small onion, very finely chopped

4 tablespoons sunflower oil
8 tablespoons white wine vinegar
1 tablespoon freshly ground cumin
2 teaspoons mustard powder
2 teaspoons freshly ground coriander seeds
1 teaspoon sugar
½ teaspoon each turmeric, paprika, ground mace and freshly ground cardamom
large pinch each cinnamon, ground cloves and cayenne

8 tablespoons toasted flaked almonds
4 tablespoons fine chopped parsley

Put the currants into a bowl, pour the sherry over and stand in a warm place to plump up for at least 2 hours.

Cook the barley, wild rice and lentils in separate pans of boiling water. Try to have everything ready at the same time. The barley will take about 40 minutes, the rice about 30 and the lentils about 20. Keep testing for doneness and as soon as just cooked, drain and turn into a big bowl. Add the onion and the plumped currants.

While the grains and lentils are cooking, make the dressing by shaking all the dressing ingredients together in a screw top jar. Dress the grain mixture while still warm then cool and refrigerate for several hours.

When ready to serve, stir in the almonds and parsley.

OUR FAVOURITE POTATO SALAD

This is an alltime winner with staff and guests alike. The tartness of the pickles is offset by the mild sweetness of the apple jelly. Try using capers or dill pickles in place of the gherkins, and for a less robust flavour substituting snipped spring onion tops for the red onion.

2¼ lb (1kg) baby new potatoes
2 tablespoons red wine vinegar
2 tablespoons olive oil
1 teaspoon each salt, pepper and sugar
4 hardboiled eggs, sliced
8 tablespoons gherkins, sliced
2 tablespoons fine chopped red onion
8-12 fl oz (250-350 ml) «mayonnaise»
2 tablespoons apple and thyme or apple and sage jelly
8 tablespoons finely chopped parsley

Steam the potatoes till just tender. Drain, and when cool enough to handle, cut into bite-sized slices. Toss immediately with the vinegar, oil, salt, pepper and sugar.

Allow to cool completely then cover with the eggs, gherkins and chopped onion. Do not stir.

Thoroughly blend the mayonnaise with the jelly and gently fold into the potato mix so that everything is well coated. Refrigerate for at least 2 hours then adjust the seasoning as required.

Gently stir in the parsley to serve.

HUNGARIAN POTATO SALAD

This is a strongly flavoured late season salad, using maincrop potatoes. It must be started the day before required. Take particular care not to over cook the potatoes.

3 lb (1½ kg) waxy maincrop potatoes
8 tablespoons red wine vinegar
4 teaspoons sugar
2 tablespoons cumin seeds
1 tablespoons caraway seeds
2 tablespoons poppy seeds

3 tablespoons capers
8½ fl oz (250 ml) soured cream
8 tablespoons set natural yogurt
salt and pepper
3 tablespoons fine chopped fresh dill, or 4 teaspoons dried dill weed

Have ready a large shallow mixing bowl. Cut the potatoes into equal sized large pieces and steam until just pierceable with a fork. Drain and slice immediately. Divide the slices into 4 roughly equal piles. Working quickly, spread one of the piles in a rough layer over the base of the bowl. Sprinkle with a quarter of the vinegar, sugar and seeds. Repeat with the remaining three piles. Cover the bowl with clingfilm and refrigerate overnight.

Next day add the capers. Blend the soured cream with the yogurt and stir into the marinated potatoes. Check the seasoning, adding a little salt or pepper if necessary. Pile into a serving bowl and sprinkle with the chopped dill.

GREEK SALAD

Serve this salad with a bowl of «baked tomato soup», a loaf of crusty bread and a bottle of chilled white wine for a superb summer evening meal.

6 fl oz (175 ml) Greek extra virgin olive oil
6 fl oz (175 ml) sunflower oil
8 tablespoons lemon juice
1 teaspoon each salt and pepper
2 teaspoons strong wholegrain mustard
1 teaspoon ground ginger
3 cloves garlic, crushed
9 oz (250 gm) young green beans, topped and cut into thirds
9 oz (250 gm) cherry tomatoes
6 fl oz (175 ml) stoneless black olives
1 cucumber, cut into ½ inch (1 cm) cubes
3 oz (175 gm) feta cheese, in ½ inch (1 cm) cubes
3 oz (80 gm) pine nuts, toasted to light gold
leaves from 1 bunch of basil, roughly torn

Start with the dressing. Put the first 7 ingredients into a clean 1 lb (450 gm) coffee jar (or similar) with a screw top. Replace the lid tightly and shake until the dressing is thick and creamy.

Steam the beans for about 5 minutes. until just cooked but still crunchy. Drain immediately and stir up with the dressing. Prick each tomato 2 or 3 times with a fork and add to the beans. Stir in the olives and refrigerate for several hours.

Toss with the rest of the ingredients just before serving.

GREEN SALAD

The easiest of salads? No, in many ways the most challenging. Simply because there can be no specific formula.

A successful green salad depends first of all on the freshest leaves and herbs available. We gather all our salad leaves and accent herbs from our Avebury gardens each morning before the dew has quite dried! The varieties we grow are carefully chosen for year round contrasts in flavour, colour and texture.

Bear these contrasts in mind when you are picking or shopping for salad greens. Look for delicate red brown Oak Leaf, for curly green or red Lollo Rosso, more robust Continuity shading from palest emerald to deep ruby, and slightly bitter Radiccio with its winedark cup shaped leaves. Mingle these red varieties with the soft spring foliage of Tom Thumb or Butter lettuce, and later on in the season with lofty Endive or flavoursome Romaine.

Accent your leaf selection with sprigs of delicately flavoured seasonal herbs. We use peppery rocket or nasturtium leaves, fragrant lemon balm, feathery chervil, golden and green marjoram, savory and white or purple flowering thyme. In full summer add chive blossoms, marigold petals or vibrant orange and scarlet nasturtium flowers.

Carefully wash and dry your salad leaves tearing (never cut) any large ones into bite sized pieces. Arrange leaves and accents in a wide shallow serving bowl. Dress only with a drizzle of walnut or hazelnut oil, a sprinkle of lemon juice and a little salt. Toss gently just to coat the leaves and serve immediately.

MATCHSTICK SLAW WITH RED LEICESTER

This is an interesting variation on standard coleslaw. Instead of cabbage we use celeriac (for a summer version, you can use thin diagonally sliced celery or young courgettes) and Red Leicester cheese replaces the ubiquitous carrot. All the ingredients are cut into julienne sticks (about 3 times the thickness of a standard matchstick) rather than grated, so the salad won't go soggy. Apple and horseradish add sparkle!

lemon juice (to prevent discolouration)
1 largish celeriac (about 1¼ lb/600 gm)
2 large or 3 medium Cox apples
2 tablespoons lemon juice
9 oz (250 gm) Red Leicester cheese
8 tablespoons «mayonnaise»
1 tablespoon honey mustard (available at speciality shops)
3 tablespoons prepared horseradish and dill (available at speciality shops)

Have ready a bowl of cold water to which a good splash of lemon juice has been added. Peel the celeriac and with a very sharp knife cut into matchsticks. Put the matchsticks into the water.

Core the apples and cut these into matchsticks too. Put into a separate large bowl and sprinkle with the 2 tablespoons lemon juice.

Cut the cheese into similar sticks and add to the apples. Drain the celeriac well and add to the apples and cheese.

Mix all the dressing ingredients together and stir into the salad. Check to see if salt and pepper are needed before serving.

BROCCOLI & CAULIFLOWER WITH SMOKED CAERPHILLY

1 large cauliflower
1 bunch broccoli, about 2 large compact heads
2½ oz (150 gm) cashew halves, toasted to golden brown
210 oz (75 gm) smoked Caerphilly cheese, cut into ¼ inch (½ cm) cubes
2 tablespoons wholegrain mustard
8-12 fl oz (250-350 ml) «mayonnaise», made with lemon juice, not vinegar

Bring a large pan of water to the boil. Have ready a large bowl of iced water.

Break the cauliflower and broccoli into tiny florets no more than 1 inch/2cm in diameter. Discard the cauliflower stalk but reserve the broccoli stalks. Peel these stalks with a sharp knife and thinly slice the fleshy interior. Blanche the florets and stalk slices for 30 seconds in the rapidly boiling water. Drain and immediately refresh in the iced water. Turn into a big mixing bowl.

Stir in the toasted nuts and the cheese cubes. Mix the mustard with the mayonnaise and fold into the salad to coat everything generously.

MINTED BULGAR

Bulgar, or cracked wheat requires no cooking or lengthy soaking, making it a very convenient base for a quick salad. This one is Moroccan inspired. Make it in summer when garden mint, parsley and naturally ripened tomatoes are plentiful.

12 fl oz (350 ml) bulgar wheat
boiling water
3 fl oz (75 ml) lemon juice
2 tablespoons light soya sauce

1 bunch spring onions, thinly sliced (both green and white parts)
4 fat cloves garlic, crushed
3 tablespoons olive oil
3 tablespoons sunflower oil
1 teaspoon pepper
6 large, firm, ripe tomatoes, chopped medium fine
1¼ pints (750 ml) flat leaved parsley, roughly chopped
8 fl oz (250 ml) mint leaves, roughly chopped
3½ oz (100 gm) peanuts, toasted till just brown

Put the bulgar into a shallow bowl and pour over enough boiling water just to moisten. There should be no standing water. Add the lemon juice and soya sauce, stir well and leave to stand for 20 minutes. The texture should be crunchy but chewable. If too dry add a tiny bit more water and leave to stand for a further 5 minutes.

Add the rest of the ingredients. Mix well and refrigerate for 1 hour for the flavours to merge. To serve, check the seasoning and add salt, and extra pepper and lemon juice if required.

ORIENTAL MAGIC

This is a strong, full flavoured salad and best served alone rather than as part of a buffet combination. Pair with a bowl of plain steamed brown rice for a simple and delicious summer supper. Take particular care when cutting the vegetables and fruit, the contrasting shapes are as essential to this salad as the crunch of the water chestnuts!

small knob fresh ginger, peeled
2 large cloves garlic, peeled
2 tablespoons lemon juice
1 tablespoon rice wine vinegar
2 tablespoons sunflower oil
1 tablespoon toasted sesame oil
2 tablespoons dry sherry
1 tablespoon clear honey
2 tablespoons tamari
½ teaspoon Chinese 5 spice
½ teaspoon white pepper

9 oz (250 gm) block firm original tofu
1 tablespoon toasted sesame oil
1 tablespoon tamari

1 large or 2 small red peppers, seeded and cut into thin strips
1 small green pepper, seeded and cut into thin strips
3 oz (175 gm) mushrooms (preferably brown) sliced vertically
4½ oz (125 gm) baby corn, sliced lengthwise into 4
1 bunch radishes, trimmed and sliced into thin rounds
½ lb (225 gm) can water chestnuts,
drained and sliced into thick rounds
½ medium pineapple, cut into ½ inch (1 cm) dice
2 small courgettes, quartered lengthwise then very thinly sliced diagonally
generous handful mung bean or lentil sprouts

Process the ginger and garlic together then add the next 9 ingredients. Process till well blended and set aside. Any unused dressing will keep for up to a week refrigerated.

Cut the tofu into ½ inch (1 cm) cubes. Heat the sesame oil in a shallow frypan till just beginning to smoke. Add the tofu and the tamari and fry on high heat until all the liquid has been absorbed and the tofu is nicely browned. Allow to cool.

Put all the prepared vegetables and fruit except the bean sprouts into a large bowl. Add the tofu and stir in enough dressing to coat generously. Refrigerate for 1 hour. Check the seasoning, adding a little salt if necessary. Serve with the bean sprouts on top.

SMOKY SPINACH SALAD

A perfect appetizer for a late spring supper when new season spinach has just grown big enough to cut. Equally good served chilled as part of a buffet selection.

9 oz (250gm) baby spinach leaves, or spinach thinnings
1 large Cox or Granny Smith apple
1 teaspoon lemon juice
2 teaspoons currants
2 teaspoons olive oil
1 teaspoon lemon juice
1 teaspoon strong wholegrain mustard
½ teaspoon each salt and pepper
9 oz (250gm) packet smoked tofu
2 tablespoons olive oil
1 tablespoon paprika
½ teaspoon freshly ground dried chillis, or ½ teaspoon cayenne pepper
3 tablespoons flaked almonds, toasted till golden

Wash and dry the spinach leaves, discarding any stalky bits, and put in a large bowl. Quarter and core the apple, slice into thin half moons and toss with the lemon juice. Add to the spinach. Stir in the currants.

Beat together the oil, lemon juice, mustard, salt and pepper and stir into the spinach mix to coat everything thoroughly.

Cube the tofu into small bite pieces and toss in a bowl with the oil, paprika and chilli. Heat a dry frypan and fry the tofu, stirring all the time until brown on all sides.

Toss with the spinach mixture and serve immediately sprinkled with the toasted almonds.

MEDITERRANEAN PASTA WITH PARMESAN

Naturally coloured tricolore pasta shapes studded with herbs, emerald beans and purple black olives evoke memories of many a balmy Mediterranean sunset. Only genuine Parmigiano-reggiano will do for this recipe and splurge on the very best olives, oil and vinegar you can find, it's worth it!

9 oz (250 gm) pasta spirals or shells (preferably tricolore)
7 fl oz (200 ml) Italian extra virgin olive oil
3 fl oz (75 ml) top quality red wine vinegar
1 teaspoon each salt and pepper
1 teaspoon strong wholegrain mustard
1 teaspoon freshly ground coriander seeds
2 large cloves garlic, crushed
9 oz (250 gm) young French beans, topped and halved
2 red peppers, seeded and cut into ¼ inch (½ cm) cubes
2 oz (50 gm) pimento stuffed olives, sliced into thirds
3½ oz (100 gm) whole large black olives
8 tablespoons coarsely chopped flat leaved parsley
2½ oz (75 gm) freshly grated Parmesan
1 tablespoon poppy seeds

Cook the pasta to just 'al dente' in lots of fast boiling water to which a dash of olive oil has been added. Drain and refresh immediately under running cold water. Transfer to a large bowl.

While the pasta is cooking make the dressing. Put the oil, vinegar and seasonings into a screw top jar and shake vigorously with the lid in place.

Steam the beans for about 4 minutes until barely tender and still crunchy. Drain and while still hot tip into another bowl and coat with some of the dressing. Allow to get cold then add to the pasta.

Stir in the peppers and both types of olive. Moisten everything well with dressing and chill for 1 hour.

To serve, stir in the parsley, Parmesan and poppy seeds and make a final check on the seasoning.

CAESAR SALAD

This salad is extremely popular all over north America, where it is almost invariably made with Romaine, a delicious long leaved lettuce, similar in appearance to an English Cos. It took us ages to get the dressing just right, but here is the formula, at last! It makes enough for 2 salads, and will keep for 2-3 days refrigerated. For a blue cheese Caesar, replace the Cheddar with a not too strong blue cheese such as Dolcelatte. For a totally non-authentic, but nevertheless delicious Caesar, replace half of the Cheddar with crumbled mature blue Stilton!

4 day-old bread rolls
2 oz (55 gm) butter
2 tablespoons olive oil
3 cloves garlic
1 egg
6 fl oz (160 ml) olive oil
3 fl oz (80 ml) white wine vinegar
2½ oz (75 gm) golden granulated sugar
1 teaspoon mustard powder
1 teaspoon salt
1 teaspoon dried marjoram or oregano
1 tablespoon tamari
1 tablespoon lemon juice
dash of Tabasco
3½ oz (100 gm) Cheddar, grated
1 or 2 Cos lettuces, or enough for 8 people

First make the croûtons. Trim the bread rolls and cut into neat ½ inch (1½ cm) cubes. You need about 18 oz (500 gm) bread cubes in all. Put into a bowl. Melt the butter with the olive oil, and pour over the bread cubes, stirring gently to coat as many as possible without breaking them up. Arrange the buttered cubes in a single layer on one or more lipped baking sheets, and bake in a slow oven, shaking occasionally, until they are crispy. Cool before adding to the salad.

Meanwhile, make the dressing. Process the garlic, then add the next 7 ingredients to the processor bowl. Process until thick, and scrape out into a large mixing bowl. Stir in the tamari and lemon juice, and the Tabasco. Finally, fold in the cheese. Refrigerate the dressing until ready to use.

Tear the well-washed trimmed lettuces into bite sized pieces, and toss with the cooked croûtons. Toss with just enough dressing to coat everything. Serve as soon as possible so that the croûtons stay crisp.

the pasta when ready and immediately refresh under cold running water. Tip into a mixing bowl. Add the citrus fruits and the prepared peppers and stir well.

Put all the dressing ingredients into a big screw top jar and shake well. Dress the salad generously and refrigerate for at least 1 hour.

Immediately before serving check the seasoning and stir in the roughly torn marjoram leaves.

SPICED POTATO SALAD

Serve this to accompany curried vegetables. It looks stunning set on a bed of deep red radiccio leaves.

3 tablespoons walnut oil
2 teaspoons cumin seeds
2 teaspoons brown mustard seeds
1 teaspoon fenugreek seeds
3 medium onions, finely diced
2 stalks celery, finely sliced
1 tablespoon turmeric
½ teaspoon cayenne pepper
2 teaspoons freshly ground coriander seeds
3¼ lb (1½ kg) small, flavourful new potatoes
4 heaped tablespoons top quality mango chutney
2 tablespoons lemon juice
about 8½ fl oz (250 ml) set natural yogurt
handful snipped chives

GOLDEN PASTA

A sharp and refreshing citrus drenched pasta salad with a hint of spice. Try to use golden marjoram rather than the more usual green for the sake of the colour palette. It's very easy to grow!

9 oz (250 gm) penne with basil
1 large orange
1 grapefruit
2 yellow peppers, seeded and cut into narrow strips
2 orange peppers, seeded and cut into narrow strips

8½ fl oz (250 m) olive oil
8 tablespoons (125 ml) cider vinegar
reserved juice from citrus fruits
½ teaspoon cayenne pepper
1 teaspoon freshly ground coriander
1 teaspoon freshly ground cumin seeds
1 teaspoon each salt and pepper
4 fl oz (100 ml) loosely packed golden marjoram leaves

Cook the pasta until just 'al dente' in a large pan of rapidly boiling water to which a dash of olive oil has been added to prevent sticking. Meanwhile, peel, segment, seed and roughly chop the orange and grapefruit, reserving the juice that comes out (a chopping board with a groove all round is easiest for this). Drain

Heat the walnut oil in a large frypan until just beginning to smoke. Toss in the cumin, mustard and fenugreek seeds and fry till the mustard seeds begin to pop. Stir in the onion and celery and fry for 3 minutes. Stir in the remaining spices and take off the heat.

Steam the potatoes until just tender. Drain well and cut any stray large ones into bite sized pieces. While the potatoes are still hot toss with the spiced onion mixture. Allow to cool slightly then stir in the chutney, juice and enough yogurt to coat generously. Refrigerate for at least 1 hour.

Just before serving, check the seasoning and stir in the chives.

SALADE NIÇOISE

Fresh asparagus makes this salad extra special, but can be omitted when out of season. Try other mild cheeses instead of Caerphilly. This is sufficiently substantial to serve as a main course with crusty bread and a good French wine.

9 fl oz (225 ml) white wine vinegar
3 fl oz (75 ml) olive oil
2 large cloves garlic, crushed
1 teaspoon yellow mustard seed
2 teaspoons strong coarse grained mustard
1 teaspoon salt
½ teaspoon pepper

1 bunch watercress, chopped
small handful fresh basil, chopped
small handful fresh flat leaved parsley, chopped
10-12 tiny salad potatoes (eg La Ratte)
4 oz (110 gm) young French beans
5 oz (125 gm) fine asparagus
a few crisp green lettuce leaves (not Iceberg!)
4 tomatoes, each cut into 6 wedges
8 hard boiled eggs, cut into quarters lengthwise
4 oz (110 gm) pitted black olives
4 oz (110 gm) Caerphilly cheese, cut into ½ inch (1 cm) cubes

For the dressing, combine the vinegar and oil in a large bowl, and whisk in the garlic, mustards and seasoning. Stir in the herbs.

Steam the potatoes till just tender. Slice while hot and stir into the dressing. Steam and refresh the beans and asparagus, and add to the dressed potatoes, stirring gently to coat. Refrigerate until ready to serve.

Arrange the lettuce leaves in a shallow serving bowl. With a slotted spoon, remove the vegetables from the dressing, and put them on the lettuce bed. Arrange the tomato and egg wedges on top and scatter with the olives and cheese. Pour the remaining dressing over everything.

TOMATO, FRESH BASIL & HERBED CHEESE SALAD

A simple olive oil and red wine vinegar dressing can be used for this salad, but «Italian dressing» provides a more exciting touch. Sliced fresh buffalo mozzarella is a good alternative to the herbed cheese. Serve with any type of pasta dish, as a starter or as an appropriate accompaniment to any Mediterranean meal.

8 tomatoes
8 oz (225 gm) herbed cheese (eg Teifi with chives)
large handful fresh basil, chopped

Slice tomatoes in four horizontally, and slice the cheese into thin rectangular pieces of a similar size to the tomatoes. Arrange these alternately over a shallow dish. Scatter the basil over and drizzle with the dressing.

CHICORY, GRAPEFRUIT & WALNUT SALAD

Here made with balsamic dressing: «green aïoli» is good as a dressing too. This is particularly nice served on a bed of crisp, dark green lettuce leaves mixed with radiccio.

4 heads chicory
2 grapefruit
8 oz (225 gm) toasted walnut halves
2 fl oz (50 ml) balsamic wine vinegar
2 fl oz (50 ml) lemon juice
2 fl oz (50 ml) sunflower oil
½ teaspoon salt
1 heaped tablespoon chopped chives

Slice chicory. Peel and slice grapefruit. Mix both with walnuts.

Whisk together all the dressing ingredients and coat the salad thoroughly (stir in well). Serve immediately after dressing as chicory tends to go translucent if left for any time.

PEAR, CHICORY AND STILTON SALAD WITH TARRAGON MUSTARD VINAIGRETTE

Pears and Stilton were created for each other and this pungent salad makes a stunning appetizer for an early autumn dinner party. Only use chicory in prime condition as chicory past its prime tends to be overly bitter. Fresh French tarragon leaves are essential here. A single supermarket package is well worth the expense.

3 tablespoons olive oil
4 tablespoons tarragon vinegar
2 teaspoons sugar
1 teaspoon coarse grained mustard
½ teaspoon each salt and pepper
1 small red onion, very finely chopped
4 small to medium heads chicory, root ends trimmed
1 tablespoon lemon juice
3 large, firm, ripe pears
3 oz (75 gm) pecan halves, toasted
4 oz (200 gm) Stilton, hand crumbled
leaves from 1 bunch fresh tarragon, finely chopped
seedless black grapes (optional)

Beat all the dressing ingredients together in a bowl until thick and creamy. Fold in the fine chopped onion.

Slice the chicory thinly crosswise, put into a larger bowl and sprinkle with the lemon juice. Core and quarter the pears, slice into thin moons and add to the chicory. Stir in the nuts, Stilton and tarragon and moisten everything with the dressing. Serve garnished with small clusters of seedless grapes for maximum visual impact.

FENNEL AND ORANGE SALAD

A refreshing summer salad with subtly different peppery accents.

2-3 small fennel bulbs (about 18 oz/500gms)
1 tablespoon lemon juice
2 small red onions
2 oranges
bunch of fresh mint (small handful of leaves)
3 tablespoons olive oil
2 tablespoons fresh orange juice
2 tablespoons tarragon vinegar
1 tablespoon coriander seeds, pan toasted till smelling toasty
1 teaspoon salt
1/2 teaspoon pepper
1 bunch watercress, leaves only

Trim the root end and stalky bits off the fennel, setting aside the feathery tops. Thinly slice crosswise and toss with the lemon juice. Peel and quarter the red onions and thinly slice. Peel, seed and slice the oranges, and cut each slice into quarters. Mix the prepared fennel, onions and fruit with the mint leaves in a large bowl. In another bowl beat together the oil, orange juice and vinegar. Grind the coriander seeds in a coffee grinder or with a pestle and mortar and add to the dressing mix with the salt and pepper. Toss the salad with the dressing.

SOUPS & APPETIZERS

Illustrations by Karen Goddard

POTATO & BLUE CHEESE GNOCCHI

Gnocchi, little dumplings originating in Italy can be made from quite a range of basic ingredients. We have made gnocchi with semolina, spinach and cream cheese, choux paste, and as in this recipe - potatoes. Gnocchi are generally poached in a simmering broth and then served with a sauce, or drained and baked with lots of butter and cheese.

Although not exactly Italian, these are brilliant made with Stilton. Use Dolcelatte for the authentic touch. Serve warm with a topping of «rich tomato sauce» and garnish with toasted halved walnuts.

18 oz (500 gm) floury potatoes, eg Maris Piper
1 tablespoon olive oil
2 teaspoons salt
1 teaspoon pepper
4 eggs, well beaten
5 oz (150 gm) blue cheese, grated
10 oz (300 gm) wholewheat flour
4-5 pints (2-3 l) stock

Cut the potatoes into even sized pieces and boil till soft. Drain and return to the dry pan to evaporate any excess moisture. Mash in the pan with the olive oil, salt and pepper. Mix in the eggs, then the cheese, then work in the flour. The mixture will be stiff but still slightly sticky. Turn out onto a lightly floured board and knead briefly until smooth. The mix will still be a bit sticky, but don't be tempted to add more flour. Wrap in cling film and chill for 1 hour.

Bring the stock gently to boil. Meanwhile, set out your stand. Throw a handful of flour into a large plastic bowl (for flouring hands) and lightly dust a clean tray with flour. Take potato mix from fridge, flour hands and pick up a lump the size of a walnut. Roll into a ball and put on the prepared tray. Continue until all mix is gone, flouring hands repeatedly, and you have about 30-36 gnocchi.

Drop the little dumplings, about 12 at a time, into the boiling stock. More will reduce the stock temperature too much and cause havoc with the cooking time. When the very first precocious gnocchi has risen to the surface, start timing. 5 minutes later remove all the gnocchi with a slotted spoon and keep warm, whilst you cook the rest in similar fashion. Make sure the stock is boiling before adding the subsequent batches.

CREAM OF SORREL SOUP

Sorrel is similar to spinach in appearance, but has a different and stronger flavour. We grow lots of sorrel. Being a perennial, it continues to produce quantities of useful leaves after our spinach has gone to sleep for the winter. This recipe can be varied according to what leafy green vegetables you have available. Substitute spinach for sorrel or use half of each. Exchange some or all of the sorrel with savoy cabbage or curly kale. Sorrel and ruby chard make another excellent combination!

2 onions, roughly chopped
4-6 large cloves garlic, crushed
2 tablespoons olive oil
½ teaspoon grated nutmeg
1 tablespoon caraway seed
4 potatoes, roughly chopped
1 pint (500 ml) dry white wine
2 pints (1 l) light stock (2 teaspoons vegetable concentrate in boiling water)
18 oz (500 gm) sorrel leaves, stalks & ribs removed

8½ fl oz (250 ml) cottage cheese
8 tablespoons soured cream
salt and pepper

Cook onions and garlic gently with the oil for 10 minutes, covered, stirring occasionally. Add nutmeg, caraway and potatoes, and stir so everything is thoroughly mixed. Add wine and bring to the boil, uncovered. Add the stock, replace the lid and simmer until the potatoes are tender. Remove from the heat and stir in the sorrel. Cool slightly, then puré.

Blend together the cottage cheese and soured cream, and beat this into the soup. Season, and reheat gently to serve. Do not boil.

BAKED TOMATO SOUP

Use only rich, red, very ripe tomatoes for this recipe. Garden ripened are best. Fresh herbs will give the better flavour, but dried still make a yummy soup! Crème fraîche can be substituted for fromage frais.

1 extra large onion, finely chopped
4 fat cloves garlic, finely sliced
2 lb (900 gm) ripe tomatoes, halved
3 tablespoons finely chopped fresh oregano
(or 1 tablespoon dried)
12 sprigs basil, leaves only, roughly torn
(or 1 tablespoon dried)
1 teaspoon each salt and freshly ground
black pepper
1½ tablespoons olive oil
8 tablespoons red wine
1½ pints (850 ml) stock
8 tablespoons tomato paste
6 oz (170 gm) fromage frais
basil sprigs or chopped parsley to garnish

Scatter the onion and garlic over the base of a clean, dry roasting pan. Put the tomatoes, cut side down, on top of the onion and scatter with the herbs. Sprinkle with the seasonings and drizzle everything with the olive oil. Bake in a very hot (225°) oven for about 20 minutes until the tomatoes are soft and their skins beginning to blacken.

Remove from the oven and scrape everything into a processor or blender. Do this in batches if necessary. Blend to a smooth purée. Put this into a large, clean pan, and add the wine, stock and tomato paste. Whisk well to combine and reheat gently on the stove top. When the soup reaches simmering point whisk in the fromage frais, and serve garnished with the basil or parsley.

CURRIED GOLDEN COURGETTE SOUP

2 oz (55 gm) vegetable ghee
1 tablespoon cumin seed
1 large onion, finely chopped
3 cloves garlic, crushed
3 large yellow courgettes
½ teaspoon cayenne pepper
1 heaped teaspoon freshly ground
coriander
1 teaspoon garam masala
1 tablespoon turmeric
3 tablespoons lemon juice
1¾ pints (1 l) stock
salt and pepper
4 oz (110 gm) creamed coconut

Heat ghee and place cumin seeds into the hot liquid. Allow the seeds to pop before adding the onion and garlic. Cook gently until soft. Then cut courgettes into half moons and sauté in the same pan. Add the cayenne, coriander, garam masala and turmeric, and coat the courgettes thoroughly. Add lemon juice and stock, and cook soup until the courgettes are soft and flavours are fully developed. Season to taste.

Blend the creamed coconut to a smooth paste with a little warm water, and stir thoroughly into the soup just before serving.

TOMATO, APPLE & CREAM CHEESE SOUP

This is a bright and cheerful soup, very popular with our younger guests!

1 onion
4 dessert apples, cored
12 tomatoes
1¾ pints (1 l) stock
handful chopped parsley
2 tablespoons tomato paste
3 tablespoons cream cheese
salt and pepper

Chop the onion, slice the apples and quarter the tomatoes. Place into a pan with the stock and bring to the boil. Then simmer on a very low heat to release all the flavours. The tomatoes and apples will become very soft.

Add the parsley and tomato paste and stir in thoroughly. Puré all the ingredients then return to the pan and over a low heat, add the cream cheese and allow it to melt slowly. Season the soup before serving with salt and freshly ground black pepper.

CANADIAN SPLIT PEA WITH RED WINE

Again, the flavours in this soup are best appreciated if it is made the day before required, refrigerated overnight and reheated to serve.

12 oz (350 gm) green split peas
12 oz (350 gm) onions, finely chopped
4 carrots, finely chopped (preferably in a processor)
a few bay leaves
2½ pints (1½ l) stock
1½ teaspoons freshly ground allspice berries
small bunch fresh thyme, tied with string (or 1 teaspoon dried)
6 tomatoes, roughly chopped
8 tablespoons red wine
2 tablespoons maple syrup
3 tablespoons red wine vinegar

Put the first seven ingredients into a lidded soup pot and bring gently to the boil. Simmer for 20 minutes.

Add the tomatoes and wine, and simmer 20 minutes more, or until the peas are very soft. Remove from heat, cool and refrigerate. The next day, remove the fresh thyme, if used, and reheat gently with the maple syrup and vinegar stirred in.

ROAST SWEET POTATO, CELERY & APPLE SOUP

Roasting the sweet potatoes first gives this soup an unusual nutty taste. It is best made the day before required to allow the flavours to intensify. Good to take in a flask on a winter walk, or serve in steaming mugfuls round the bonfire!

4 sweet potatoes (c 1¾ lb/800 gm)
salt
2 oz (50 gm) margarine
2 onions, roughly chopped
5 or 6 sticks celery, roughly sliced
2 teaspoons freshly ground coriander
1 teaspoon freshly ground allspice
3 tart eating apples, cored and sliced
2¼ pints (1300 ml) stock

Scrub the potatoes and stab liberally with a fork. Rub the skins all over with salt and bake at 200° for 45 minutes, until soft.

Meanwhile melt the margarine and sauté the onion and celery with the spices until the onion is transparent. Add the apple and stock. Roughly chop the roast sweet potato and add to the pan. Cover with a tight fitting lid and simmer for about 30 minutes, or until everything is soft. Process to a smooth texture, then cool rapidly and refrigerate, covered, overnight. Reheat gently to serve.

PATÉ TRICOLORE

Broccoli, cauliflower and red peppers give this paté the colours of the Italian flag. It makes a wonderful cold starter, served thinly sliced with «roast pepper relish» on the side: or serve warm in a little pool of sieved «rich tomato sauce» or «golden tomato sauce».

8 oz (225 gm) broccoli
1 teaspoon dried dill weed
1 teaspoon dried thyme
handful fresh chopped parsley
2 oz (55 gm) Cheddar, grated
½ teaspoon salt
2 eggs, beaten
8 oz (225 gm) cauliflower
¼ pint (150 ml) milk

1 teaspoon grated nutmeg
2 oz (55 gm) cream cheese
½ teaspoon salt
2 eggs, beaten

2 red peppers
2 cloves garlic
2 oz (55 gm) onion, very finely chopped
2 tablespoons tomato paste
½ teaspoon salt
½ teaspoon paprika
2 eggs, beaten

Prepare the mixes for each layer in turn. First, steam the broccoli until crisp-tender. Puré. Add the rest of the ingredients and mix well.

Next cook the cauliflower in the milk with the nutmeg. Puré with the cooking milk. Add the other ingredients and mix well.

Last, roast the peppers whole in the oven until soft and dark – about 15-20 minutes. Take them out and put into a paper bag until they are cool enough to handle. Remove the skin and pips, and puré the flesh. Mix in the rest of the ingredients.

Take a 2 lb (1 kg) loaf tin and line well with baking parchment. Pour in the broccoli mix. Very carefully spoon cauliflower mix over, keeping them separate. Top with the pepper mix. Cover with another piece of parchment, then seal with foil. Bake at 160° for 1½ hours. If you are serving warm, leave to stand for a few minutes to set properly, or cool completely in the tin.

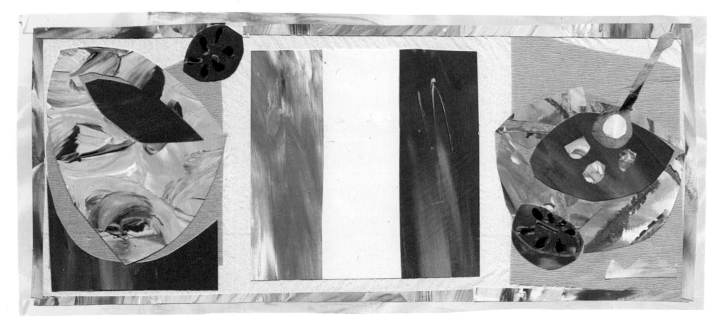

MIDSUMMER PEA & ELDERFLOWER SOUP WITH MINT

Make this wonderfully fresh tasting soup at the height of summer, when the elderflower is in blossom and your garden is bursting with young and tender vegetables. It is important to add the mint right at the end of the cooking time to preserve its full flavour and freshness.

2 oz (50 gm) butter
1 onion, chopped
2 potatoes, thinly sliced
4 oz (100 gm) crisp lettuce leaves
6 oz (150 gm) mangetout, weighed after topping
1 teaspoon salt
½ pint (300 ml) elderflower wine
2 pints (1100 ml) stock
9 oz (250 gm) shelled peas
large handful fresh mint leaves
3 fl oz (80 ml) double cream
mint sprigs and elderflowers to garnish

Melt the butter in a lidded pan and gently cook the onion till transparent. Lay the potato slices over the onions and cover with the lettuce leaves. Scatter the mangetout over the lettuce. Sprinkle with the salt and pour the wine over. Cover tightly and cook on very low heat for 15 minutes.

Add the stock and simmer, still covered, 15 minutes longer. Uncover and add the peas and mint and cook for a further 5 minutes. Cool slightly, then process till smooth. Return to the pan, add the cream, and reheat gently (do not boil). Serve garnished with sprigs of mint and elderflowers broken into florets.

PAN BAGNA

For our tenth anniversary celebratory evening openings we made up our normal «magic bread» mixture into half sized rolls, and topped them with a knob of dough. When taken to the tables they looked like a troop of little snowmen! Snowmen appear here in our version of this snack dish, popular along the Côte d'Azur. They make an unusual starter for a light summer meal (perhaps a frittata with a green salad?). They are ideal for picnics and can also be served with a smooth soup (eg «leek & avocado soup with lime») for a perfect simple lunch or supper. Regular rolls can be used instead of snowmen, but they do add an unusual touch.

1 quantity «magic bread», rolled into 12 snowmen and baked at 160° for about 15 minutes

large bunch parsley, chopped
2-3 cloves garlic, crushed

2 tablespoons lemon juice
3 tablespoons olive oil
salt and pepper

3½ oz (100 gm) pitted black olives, roughly chopped or halved
3 red peppers, roasted, skinned and cut into squares
6 tomatoes, seeded and roughly chopped
2 tablespoons capers
bunch watercress, roughly chopped (leaves only)
3-4 oz (75-100 gm) freshly grated Parmesan cheese

When bread rolls are cold, cut in half cross-wise and remove the middles to leave a ½ inch (1 cm) shell.

Process the parsley, garlic, lemon juice and a quarter of the bread middles (save the rest for breadcrumbs), and with the processor still running, stream in the olive oil. Season and reserve: this is your dressing.

Gently stir together the prepared olives, peppers, tomatoes, capers, cress and Parmesan to make the filling.

Mix half the dressing into the filling, and spread the rest over the insides of the hollowed rolls. Spoon in the filling and reassemble. Wrap each roll in foil, and refrigerate several hours or overnight, so the flavours can develop. Serve cold.

CAULIFLOWER & CUMIN SOUP

This is a delicate and delicious soup. For a more substantial version, cook a couple of chopped medium potatoes in the stock along with the cauliflower.

2 tablespoons soft margarine
1 tablespoon cumin seed
1 onion, chopped
1½ lb (700 gm) cauliflower florets
1 tablespoon ground cumin
1¾ pints (1 l) stock
salt and pepper

Heat margarine. When hot, add the cumin seeds and allow them to open and release their flavour into the margarine. Then add the onion and sauté until transparent. Add to this the cauliflower, ground cumin and stock, and simmer until the cauliflower is cooked. Puré, and season with salt and pepper before serving.

GREEN AÏOLI WITH CRUDITÉS

Crudités served with this gorgeously coloured, rich, garlicky mayonnaise make the perfect starter to a light Mediterranean style meal. Serve the aïoli in a bowl surrounded by a selection of vegetables, such as individual chicory leaves, carrot matchsticks, caulifloretes, celery strips, yellow and red cherry tomatoes with their stems on, cucumber strips or half moons, thinly sliced fennel, kohlrabi matchsticks, whole tiny button mushrooms, radish flowers (soaked in iced water to open), courgettes in matchsticks or diagonal slices.

2 cloves garlic
3 spring onions
handful fresh basil
handful fresh parsley, stalks removed
1 egg
¼ pint (150 ml) olive oil
¼ pint (150 ml) sunflower oil
2 fl oz (50 ml) lemon juice
pinch cayenne pepper
salt and pepper

Process the garlic, then add the spring onions, including all the green parts which help give this aïoli its colour. Add the basil and parsley and process again.

Add the egg to the mixture and set the processor going. Slowly pour in the olive oil and sunflower oil so that a mayonnaise style dressing is formed. Add the lemon juice and continue to process for a few seconds. Remove from the machine and season with a pinch of cayenne and some salt and freshly ground black pepper.

SMOKED CHEESE BLINIS

Also called blintzes, blinis are traditionally made with an egg enriched
yeast dough, fried like American pancakes and served with a topping of
soured cream or crème fraîche. Blinis
can also be made with a regular
pancake batter using buckwheat flour.
Here, they are fried just like crêpes, but
on one side only, then filled and folded
like envelopes, oven baked and served
with soured cream and relish.

1 quantity «buckwheat pancakes»
16 carrots
2 oz (55 gm) butter
1 tablespoon dried dill
1 teaspoon ground nutmeg
salt and pepper
4 eggs, hard boiled
11 oz (310 gm) smoked cheese (eg smoked Caerphilly)

Mix the batter and leave in fridge whilst
preparing the filling.

Chop the carrots into small pieces and
boil until soft enough for mashing. Drain
and mash with the butter, dill, and
nutmeg and season with salt and pepper.
Peel and finely chop the eggs and cube the
smoked cheese into small ½ inch (1 cm)
pieces. The cheese and eggs can then be
stirred into the carrot mixture.

Make pancakes in normal way, but
cook on one side only. Put a spoonful of
carrot mixture in the centre of each of the
uncooked sides, and fold from four directions to make 8 parcels. Use a dab of
water to seal if necessary. Put in a lightly
oiled baking dish and brush the tops with
oil. Cover with foil and bake at 190° for
30 minutes or until heated right through.

Serve with dilled soured cream on top,
and «roast pepper relish» on the side.

MILLET & CHEDDAR WEDGE

This can be eaten hot with vegetables, but we usually serve it as a cold savoury with chutney and a salad. It will keep well in the fridge – ideal for picnics!

1 lb (450 gm) millet seed
1 pint (550 ml) water
1 red pepper
1 onion
2 tablespoons chopped fresh parsley
1 lb (450 gm) Cheddar, grated
1 tablespoon turmeric
1 teaspoon salt
2 tablespoons rhogan josh
4 eggs

Cook the millet in the water until it becomes quite soft, and all water is absorbed. It will still be a little crunchy, but will finish cooking in the oven.

Finely chop or process the red pepper and onion and place into a bowl with the millet and all the other remaining ingredients except the eggs. Beat the eggs and then stir into the mixture and put all into a greased 10 inch (25 cm) flan dish lined with baking parchment. Bake at 160° for approximately 35 minutes, until set and light gold.

PUMPKIN & COCONUT SOUP

1 onion, chopped
2 teaspoons cinnamon
2 teaspoons ground ginger
1 teaspoon freshly ground allspice
½ teaspoon freshly grated nutmeg
2 lb (900 gm) pumpkin, weighed after peeling and seeding, cubed
1¾ pints (1 l) light stock
4 oz (110 gm) creamed coconut

Sauté the onion with all the spices till softening, then add the pumpkin. Cook for 5 minutes. Add stock and bring to the boil. Cut the creamed coconut into pieces and drop into the pan. When coconut melts, take off the heat. Puré the soup when cool, and reheat gently for serving.

CORN, POTATO & PARSLEY CHOWDER

Corn (sweetcorn) is easy to grow, although it does require quite a lot of space. Start it in the greenhouse and plant out when all danger of frost is past. Each plant should yield 3-4 luscious cobs, which should be picked and rushed immediately to the steamer or oven for eating straight from the cob with lots of butter and pepper. This recipe is a good way of using end of season corn (if you have any left, that is), or shop bought sweetcorn, which just isn't the same thing.

1 lb (500 gm) waxy potatoes, scrubbed clean and cut into ¼ inch (½ cm) dice
2 pints (1150 ml) stock
1 large onion, finely chopped
4 fat cloves garlic, crushed
4 large celery sticks, finely sliced
1 each green and red peppers, seeded and diced
14 oz (400 gm) sweetcorn, stripped from the cob
1-2 fresh chillis, seeded and very finely chopped (no more than ½ oz/15 gm before seeding)
1 tablespoon cumin seed
1 tablespoon dried oregano
2 teaspoons dried basil
½ oz (15 gm) butter
½ pint (300 ml) dry white wine
7 fl oz (200 ml) double cream
at least 8 tablespoons finely chopped parsley
salt and pepper

Cook the potatoes in the stock until just tender. Reserve the potatoes and the cooking liquid.

Put all the other vegetables and seasonings in a pan with the butter and cook on gentle heat for 8-10 minutes, or until softening. Add the wine and cook 1 minute more. Add the reserved potatoes and stock. Cover and simmer very gently for 30 minutes. Remove pan from the heat, cool and refrigerate overnight to allow the flavours to develop.

The next day, puré half the mixture and reheat everything with the cream and parsley. Do not boil! Season to serve with a little salt and plenty of pepper.

BROCCOLI & STILTON SOUP

1½ lb (700 gm) broccoli
1 onion, chopped
1 tablespoon dried sage
1¾ pints (1 l) stock

6 oz (170 gm) blue Stilton, grated
freshly ground black pepper

Floret the broccoli and put the florets to one side. Thinly slice the tender parts of the broccoli stems, and put these in a pan with the onion, sage and stock. Simmer until everything is soft. Add the broccoli florets and continue to simmer 2-3 minutes, until the florets are crisp-tender but still bright green.

Puré the mixture and return to the pan. Add the Stilton and heat gently, stirring continuously until the cheese has melted. Add pepper to taste and serve immediately.

LEEK & AVOCADO SOUP WITH LIME

This autumn soup has a fresh, summery tang. Delicious served hot or iced.

6 fat leeks, trimmed and thinly sliced
zest of 2 limes
2½ pints (1½ l) stock

2 large avocados, stoned and peeled
juice of 2 limes
salt and pepper
dash of Tabasco
mint sprigs
lime slices

Put the leeks and lime zest in a large lidded pan and cover with the stock. Cover and simmer until the leeks are tender. Puré the leeks with all the liquid and return to the pan.

Blend the avocado with the lime juice to a smooth purée, and stir into the soup. Season (Tabasco optional). Serve immediately, or chill and serve over ice cubes, garnished with mint and lime.

RED PEPPER & TOMATO SOUP

3 tablespoons olive oil
1 large or 2 medium onions, finely chopped
4 cloves garlic, thinly sliced
3 red peppers, cut into thin strips
6 tomatoes, chopped
1¾ pints (1 l) stock
2 tablespoons tomato paste
handful fresh chopped basil
salt and pepper

freshly ground allspice

Heat olive oil and sauté the onion and garlic until tender. Add pepper strips. When these begin to soften, add the tomatoes, stock, tomato paste, and basil and season with salt and pepper.

Cook gently until the flavours mingle and the soup thickens. Check the seasoning before serving, and serve sprinkled with a pinch or two of allspice.

DOLMADES

A standard packet of vine leaves contains about 50 leaves, so this is a good recipe to make for a crowd, perhaps for a summer buffet party. The quantity of filling mixture here will stuff a whole packet of leaves with a couple of tablespoons left over for you to eat as a reward for patience! Dolmades are best eaten cold, and are especially good with a dish of cucumber mixed with Greek style yogurt and mint, on the side. Serve 2 or 3 as an appetizer.

8 oz (227 gm) packet of vine leaves in brine
7 oz (200 gm) long grain brown rice
2 tablespoons olive oil
1 large onion, finely chopped
4-6 fat cloves garlic, crushed
1 teaspoon cinnamon
7 fl oz (200 ml) dry white wine
2 large tomatoes, seeded and finely chopped
zest of 2 lemons and juice of 1
2 oz (50 gm) currants
2½ oz (70 gm) toasted pine nuts
4 tablespoons finely chopped fresh mint
2 tablespoons tomato paste
salt and freshly ground black or white pepper

Cover the vine leaves with boiling water. After 5 minutes, drain carefully and set aside.

Cook the rice in lots of boiling water till just tender. Drain and refresh under cold water, then tip into a mixing bowl. Heat the olive oil on high heat and sauté the onion and garlic with the cinnamon for 2 minutes. Add half the wine and continue to sauté until all the liquid has evaporated. Remove from heat, cool slightly, then add to the rice.

Add all the rest of the filling ingredients. Mix well and season to taste. Lightly oil a 3-4 inch (8-10 cm) deep lidded baking dish. Begin to separate the vine leaves and lay the first one on a board with the stem end towards you. Put a heaping teaspoon of filling in the centre and turn up the bottom two lobes. Next fold in the sides to cover the filling. Now roll up tightly from the bottom, and place each roll seam side down in your baking dish. Continue to fill and roll, packing the leaves in tightly as you go until all are used up. Make a second layer if necessary. Pour the remaining wine over all and cover the dish tightly with foil. Put the lid on and bake at 150° for 35 minutes. Cool in the dish with the lid and foil in place. Refrigerate till serving time.

GERMAN POTATO & ONION SOUP

For a richer soup, use half double cream and half milk at the last stage.

---

1 oz (30 gm) margarine
4 fat cloves garlic
1½ lb (700 gm) mixed red and white
onions, chopped
1½ tablespoons celery seed
1 tablespoon caraway seed
1 tablespoon cumin seed

1½ lb (700 gm) new potatoes, sliced
⅓ pint (190 ml) dry white wine
2 pints (1150 ml) stock
2 teaspoons salt
1 teaspoon freshly ground black pepper

---

1 pint (550 ml) milk
bunch spring onions, thinly sliced

Heat margarine in a deep, large pan. When bubbly, add the garlic, onions and spices. Reduce heat and sauté about 10 minutes, until the onion is softening.

Add potatoes, wine, stock and seasonings. Cover pan and simmer on low heat for about 25 minutes until potatoes are tender.

Take pan off heat and cool slightly. Puré the soup in batches in processor or blender until smooth. Return the purée to the pan and reheat gently with the milk. Do not boil. When the soup is hot, ladle into bowls and serve garnished with the fine sliced spring onions.

SPICED BUTTERBEAN & LEMON SOUP

This soup is best made in advance, refrigerated overnight to allow the flavours to develop, and heated through gently for serving.

---

1 lb (450 gm) butterbeans
1 large onion, chopped
2 pints (1100 ml) stock
zest of 2 lemons

1 teaspoon cayenne pepper
juice of 2 lemons
1¾ pints (1 l) stock
salt and pepper

Cook together the dry butterbeans with the onion, stock and lemon zest until the beans are soft.

Add cayenne pepper, lemon juice, the rest of the stock and salt and pepper. The soup can then either be left as it is with whole beans, or can be puréed partially or totally to give a thicker texture.

MAIN DISHES

Illustrations by Felicity Bowers

ORIENTAL SPRING ROLLS WITH LIME-GINGER SAUCE

In 1992 we brought some kaffir limes back from Thailand. We planted the seeds, and in our tenth anniversary year we were able to feature the leaves from our baby trees in one of our evening menus. They are used in oriental dishes much as bay leaves are in the west (but with very different effects!). As knobbly skinned kaffir limes are well nigh unobtainable in Britain, we use regular limes for the sauce for our spring rolls.

When making the filling for the rolls, it's essential to have everything prepared and to hand before you start any cooking. For this, and for all recipes which involve stir frying, it's best to use a wok. The shape of the wok ensures rapid, even cooking to retain every scrap of flavour. Served with «pineapple-cashew rice» and a side dish of melon balls and ginger (see «sambals»), oriental spring rolls make for a spectacular dinner party!

5 oz (150 gm) smoked tofu
225 gm can water chestnuts, drained and sliced
1 tablespoon tamari

4 carrots, cut into small cubes
1 tablespoon toasted sesame oil
1 tablespoon sunflower oil
4½ oz (125 gm) shiitake mushrooms, thinly sliced vertically
9 oz (250 gm) chestnut mushrooms, thinly sliced vertically
2 tablespoons light soya sauce

1 tablespoon toasted sesame oil
1 tablespoon sunflower oil
2 bunches spring onions, finely sliced
6 cloves garlic, crushed
1 oz (30 gm) knob fresh ginger, peeled and grated
¼ teaspoon freshly ground chilli
2 tablespoons light soya sauce
1 teaspoon sugar
½ teaspoon freshly ground black pepper
9 oz (250 gm) sugar snap or mangetout, topped and thinly sliced diagonally
7 oz (200 gm) beansprouts
½ teaspoon salt

24 sheets filo pastry
sunflower oil for brushing

Put tofu and water chestnuts in a small bowl and sprinkle with the tamari. Mix thoroughly to coat. Keep to hand.

Blanch the carrots for 2 minutes in rapidly boiling water. Drain and refresh.

Heat the first oils together in your wok till they just begin to smoke, and add the shiitake mushrooms. Stir fry 30 seconds, then add the chestnut mushrooms and the light soya sauce, and stir 30

seconds more. Tip into a bowl and reserve.

Return the wok to the heat and add the second batch of oils. When really hot, toss in the spring onions, garlic, ginger and chilli. Stir just to coat, then add the blanched carrots with the light soya sauce and the sugar and pepper. Stir vigorously for 1 minute then tip in the water chestnuts and tofu, the reserved mushrooms with their cooking juices, and the peas. Stir for 30 seconds more. Add the beansprouts and stir for a final 30

LIME-GINGER SAUCE

2 tablespoons sunflower oil
1 tablespoon toasted sesame oil
3 large leeks, trimmed and thinly sliced
2 oz (55 gm) knob fresh ginger, peeled
and grated
4 fat cloves garlic, crushed
7 fl oz (200 ml) medium sherry
zest of 3 limes
1¼ pints (750 ml) stock

juice of 3 limes
2 tablespoons light soya sauce
2 teaspoons sugar
½ tablespoon tamari
½ teaspoon freshly ground white pepper
1 tablespoon arrowroot
cold water

Heat the oils in a heavy based pan and gently sauté the leeks, ginger and garlic for 5 minutes. Add the sherry, lime zest and stock. Cover the pan and simmer on very low heat for 30 minutes until everything is very soft.

Push this sauce through a fine sieve extracting as much liquid as possible. Return to the pan, and stir in the lime juice, soya sauce, sugar and tamari. Bring slowly back to simmering point. Slake the arrowroot with a little cold water and stir into the simmering liquid. Cook gently to a glossy sauce. Adjust the seasoning with pepper or sugar as required and serve warm.

seconds. Remove immediately from the heat and sprinkle with salt.

Cool as rapidly as you can before filling the rolls. Have ready an oiled heat-proof serving dish. Lay 1 sheet of filo pastry flat on a board and lightly brush with oil. Lay a second sheet on top and brush. Top with a third sheet. Now put about an eighth of your filling mixture in a thick stripe, about 1 inch (2 cm) from the short end of your 3 sheets. Roll into a cylinder shape, tucking in the long edges as you go, to encase the filling. Lay the roll in your oiled dish. Make 7 more rolls in the same way.

Brush all 8 with oil and bake in a pre-heated 180° oven for 25-30 minutes. Pour a little lime-ginger sauce over to serve and garnish with the chopped green leaves from the spring onions. Hand the rest of the sauce separately.

MUSHROOM & SPINACH ROMANOFF

This tasty pasta dish is quick and easy to make. We have been known to put a couple of these together during the course of an unexpectedly busy lunch, when it was obvious that our planned 'megaliths' were going to run out. It's a good one to make when unexpected guests arrive, or on any occasion when time is short. By the way, children love it!

12 oz (340 gm) tagliatelle verde
2 cloves garlic, crushed
4 tablespoons olive oil
1½ lb (700 gm) button mushrooms, thinly sliced
1 lb (450 gm) spinach, chopped
2 oz (55 gm) wholewheat flour
1 pint (550 ml) milk
handful fresh basil, chopped
salt and pepper
1½ lb (700 gm) cottage cheese
1 teaspoon freshly ground pepper
2 cloves garlic, crushed
handful parsley, finely chopped
½ teaspoon cayenne pepper

Cook tagliatelle in boiling water with a little oil to keep it from sticking to the pan or to itself until just al dente. Drain immediately and refresh.

Sauté garlic in the oil for 2-3 minutes, add the mushrooms and dry fry them: a little water may be needed to prevent

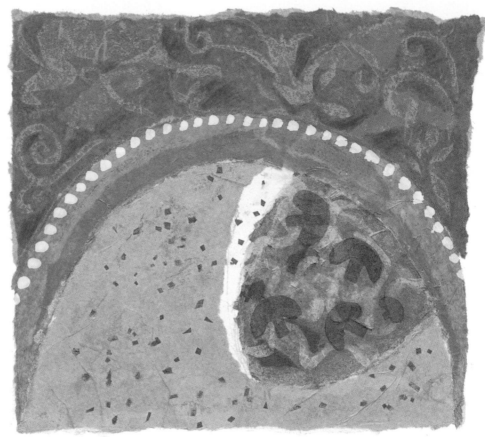

them sticking. Add the spinach and cook quickly, stirring continuously so the spinach stays green. Stir in the flour and cook for a couple of minutes before adding the milk a bit at a time to produce a thin sauce. Add the basil and season to taste. Stir in the tagliatelle and put into an oiled dish.

Mix together the cottage cheese and other ingredients for the topping and spread over the tagliatelle. Bake at 180° for 30-35 minutes.

RED PEPPER & FRENCH BEAN ROMANOFF

Cook 1 lb (450 gm) beans, cut into 1 inch (2-3 cm) sticks, in boiling water until just tender and still green. Sauté 3 red peppers – cut into strips – in oil, instead of mushrooms. Add beans at point where spinach was added and continue recipe as above.

88

CHESTNUT & ORANGE FILO PURSES

These richly filled golden bundles are perfect for winter parties. Serve with just a touch of «dark mushroom cognac sauce» and surround with a mixture of lightly steamed and roast baby vegetables. Or for the centrepiece of your Christmas dinner serve a duet of filo purses, one chestnut and orange and one «Brie and cranberry».

1 lb (450 gm) dried chestnuts
juice and zest of 2 oranges
1 onion, finely chopped
1 teaspoon dried sage
salt and pepper
c 16 sheets filo pastry
3-4 oz (85-110 gm) butter, melted

Soak the chestnuts for 8 hours, then cook in the soaking water until tender. Grate or puré the nuts and mix with enough orange juice to make the mix soft but not sloppy. Add the zest, onion and sage, and mix well. Season.

Cut the filo pastry in half, so you have smaller rectangles. Lay four pieces across each other, brushing each piece with a little butter, so you end up with a circle. Place ⅛ of the mix in the centre of the first circle. Gather up the edges, and pinch together at the 'neck'. Repeat everything seven more times. Brush the outsides with butter, and bake at 180° for 25 minutes, or until golden.

CELERY & PECAN CAKES

These are especially good with «celery & Stilton sauce», «basil topped tomatoes» and «magic mash». Serve with «apple sauce» for a light snack; or lay on top of half a lightly toasted roll spread with «spiced tomato sauce», sprinkle with grated cheese and pop under a hot grill to melt the cheese. Cover with the other half of the toasted roll and enjoy a really superior cheeseburger!

1 lb (450 gm) pecans
sunflower oil
2 onions, finely processed
1 head celery, finely processed
8 oz (225 gm) breadcrumbs
1 teaspoon dried thyme
1 teaspoon dried sage
salt and pepper

Keep back 16 fine pecans, and toast the rest lightly in the oven. Cool, then process.

Heat oil in a pan. Add onions and celery and sauté gently until cooked. Take off the heat. Mix together the ground pecans, celery mix, breadcrumbs and seasonings. Shape into 16 cakes, ½-1 inch (1-2 cm) thick. Use reserved pecans to decorate. Bake on a tray at 180° for 20 minutes.

CAULIFLOWER, BROCCOLI & POTATO PIES

This is hearty fare, lightened by the zing of pesto in the potato layer, and made flavour exploding with the accompanying «celery and Stilton sauce». We make these individual pies in the bowls in which we serve our fruit salad. They measure about 4 inches (10 cm) diameter and 2 inches (5 cm) deep. This size is perfect for one person, so, for this recipe, you will need 8 similar bowls (for our potter's address, see the front of the book!).

To serve, bring the pies to the table, slightly off-centred on individual warm plates. Surround the pies with 2 or 3 different vegetable accompaniments. Choose from steamed and buttered mangetout, shell peas and/or French or runner beans (depending on the season); herb baked tomatoes; and baby carrots with butter and freshly ground coriander seed. Serve the sauce separately, on the side.

1¾ lb (800 gm) floury potatoes, eg Maris Piper
3 tablespoons «pesto»
1¼ lb (550-600 gm) small broccoli florets
1¼ lb (550-600 gm) cauliflower in very small florets
2 oz (55 gm) butter, melted
½ teaspoon ground allspice
½ teaspoon ground nutmeg
2 teaspoons salt and 1 teaspoon pepper
1 quantity «standard pastry»
1 quantity «celery & Stilton sauce»

Boil or steam the potatoes till soft. Drain and shake in a dry pan over the heat to evaporate any moisture. Mash in the pan with the pesto and set aside.

Steam the broccoli and cauliflower together till just crispy-tender. Tip into a bowl and stir gently with the butter, spices, salt and pepper. Now divide half this mix between the 8 bowls, filling each to about one third. Pack gently. Spread the pesto-potato mixture over the broccoli-cauliflower. Top with the remaining broccoli-cauliflower and pack lightly.

Roll the pastry to ¼ inch (½ cm) thick and cover the pies, dampening the rim of each bowl so its hat will stick. Bake at 160° for 35-40 minutes, until golden brown and smelling delicious.

PIES FOR THE NON STILTON LOVER

Thinly slice 6-8 oz (170-225 gm) fine Cheddar, Caerphilly, smoked Caerphilly or a melty cheese such as Teifi, and pack half the slices between the potato and the final broccoli-cauliflower layer, and the other half just under the pastry. Bake and serve as described above, but in place of «celery & Stilton sauce» serve with «rich tomato sauce».

HERBED POLENTA WITH EGGS FLORENTINE

In this recipe the polenta is fried and then baked with hard boiled eggs and garden spinach, and a special topping: here we use Cloisters, a subtly flavoured soft cheese from Gloucester. A young Camembert could be substituted, or experiment! Boil your eggs while you prepare the polenta.

2 pints (1150 ml) water
2 teaspoons salt
2 oz (55 gm) butter
11 oz (310 gm) polenta, or fine ground maize meal
4 oz (110 gm) freshly grated Parmesan cheese
¾ packed teacup finely chopped basil and/or oregano
1-2 tablespoons olive oil
2¼ lb (1 kg) spinach with stalks and tough ribs removed
½ oz (15 gm) butter
2 teaspoons freshly ground nutmeg
4 oz (110 gm) cream cheese
zest of 4 large lemons
3 onions, finely chopped
4 cloves garlic, crushed
salt and pepper
1 quantity «standard cheese sauce»
12 oz (350 gm) Cloisters cheese, chopped
1 tablespoon coarse grained mustard
1 teaspoon nutmeg
6 hard boiled eggs
Parmesan cheese

In a large pan, bring water, salt and butter to a boil, then slowly add polenta, whisking all the time. Reduce heat to simmering (or move immediately to another element on low heat) and continue to simmer for 20-30 minutes, beating frequently. When the mixture begins to leave the side of the pan, and your wooden spoon can stand up all by itself, you're ready for the next stage.

Beat in the Parmesan and herbs all at once, then spread the mix as evenly as possible, 1 inch (2 cm) thick on a cold damp surface such as a marble pastry board, or in a lightly wetted baking dish. Leave to go completely cold, then cut into rounds with a 2 inch (5 cm) scone or cookie cutter. Heat oil in a heavy pan, and fry the polenta rounds on both sides till light golden. Thinly oil a deep ovenproof dish and arrange the polenta rounds over the base, overlapping them slightly.

Wash spinach and shake off as much water as possible. Heat the butter in a heavy based large pan and vigorously stir fry the spinach with the nutmeg till the leaves just begin to wilt. Remove from pan immediately. Finely chop spinach with the cream cheese and lemon zest, preferably in a food processor. Sauté the onions and garlic until the onion is beginning to soften, and add to the spinach mixture. Season.

Make up the cheese sauce using Cloisters cheese, and add nutmeg to the seasonings at the end, substituting coarse mustard paste for the powder.

Halve the hard boiled eggs lengthwise, and lay them, cut side up, on top of the polenta. Spread the spinach mixture over the eggs, and top with the sauce. Sprinkle with a little more Parmesan, and bake at 190° for 35-45 minutes, until golden, bubbly and heated through.

DUET OF STUFFED MUSHROOMS

If you are lucky enough to have someone come to your door with field mushrooms (as happened to us once, when our gardener was returning home after some late harvesting on a neighbouring farm) you want to do something special with them. Twice.

16 large flat capped mushrooms
6 oz (170 gm) wild rice
1 onion, finely chopped
2 cloves garlic, crushed
3 tablespoons sunflower oil
1 teaspoon dried thyme
1 teaspoon grated nutmeg
2 oz (55 gm) toasted flaked almonds
6 oz (170 gm) cream cheese
chopped parsley
1 onion, finely chopped
2 cloves garlic, crushed
1 oz (30 gm) margarine
8 oz (225 gm) fresh spinach, well chopped
2 fl oz (50 ml) white wine
4 oz (110 gm) feta cheese, crumbled
handful Parmesan cheese
1 teaspoon dried marjoram
1 teaspoon dried rosemary
pepper
3 eggs

Chop the mushroom stalks and reserve the caps.

Cook the wild rice in boiling water: this takes much longer than normal rice, so allow plenty of time. Sauté onion and garlic and half the chopped mushroom stalks in sunflower oil until soft, and add the thyme, nutmeg and almonds. When the rice is cooked and cooled, mix it in with the almond mixture. Stir in well the cream cheese and parsley and spoon into 8 of the flat cap mushrooms.

For the second filling, sauté the onion and garlic in the margarine until soft, add the remaining mushroom stalks and the spinach and cook with the white wine until soft. Mix in the feta cheese, Parmesan, and herbs, and season with pepper only – the feta is salty enough. Beat the eggs and mix into the spinach mixture. Fill the remaining 8 mushrooms.

Place all the mushrooms in a shallow dish with a little oil and wine in the bottom, and cover with foil to contain the steam. Bake at 160° for 35-45 minutes, until the mushrooms are soft and filling is thoroughly cooked.

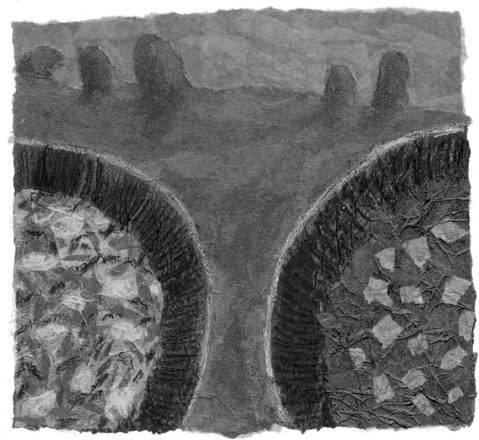

baking sheet. Bake at 160° for about 20 minutes till just firm. Do not allow to become dry. Transfer to an attractive warmed dish to serve.

POST-CAMBRIAN SAUSAGES

Derby Sausages. Substitute sage Derby for the Cheddar and add an extra ½ tablespoon of sage.

Pickwick's Sausages. Substitute ripe Stilton for half the Cheddar. Omit the sage and add instead 1 teaspoon each ground ginger and ground cloves.

London Sausages. Substitute finely chopped spinach for the parsley. Add 1 teaspoon of grated nutmeg and a generous dash of port.

Cheesy Surprise Sausages. Cut 32 sticks of smoked cheese, each 2 inches by ¼ inch (5 cm by ½ cm). Mould the regular mixture around the cheese slices when you make the sausages, taking care the surprise is well hidden!

GLAMORGAN SAUSAGES

It has become a tradition at Stones to serve these on August bank holiday Monday with «apple sauce», sauté potatoes and maple baked beans. «Cranberry & apple sauce» is also nice, and you can of course vary your accompaniments according to what is in season and the preferences of your guests.

1¼ lb (550 gm) wholewheat breadcrumbs
1 onion, very finely chopped
8 oz (225 gm) brazil nuts, chopped
12 oz (340 gm) Cheddar, grated
1 tablespoon dried sage
2 handfuls chopped fresh parsley
3 eggs, beaten
salt and pepper

Mix the breadcrumbs, onion, nuts and cheese together, bind with the eggs and season. Form into 16 sausage shapes, placing them on a parchment covered

93

MUSHROOM TOURTIÈRE

Tourtière is a French Canadian pie, traditionally eaten in the province of Québec on festive occasions such as Thanksgiving and New Year. Slow cooking is essential to bring out the flavours of the filling ingredients. Lacking the potbellied woodburning stove so common in households north of the St Lawrence River, we here cook components on very low heat. Serves 8 generously, with some left over. Delicious eaten cold for a picnic.

1 quantity «standard pastry»
12 oz (340 gm) green split peas
¾ pints (425 ml) strong stock made from
1 tablespoon concentrate in boiling water
1 scant teaspoon ground cloves
3-4 bay leaves
salt and pepper
1 oz (30 gm) vegetable margarine
1 large onion, finely chopped
2 Bramley apples, finely chopped
1 tablespoon dried sage
2 teaspoons dried thyme
2 fat cloves garlic, crushed
2 lb (1 kg) mushrooms, coarsely processed
or finely chopped
zest of 2 lemons
juice of 1 lemon
1 teaspoon salt
½ teaspoon freshly ground black pepper
1 teacup finely chopped parsley

2 tablespoons sunflower oil
2 tablespoons tamari
2 tablespoons apple juice concentrate
1 block firm tofu, pressed dry and thinly
sliced
1 egg, beaten

Line a 10 inch diameter by 1 inch deep (25 cm by 3 cm) quiche dish with pastry. Cover with cling film and refrigerate in anticipation of the filling, which consists essentially of a sandwich of puréed split peas with an apple and mushroom filling – and something special on the top.

Put split peas, stock, cloves and bay leaves in a pan with a tight fitting lid. Simmer 1-1½ hours on very low heat until the peas are soft. Check periodically and add a little more water if the mix is sticking. Remove bay leaves, and beat to a purée, seasoning to taste. Cool.

Melt the margarine and add the onions and apples with the herbs and garlic. Sauté gently until the onions are beginning to soften. Add the mushrooms and lemon zest and juice. Sauté 1 minute, stirring continuously, and season to taste. Cool and stir in the parsley.

Beat the sunflower oil with the tamari and apple concentrate. Lay the tofu slices over a shallow, lipped baking sheet and drizzle with the marinade. Turn around in the marinade for 15-30 minutes, then bake on the sheet at 160° for 15 minutes. Cool.

Divide the split pea mixture roughly in half, and put one half onto the base of the pastry shell. Strain any excess liquid from the mushroom mix (save the liquid to add to soup or salad dressing), and put this over the split pea base. Top with the remaining half of the split peas. Arrange the tofu slices over all and cover with pastry. Brush with beaten egg and bake at 160° for 45 minutes. Rest for 10 minutes before cutting into wedges. Serve with «cranberry-onion gravy» and a selection of seasonal vegetables.

½ pint (300 ml) tomato juice
2 tablespoons tomato paste
8 oz (225 gm) cannellini or haricots,
soaked overnight and cooked
2 oz (55 gm) black olives
4 oz (110 gm) peas
salt and pepper
freshly grated Parmesan cheese to serve

Melt the margarine and sauté the onion, garlic and peppers. Stir in the cabbage, tomatoes, red wine, herbs, lemon halves and bay leaves. Cover with a tight fitting lid and simmer about 45 minutes-1 hour, until vegetables are cooked and flavours are mingling. Fish out the lemon halves and discard.

Add tomato juice and paste, cooked beans, olives and peas. Season and leave the lid off the pan to allow the stew to reduce and thicken. Serve with Parmesan on the side.

MINESTRA

This aromatic Italian bean casserole is best served with a side dish of penne or other pasta shapes with pesto, and a salad incorporating, if possible, a few leaves of slightly bitter radiccio and rocket. Have available «garlic bread» and/or crostini for mopping up the juices. Remember to have your beans soaked and cooked before you start this recipe.

2 oz (55 gm) margarine
1 red onion, thinly sliced
4 cloves garlic, crushed
1 each red and green peppers, thinly sliced
6 oz (170 gm) white cabbage, chopped
8 ripe tomatoes, quartered
¼ pint (150 ml) red wine
1 tablespoon each dried thyme and
marjoram
1 lemon, halved
a few bay leaves

ASPARAGUS & FRESH HERB TART

Celebrate the short asparagus season with this lovely tart. Serve warm or cold with a salad of young mixed leaves.

1 quantity «standard pastry»
1 oz butter
1 oz wholewheat flour
½ pint (300 ml) milk
1 bay leaf
8 oz (225 gm) asparagus
6 eggs
handful fresh mixed herbs, chopped
salt and pepper
1 onion, chopped
sunflower oil
6 oz (170 gm) cream cheese

Line flan dish with pastry.

Melt the butter in a pan and add the flour. Cook for about 1 minute over a low heat. In another pan, warm the milk gently with the bay leaf and the inedible tough ends of the asparagus. Discard the bay leaf and the stalks, and add the milk slowly to the flour, stirring all the time until you have a smooth sauce. Leave to cool. Beat in the eggs and herbs, and season.

Meanwhile, sauté the onion in the oil. Chop the tender part of the asparagus stalks into pieces, leaving about 3 inches (7 cm) at the tip. Gather the tips together and tie with string. Stand in a pan with their cut ends in 1 inch (2 cm) of water. Put chopped stalks loose around the bundle. Cover and cook for about 3 minutes, till barely tender. Drain immediately.

Scatter the onion and sliced asparagus over the bottom of the lined dish. Dot cream cheese over evenly. Carefully pour over the sauce, then arrange asparagus tips on top, making a decorative pattern. Bake at 160° for 40 minutes, or until set and golden.

BAVARIAN GALETTE

For this dish you need a standard pancake mix made up into eight 8 inch (20 cm) pancakes, which you will layer up with a cabbage and a courgette filling, and lots of chopped parsley. Serve with buttered herbed noodles and a selection of garden vegetables. Butter-roast squash, runner beans, baby carrots and corn scraped from the cob make a vibrant combination!

1 quantity «standard pancakes»
1 red cabbage weighing 1¼ lb (550 gm) after trimming base core
2 large Bramley apples weighing 10-12 oz (280-340 gm) after coring
1 oz (30 gm) margarine
1 tablespoon paprika
1 teaspoon cayenne pepper
1 teaspoon salt
4 tablespoons cider vinegar
3½ oz (100 gm) sultanas

1 oz (30 gm) margarine
8 oz (225 gm) onions, finely chopped
4 fat cloves garlic, crushed
2 teaspoons dried rosemary
1¼ lb (550 gm) courgettes, diced
1 tablespoon white wine
6 oz (170 gm) Teifi (or similar), grated
¾ packed teacup finely chopped parsley

3 oz (55 gm) full fat cream cheese
¼ teacup parsley
1 teaspoon each salt and freshly ground black pepper
1 large tomato, thinly sliced

Thinly slice the cabbage and cube the apples as small as possible. Melt the margarine and add the cabbage, apple cubes and seasonings. Stir fry for 1 minute. Add the vinegar and sultanas. Reduce heat, cover and cook until the cabbage is soft (25-30 minutes). Stir occasionally and add an extra splash of vinegar if the mixture starts to stick. Remove from the pan and allow to cool. Clean the pan ready for the courgette layer.

Melt the margarine and sauté the onions and garlic with the rosemary for 3 minutes, or until the onions are softening. Add the courgettes and the wine. Cover and cook gently until the courgettes are tender. Remove from the heat and allow to cool before stirring in the cheese and the parsley.

Lightly brush a 10 inch (25 cm) quiche dish or similar with sunflower oil.

Lay your first pancake flat on the bottom of the dish and top with a quarter of the cabbage mixture making sure the filling is flat and evenly spread over the surface. Lay the next pancake on top of the cabbage, and top with one third of the courgette mixture, first squeezing it gently to remove any excess moisture. Repeat these layers until the final pancake rests flat on top of the final cabbage layer.

Pure the cream cheese with the parsley and seasonings. Spread this mixture evenly over the topmost pancake, and cover with the sliced tomatoes. Bake the galette at 180° for 35-40 minutes, or until it is thoroughly heated. Test by sticking a thin-bladed knife down the middle. If the topping starts to brown, cover lightly with foil. Cut into wedges for serving, like a cake.

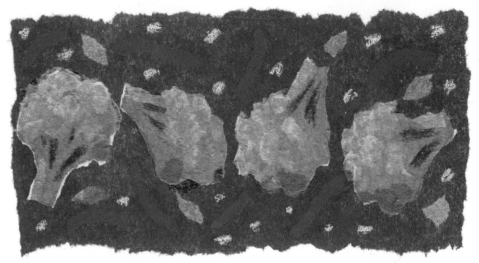

WEST COUNTRY HOTPOT

The vegetables here are cooked very slowly in a rich, creamy, cider mixture spiked with sage. The slow cooking ensures that the vegetables have time to absorb all these wonderful flavours! Serve simply with chunks of fresh baked bread to soak up the juices.

2 leeks
3 potatoes
8 oz (225 gm) pot barley
1 Bramley apple
3 parsnips
4 courgettes
3 tablespoons dried sage
salt and pepper
6 oz (170 gm) clotted cream
1 pint (550 ml) cider
¾ pint (425 ml) stock
8 oz (225 gm) Cheddar, grated

Cut the vegetables and apple into slices ⅓ inch (1 cm) thick. Layer up in sequence, starting with the leeks and putting the barley over the potatoes, in a lidded casserole.

Sprinkle sage and seasoning over, followed by the clotted cream and the cider and stock. Cook with the lid on for 2 hours at 150°. Check seasoning. Scatter cheese over the top and cook at 160° for a further 15 minutes uncovered, until golden.

BROCCOLI & COTTAGE CHEESE ROLY POLY

Try this with any of the tomato sauces, or «red pepper-almond sauce». For an unusual and delicious combination, serve with «caponata».

1 lb (450 gm) wholewheat flour
2 tablespoons baking powder
2 teaspoons salt
4 oz (110 gm) vegetable suet
2 tablespoons dried sage
2 tablespoons lemon juice
10-12 fl oz (300-350 ml) cold water
1 lb (450 gm) small broccoli florets
1 leek, finely chopped
3 oz (85 gm) butter
2 oz (55 gm) ground almonds
12 oz (340 gm) cottage cheese
pinch cayenne pepper
1 tablespoon lemon juice
salt and pepper
1 egg for brushing

For the suet pastry, thoroughly mix all the dry ingredients together. Stir in the lemon juice then add enough cold water to form a fairly firm dough. Leave to rest.

Lightly cook broccoli in boiling water until just tender, and still green. Refresh. Sauté the leek in butter until soft. Mix together the leek, broccoli, almonds, cottage cheese, cayenne pepper and lemon juice, and season to taste.

Follow the rolling, filling and rolling up instructions given for «mushroom & spinach roly poly». Brush with beaten egg before baking at 180° for about 40 minutes until pastry is cooked through and shiny and golden. Rest before cutting in slices to serve.

FRENCH BEAN, WALNUT & STILTON LASAGNE

For this recipe you need an attractive 3–4 inches (8-10 cm) deep oblong ovenproof dish, about 12 inches long and 5-6 inches wide (30 cm by 14 cm).

olive oil
12 strips wholewheat or spinach lasagne
12 oz (340 gm) walnuts, toasted
1 lb (450 gm) French beans, tailed and halved
1½ pints (850 ml) milk
3 bay leaves
1 onion studded with cloves
4 oz (110 gm) butter
4 oz (110 gm) wholewheat flour
1 teaspoon cayenne pepper
4 oz (110 gm) blue Stilton, grated or crumbled
salt and pepper
8 tomatoes, sliced
handful fresh basil
4 oz (110 gm) blue Stilton, grated or crumbled
handful Parmesan cheese

Bring a large pan of water to a rolling boil. Add a splash of oil to prevent the lasagne strips sticking to the pan or to each other. Carefully lower the strips one by one into the water. Cook until al dente (about 20 minutes), occasionally gently lifting the strips with a wooden spoon. Drain and refresh under cold running water.

Whilst the lasagne is cooking, toast the walnuts (if you don't already have some toasted) and steam the beans till crunchy-tender. Warm the milk with the bay leaves and onion ready for the sauce.

Melt the butter and stir in flour and cayenne to make a roux. Cook this for a couple of minutes before gradually adding the strained, warm milk a bit at a time: a balloon whisk helps to ensure a smooth sauce. Add the 4 oz of Stilton and season.

Lightly oil the dish and cover the base with 4 of the cooked lasagne strips, slightly overlapping. Next spread a third of the sauce over the strips. Sprinkle with half the beans and half the nuts. Top this layer with half the tomatoes, half the basil and half the other 4 oz of Stilton. Repeat these layers in the same order, starting with 4 more strips of lasagne. Now cover with the remaining 4 strips, and spread with the rest of the sauce. Sprinkle with the Parmesan and bake at 180° for 45 minutes, until cooked through and golden on top.

99

AUBERGINE & SMOKED CHEESE RAVIOLI

For this dish choose aubergines that are long and thin, so you get the right shaped slices. You will need some toothpicks to secure the ravioli rolls.

4 largish aubergines
salt
olive oil
1 egg, beaten
4-6 slices stale bread, grated or processed
1½ oz (40 gm) butter
2 onions, roughly chopped
2 fat cloves garlic, crushed
1 teaspoon ground mace
1¾ lb (800 gm) spinach, roughly shredded
11 oz (320 gm) smoked Caerphilly cheese, cut into 16 3 by ¼ inch (8 by ½ cm) sticks
1 pint (550 ml) «rich tomato sauce» or «tomato garlic sauce»
4 oz (100 gm) freshly grated Parmesan cheese

Cut the stem ends off the aubergines, and a thin sliver from each base. Stand up on the base, and cut a thin slice from two of the long sides. Throw all the bits away. Now slice the trimmed aubergines vertically into ⅓ inch (¾ cm) slices. You need 16 slices in all, but don't make them thicker as they will be too hard to roll. Spread all the slices on a wire rack, and put the rack on a large lipped tray. Sprinkle with salt and let stand 1 hour. Now rinse the slices under cold running water, then pat dry with a clean tea towel.

Preheat the oven to 190°. Drizzle a little olive oil onto 2 or 3 baking sheets (you need enough room to lay out all the aubergine slices in a single layer) and put the oiled sheets in the oven. Have ready the beaten egg and breadcrumbs, each in a wide bowl. When the oil begins to smoke, remove the sheets from the oven. Quickly dip the aubergine slices in the beaten egg to coat all sides, then into the crumbs. As you coat them, lay them flat on the hot baking sheets. When all are coated, return the sheets to the oven and bake for 10-15 minutes or until the aubergine is bendy. Remove from the oven and reserve.

Whilst the aubergine is baking, start the spinach purée. Melt the butter in your largest lidded pan. Add the onion, garlic and mace. Stir and cook, covered, on gentle heat 8-10 minutes or until the onion is translucent. Uncover the pan and increase the heat to high. Add the spinach, stirring as you add. As soon as the spinach begins to wilt, remove from heat and puré everything.

Lay your baked aubergine slices on a large board. Spread all the slices with an equal amount of spinach purée. Pile four smoked cheese sticks crossways in the centre of each slice and roll up from the short end. Secure with a toothpick.

Pour three quarters of the tomato sauce into a baking dish and pack the aubergine ravioli on top. Cover with the remaining sauce and scatter with the Parmesan. Foil and bake at 190° for 20 minutes. Remove the foil and bake a further 5 minutes, or until everything is bubbling and exquisitely golden.

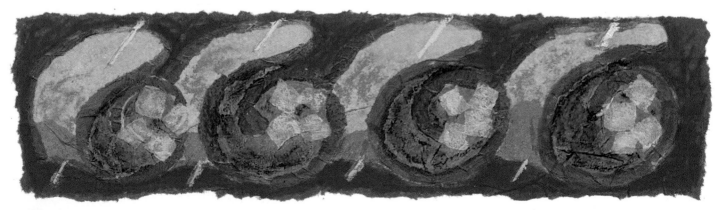

Sauté onion, garlic and pepper in oil. When onion starts to soften, add tomatoes, and continue to cook until they form a sauce – about 15-20 minutes. Add tomato paste, oregano and seasonings.

Meanwhile, cook pasta in plenty of boiling water till al dente. Drain and refresh in cold water.

Cut the aubergine into rounds ½ inch (1 cm) thick. Lay on a baking sheet. Brush with oil and bake at 180° for 10 minutes.

Mix the Cheddar and cottage cheese together in a bowl with the cayenne and salt.

Put half the sauce in the bottom of an ovenproof dish. Arrange the aubergine slices over. Then spoon in half the cheese mixture, followed by all the raw spinach. Next the pasta, then the rest of the sauce, and lastly the remaining cheese. Sprinkle with the mozzarella. Bake at 180° for 40 minutes.

AUBERGINE & SPINACH PASTICCIO

This is a light pasta dish ideal for a summer lunch. Serve with garlic bread or crostini and a salad, or for a more elaborate meal, with «rosemary, red onion & tomato focaccia».

2 onions, chopped
4 cloves garlic, crushed
1 red pepper, diced
sunflower oil

1½ lb (700 gm) tomatoes, chopped
2 tablespoons tomato paste
handful fresh oregano (or 1 tablespoon dried)
salt and pepper
8 oz (225 gm) pasta shells
1 aubergine
sunflower oil
8 oz (225 gm) Cheddar, grated
1 lb (450 gm) cottage cheese
¼ teaspoon cayenne pepper
¼ teaspoon salt
8 oz (225 gm) fresh spinach, roughly chopped
3-4 oz (85-110 gm) mozzarella, grated

101

TOMATO, MUSHROOM & COURGETTE SHOO PIE

1 quantity «savoury choux pastry»
2 oz (55 gm) butter
2 onions, chopped
4 cloves garlic, crushed
4 courgettes, thickly sliced
1 lb (450 gm) button mushrooms
1½ lb (700 gm) tomatoes, chopped
8½ fl oz (250 ml) red wine
4 tablespoons tomato paste
handful fresh basil (or 1 teaspoon dried)
salt and pepper
4 oz (110 gm) Cheddar, grated

Follow the choux pastry recipe for profiteroles, bake and cool.

Melt butter in a pan and add onion and garlic. Sauté till soft. Add courgettes and mushrooms and cook for 1-2 minutes. Add tomatoes, wine and tomato paste, and reduce to a thick sauce. Add herbs and seasonings. Transfer to an ovenproof dish. Top with the profiteroles, and sprinkle with Cheddar. Bake at 160° for 25 minutes.

STONES' PAELLA

This has all the essential flavours of a traditional Spanish paella. Ideally it should be assembled in a handled paella pan (24 inches/60 cm or more in diameter and about 2 inches/5cm deep), but a very wide heavy frypan or a shallow flat-based wok can be substituted. The quantities and varieties of vegetables can be varied according to what is in season, the only critical part of this recipe being the rice cooking. Garnish attractively and serve straight from the pan with a glass (or two) of sangría or rioja!

4 oz (100 gm) flageolet beans, soaked overnight
12 fl oz (350 ml) tomato juice
8 fl oz (250 ml) dry white wine
3 fl oz (80 ml) lemon juice
12 fl oz (350 ml) stock
1 teaspoon (1 gm) saffron strands
16 fl oz (500 ml) long grain brown rice
5 oz (140 gm) French beans, tailed and halved

3-4 tablespoons olive oil
1 whole garlic bulb, peeled and thinly sliced
1 large Spanish onion, finely chopped
4 carrots, thinly sliced diagonally

1 each red, green and yellow peppers, seeded and diced into ½ inch (1 cm) squares
6 oz (170 gm) pack frozen petits pois, thawed (or same fresh)
4 oz (100 gm) flaked almonds, toasted
8 firm, ripe tomatoes, cut in wedges
4 oz (100 gm) pitted black olives
4 fl oz (100 ml) each finely chopped mint and parsley

salt and pepper
lemon juice
1 large lemon cut into thin wedges
4 hard boiled eggs, each cut into 8 wedges (omit for a vegan dish)
sprigs of fresh mint

First drain and rinse the flageolets, cover with fresh cold water and boil until just tender. Drain again.

Next, bring the tomato juice, wine, lemon juice, stock and saffron to a boil and throw in the rice. Reduce the heat to very low. Cover the pan and simmer gently until the rice is almost tender (about 45 minutes). Check occasionally and add a little water if necessary. Remove from the heat and leave to stand, covered, for 10 minutes, by which time the rice should be perfectly cooked and all the liquid absorbed.

While the rice is simmering, steam the French beans till crunchy-tender. Refresh and set aside.

In a paella pan, or your best substitute, warm the olive oil and add the garlic slices. Stir occasionally over very gentle heat until browning. Remove with a slotted spoon and set aside. Increase the heat to high and stir fry the onion and carrot in the remaining garlic flavoured oil for 2 minutes. Add the peppers and continue stirring for a further 1 minute. Add the saffron rice, the flageolets, the peas, French beans and reserved garlic and stir until everything is heated through. Stir in half of the toasted almonds, half the tomatoes and olives (save the rest for garnish) and all the mint and parsley.

Take off the heat and season to taste with salt, freshly ground black pepper and lemon juice. Stir well and scatter with the remaining almonds. Serve straight from the paella pan, garnished with the reserved tomatoes and olives, lemon and egg wedges and the mint sprigs.

BROCCOLI & MUSHROOM GOUGÈRE

1 quantity «savoury choux pastry»
1 oz (30 gm) butter
1 onion, chopped
2 oz (55 gm) button mushrooms
1 small courgette, sliced
10 tomatoes, chopped
pinch dried basil
6 tablespoons soured cream
salt and pepper
8 oz (225 gm) broccoli, trimmed
1 lb (450 gm) button mushrooms
2 oz (55 gm) butter
4 oz (110 gm) Cheddar, grated
1 egg, beaten

Make the pastry mix and bake in a ring shaped tin. When it is cold (you can bake this the day before you need it), knock the ring out of the tin and cut it in half horizontally. Hollow out any soft middle, and discard, or nibble! Now make the sauce.

Melt the butter in a pan and sauté onion gently. Add mushrooms and courgette, and cook till tender. Add tomatoes and cook until broken down to form a sauce. Add basil and cool. Puré and add the soured cream and season. Reheat gently, and keep warm.

Steam the broccoli until just tender. Sauté three quarters of the mushrooms in a similar proportion of the butter, then mix with the broccoli and about half a cupful of the sauce.

Put half of your hollowed ring, hollow side up, into a lightly oiled quiche dish, and fill with the mushroom broccoli mix. Sprinkle with half the Cheddar then cover with the other half of the ring, hollow side down. Brush the ring with the beaten egg and sprinkle with the rest of the cheese. Bake in a preheated 160° oven for 20 minutes. Meanwhile, sauté the remaining mushrooms in the rest of the butter. When the gougère is cooked, pile the sautéed mushrooms in the centre and surround the whole creation with a little of the reserved sauce. Hand the rest of the sauce separately.

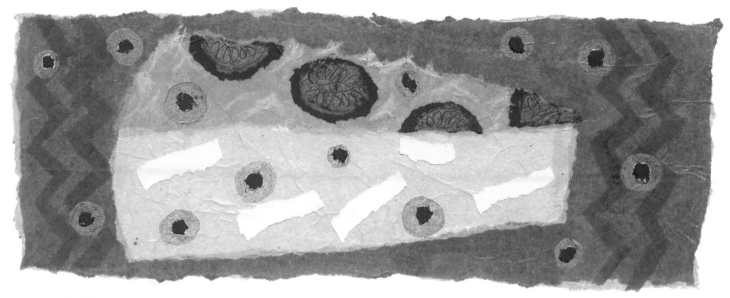

TORTILLA ESPAÑOL

In Spanish speaking America, a tortilla is a flat, very thin cake made of maize meal or wheat flour, or sometimes a combination of both. In Spain, a tortilla is an omelette packed with lots of exciting extras. We make tortilla Español the same way we make our frittatas. The melting soufflé surround provides a perfect contrast to the hidden textures within.

6 eggs, separated
2 tablespoons chopped fresh marjoram (or 1 tablespoon dried)
2 tablespoons paprika
1 tablespoon olive oil
½ teaspoon each salt and freshly ground black pepper

4 tablespoons olive oil
3 potatoes, sliced and boiled till half-cooked
1 teaspoon salt
1 large Spanish onion, sliced
4 cloves garlic, crushed
4 oz (100 gm) pimento stuffed olives, sliced
2 tomatoes, seeded and chopped
2 tomatoes, sliced
pinch of pepper

Beat the egg yolks in a bowl with the marjoram, paprika, oil and seasonings. Beat the egg whites separately till very stiff. Set aside.

Heat the 4 tablespoons of olive oil in a large frypan, and when the oil begins to smoke, add the potato slices and salt. Fry quickly until golden brown all over, then remove with a slotted spoon and set aside momentarily. Add the onion and garlic to the pan, and again fry quickly until browning. Reduce the heat to medium and stir in the olives, chopped tomatoes and fried potatoes, until everything is mixed up and evenly spread.

Fold the egg whites into the yolk mixture, and carefully pour into the pan, lifting the vegetables as you pour, so the egg gets under all the filling. Turn on your grill to preheat. Cook the tortilla for 5-7 minutes until the underside is done, shaking the pan occasionally and loosening the edges with a spatula. Cover with the sliced tomatoes and sprinkle with pepper.

Pop the pan under the preheated grill and cook until the top stands in golden peaks. Serve immediately, cut into wedges. Maravillosa!

GOLDEN TEMPLE CURRY

This curry is named for a beautiful, fairy tale temple on the lakeshore at Mae Hong Son in northern Thailand, and dedicated to Yongyut Polmag, market guide and backpack chef incroyable! Serve garnished with spring onions thinly sliced lengthwise and perhaps a little dish of seeded chopped tomato sprinkled with fresh mint. «Pineapple-cashew rice» is a perfect accompaniment. Try to cut all the vegetables into even-sized pieces.

3 tablespoons cumin seed
1 tablespoon yellow mustard seed
1 tablespoon fenugreek seed
1 inch (2 cm) knob fresh ginger, roughly chopped
5 cloves garlic, peeled
1 onion, roughly chopped
zest and juice of 2 lemons
2 small fresh chillis, seeded and roughly chopped
1 tablespoon salt
1 tablespoon ground turmeric
1 tablespoon sugar

4 tablespoons sunflower oil
5 small onions, quartered
2 lb (900 gm) evenly sized small new potatoes
6 small carrots, left whole or halved
200 gm packet creamed coconut, blended with 1 pint (550 ml) hot water
3 fl oz (75 ml) light soya
1 cauliflower, in florets

2 yellow courgettes, cut into chunks
2 yellow peppers, seeded and cut into squares
extra lemon juice, sugar, salt, white pepper and light soya to season

First, toast all the seeds in a heavy frypan until the mustard seed 'pops'. Set aside. Next, process the ginger and the garlic to a coarse paste. Add the onion, lemon juice and zest and chillis, and process again. Scrape into a bowl and stir in the salt, turmeric, sugar and toasted seeds. This is the curry paste.

Heat the oil in a large, heavy lidded pan and fry the curry paste for 2 minutes. Add the onion quarters, the potatoes and carrots and fry 2 minutes more, stirring all the time. Add the blended coconut cream and light soya sauce. Cover the pan and simmer very gently until the potatoes can just be pierced with a fork. Add the rest of the vegetables, and continue to simmer, covered, about 30 minutes longer until everything is tender but not mushy. Taste, and add any extra seasoning required. Turn out into a hot serving bowl and garnish creatively.

Note. When the potatoes are tender, the curry can be removed from the heat, cooled and refrigerated overnight. The next day, add the remaining vegetables and reheat slowly for about 1 hour. Season and serve as above.

107

CORN CIRCLES

Our garden corn is ready some time after the surrounding fields of cereal and their crop circles and other alien shapes have been harvested. This recipe provides a bit of nostalgia for, and is dedicated to, all the ardent croppies who descend on Avebury and enjoy our food in June and July.

1 quantity «cornmeal pancakes», made up into 8 inch (20 cm) pancakes
½ oz (15 gm) butter
½ teaspoon cayenne pepper
1 teaspoon black pepper
1 teaspoon salt
10 oz (280 gm) leeks, finely sliced
1 lb (450 gm) sweetcorn kernels, stripped from the cobs
8 tablespoons double cream
1 small red pepper, finely chopped
6 oz (170 gm) smoked mozzarella, grated
8 oz (225 gm) runner beans, finely sliced
½ oz (15 gm) butter
6 oz (170 gm) onion, finely chopped
1 teaspoon celery seed
1 tablespoon wholewheat flour
8 tablespoons milk
4 eggs, hard boiled
1½ tablespoons capers
1 teaspoon ground mace
salt and pepper
2 oz (55 gm) Caerphilly cheese, grated
2 tablespoons parsley, finely chopped
5 tablespoons double cream
4-5 baby corn cobs, halved lengthwise

Once you have made your pancakes, you have two filling mixes to prepare, one with yellow corn and one with green beans. For the first, melt butter on gentle heat and add the seasonings and leeks, and cook until the leeks are softening, but still bright green. Stir in the corn and cream. Stir for 1 minute. Add the red pepper and stir for 3 minutes more. Remove the pan from the heat and stir in the mozzarella.

Next, blanch the runner beans for 2 minutes and refresh under a cold tap. Set aside. Melt butter on low heat and add the onion and celery seed. Cook gently until the onion is soft. Stir in the flour and cook 1 minute. Gradually add the milk and stir until the sauce is thick. Take off heat and stir in the beans. Put the hard boiled eggs into the processor with the

capers and mace, and process to a smoothish paste. Stir this paste into the onion bean mixture and season.

Brush a 10 inch (25 cm) shallow dish lightly with oil, and lay your first pancake flat on the base of the dish. Top with a quarter of the corn mixture, and then the second pancake. Top with the second quarter of the corn mix and the third pancake. Next comes a bean layer. Take half the mix, and spread. Make sure with each layer that you spread the filling evenly and keep it flat. Add another pancake, another corn layer, another pancake and the final bean layer. Top with the sixth pancake and the final layer of corn filling. Cover with the seventh pancake.

For the topping, process the Caerphilly with the parsley and cream. Spread evenly over the topmost pancake in your stack. Arrange the baby corn halves around the corn circles like the spokes of a wheel. Bake at 180° for 35-45 minutes, until heated right through. Test by sticking a knife into the middle.

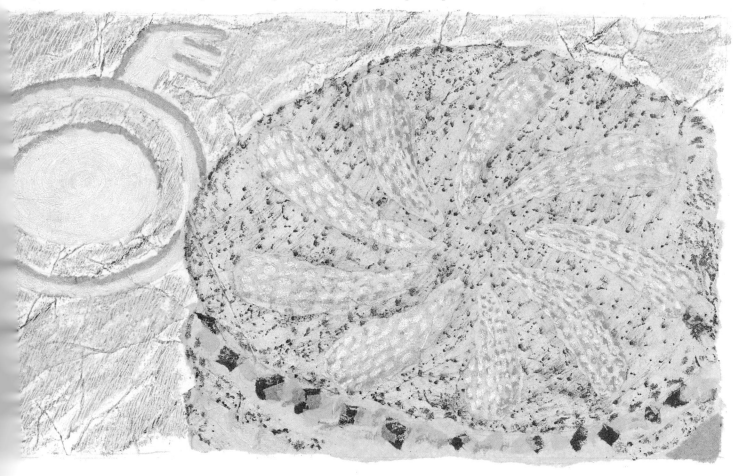

4 tablespoons tomato paste
handful fresh dill
salt and freshly ground pepper
8 sheets filo pastry
olive oil for brushing

Heat oil and sauté the onion and garlic. Add aubergines, peppers and courgettes to the pan. Cook for a few minutes longer before adding the tomatoes, tomato juice and paste, and dill. Allow this to simmer until the vegetables are all soft and the flavours released. Season and leave to cool slightly.

Brush one sheet of filo pastry with oil and lay across one half of a quiche dish (10 inch/25 cm). Place another oiled sheet over the other half of the dish, ensuring that some of the pastry is over-hanging. A third oiled sheet of filo should cover the join in the middle of the first two sheets. Half the ratatouille mix can then be piled into the dish.

Oil two more sheets of filo and cover the ratatouille with these, tucking in their edges. Spoon in the remaining ratatouille. Then oil the last three sheets of filo and arrange these over the top ensuring all the sauce is covered. All the stray edges of filo can then be scrunched together around the rim of the dish. Brush with oil all over and cook in a hot oven (200°) until golden and crispy on the top – about 15 minutes.

RATATOUILLE FILO PIE

Bring your oven up to temperature before putting in the pie, and serve it hot with warm «butterbean hummus» and a Greek salad of feta cheese and olives.

4 tablespoons olive oil
1 large onion, finely chopped
2 cloves garlic, crushed
2 aubergines, chopped
1 red pepper, chopped
1 green pepper, chopped
4 courgettes, sliced
10 ripe tomatoes, chopped
10 fl oz (300 ml) tomato juice

BRIE & CRANBERRY FILO PARCELS

These parcels are best served immediately, crisp and golden brown, with the Brie and cranberries melted together inside. Serve as a starter with a little salad and «herbed crème fraîche», or as a main course with vegetables and a rich red wine. Fresh cranberries are only available around Christmas time. They freeze perfectly, so we buy lots then, and use throughout the winter and early spring.

14 oz (400 gm) fresh or frozen cranberries
1 tablespoon muscovado sugar
1 tablespoon cinnamon
1 lb 10 oz (740 gm) Brie
24 sheets filo pastry
3 oz (85 gm) butter, melted

Soften the cranberries with 2 tablespoons water and the sugar and cinnamon.

Cut the Brie into eight equal chunks. Next cut, butter and lay out the filo pastry as for «chestnut & orange filo purses», but adding an extra layer of pastry rectangles. Put 1 chunk of Brie and a teaspoon of the softened cranberries (ie ⅛ of the mixture) in the centre of the first circle. Gather up the edges and pinch at the 'neck'. Make sure the filling is sealed in well. Make seven more parcels, brush with butter and bake at 180° for 25 minutes.

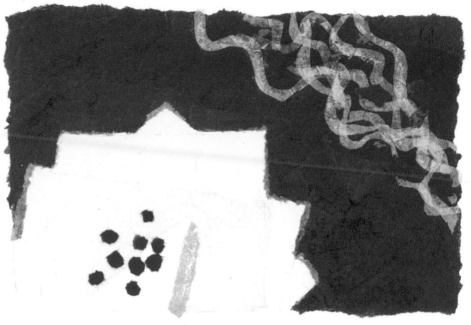

SUN DRIED TOMATO & WALNUT TAGLIATELLE

Good with olive bread and a really crisp green salad with fresh garden herbs.

2 oz (55 gm) butter
1 large onion, chopped
1 oz (30 gm) sugar
4 cloves garlic, crushed
8½ fl oz (250 ml) white wine
large sprig rosemary, stripped
salt and pepper

3 oz (85 gm) sun dried tomatoes, soaked in warm water
4 oz (110 gm) walnuts, toasted
12 oz (340 gm) tagliatelle
4 oz (110 gm) fresh Parmesan, or other hard cheese, grated
4 oz (110 gm) mozzarella, grated

Melt butter in a pan. Add onion and sugar and caramelise over a low heat. Add garlic, wine and rosemary and reduce by one third. Season.

Drain and chop the tomatoes and add to the sauce. Stir in the walnuts and keep everything warm.

Meanwhile, cook the pasta al dente. Toss the hot, cooked pasta with the sauce and serve immediately topped with the cheese.

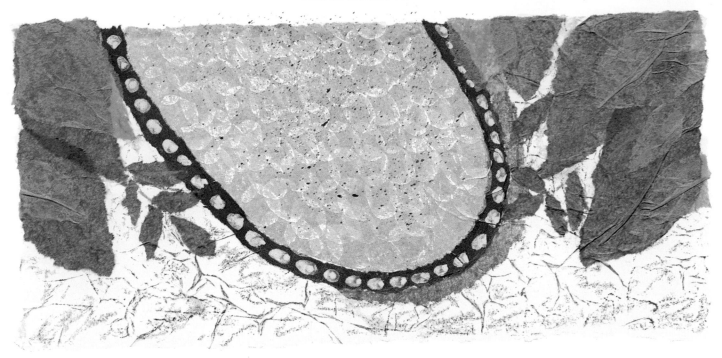

SPINACH & STILTON BOULANGÈRE

Celebrate the first new potatoes and youngest, freshest leaves with this early summer bake.

3 lb (1⅓ kg) new potatoes, sliced
1 oz (30 gm) butter
3 lb (1⅓ kg) fresh spinach
1 teaspoon freshly ground nutmeg
2 oz (55 gm) butter
2 onions, chopped
4 large cloves garlic, crushed
3 sticks celery, sliced

4 oz (110 gm) wholewheat flour
1 tablespoon coarse grained mustard
10 fl oz (300 ml) milk
10 fl oz (300 ml) double cream
8 oz (225 gm) strong blue Stilton, grated or crumbled
salt and freshly ground black pepper
1 oz (30 gm) butter
2 tablespoons sesame seed
2 tablespoons poppy seed

Boil potatoes till slightly under-done.

In a large pan, melt the first oz (30 gm) of butter and add the spinach, with only the water clinging to the leaves, and the nutmeg. Stir quickly, and when the leaves are just wilting, remove from the heat. Drain any excess liquid and roughly chop.

Next, melt the second butter and sauté the onion, garlic and celery till soft. Mix in the flour and cook for a minute. Stir in the mustard, then gradually add the milk and cream, and cook to give a thick sauce. Add the Stilton and chopped spinach. Season and turn into a large buttered baking dish.

Lay the potato slices neatly on top of the spinach mixture and season with a little more salt and pepper. Dot with the last butter, sprinkle with the seeds and bake for about 35 minutes in a 180° oven until the potato is golden and crisp.

TORTA MEXICANA

Cut the hot torta into wedges like a cake to reveal the layered colours of your labours, and serve with extra soured cream or «guacamole». Confused engineers might find the illustration helpful!

1 quantity «cornmeal pancakes» made into 6 in a 10 inch (25 cm) pan
¼ quantity «refritos»
14 oz (400 gm) floury potatoes
4 tablespoons soured cream
4 eggs, hard boiled and mashed or processed
1 oz (20 gm) fresh coriander, finely chopped
salt and pepper
sunflower oil
18 oz (500 gm) Cheddar, grated
1 papaya, peeled, seeded and cut into thin moons

Roughly process all the refritos and set aside.

Boil the potatoes until tender. Drain and mash with the soured cream, mashed egg and coriander. Season.

You are now ready to assemble your torta. Oil a 10-12 inch (25-30 cm) round ovenproof dish and lay your first pancake flat on the base. Spread a third of the bean mix evenly over the pancake, repeat with a quarter of the cheese and top with the second pancake. Cover with half the potato mix and another pancake. Now repeat the bean and cheese layers, a fourth pancake, the rest of the potato and a further pancake. Cover this with the rest of the beans. Lay out papaya slices on the bean mix (saving some for the top). Cover with half the remaining cheese and the last pancake. Finally, scatter the last of the cheese on top and arrange the reserved papaya moons on the cheese.

Bake at 180° for 35-40 minutes.

MARROW & CHESTNUT HOTPOT

Long, slow cooking is essential to bring out all the flavours in this delicious hotpot. If you're making it for lunch, cook your chestnuts the day before. If for dinner, soak them overnight and cook the same day. If you are going out for the day, you can cook this for a longer time at a lower temperature. It's a warming dish to come home to after a walk through the autumn leaves! Use margarine throughout instead of butter, if you like. You can omit the wine and use all stock if you really must, and you can add additional vegetables according to what you have on hand. A little chopped kale is very nice!

1 lb 4 oz (570 gm) dried chestnuts
zest and juice of 4 oranges
½ pint (300 ml) dry white wine
1-1½ pints (550-850 ml) stock
1 oz (30 gm) butter/margarine
4 carrots, sliced ¼ inch (½ cm) thick
3 fat sticks celery, sliced ¼ inch (½ cm) thick
3 onions, cut into wedges
1 oz (30 gm) butter/margarine, softened
2 baking size potatoes, sliced as thinly as possible
2 tablespoons each chopped fresh thyme and sage, or 1 tablespoon dried
1 thin skinned marrow, halved lengthwise, seeded and sliced ½ inch (1 cm) thick

2 tablespoons coarse grained mustard
½ oz (15 gm) butter/margarine, chopped
1 teaspoon salt
½ teaspoon pepper

Soak the chestnuts for several hours or overnight with the orange zest and juice, the wine and just enough stock to cover. Next day, bring the chestnuts with their soaking liquid to the boil. Lower heat and simmer gently for 20 minutes. Remove from heat and reserve everything.

Next melt the butter, and gently sauté the carrot slices for 5 minutes. Add the celery and onions, and continue to sauté, very gently, 10 minutes more.

Generously butter a deep, lidded 6-8 pint (3½-4½ l) casserole dish and line all over with potato slices (they should stick to the sides). Divide the remaining potato slices into 2 heaps and set aside. Spread half the carrot mix over the potato lined base and sprinkle with half the thyme and sage. Using a slotted spoon, fish half the chestnuts from the cooking liquid and scatter over the vegetables. Cover the chestnuts with half of the marrow slices, then half of the reserved potatoes (both neatly arranged!). Spread 1 tablespoon of the mustard over the potatoes.

Now repeat: carrot mixture, herbs, chestnuts, carefully arranged marrow then potato, one more time. Pack everything down with the palm of your hand.

Make up the chestnut cooking liquid to 1 pint (570 ml) with stock. Pour this over the hotpot and dot the last exposed potato layer with the remaining mustard and the ½ oz of butter bits. Sprinkle the seasonings over. Cover the casserole tightly with foil, then put the lid on. Cook for 1½-2 hours in a 150° oven, until everything is tender. Remove the lid and foil and cook for 10-15 minutes longer to brown the top. Serve straight from the casserole dish.

PENCARREG & WALNUT ROAST

Pencarreg is a fine flavoured Brie obtainable from speciality cheese stores. Use before it ripens fully: you want it to melt, not pour! Decorate with dessert apple moons if you like, before baking. Serve this intriguing roast with «dark mushroom & cognac sauce», or «rich tomato sauce» and vegetables such as rosemary or «lemon roast potatoes», a carrot purée and buttered garden beans.

1 large onion, chopped
4 cloves garlic, crushed
1 head celery, chopped
3 tablespoons sunflower oil
3 large carrots, grated
1 lb (450 gm) toasted walnuts
1 tablespoon dried sage
1 lb (450 gm) wholewheat breadcrumbs
salt and pepper
6 eggs, beaten
1 lb (450 gm) Pencarreg, thinly sliced
2 Bramleys, thinly sliced

Sauté the onion, garlic and celery in oil until soft. Add the carrot and a little water to prevent sticking, and cook until the carrot is soft.

Process or roughly crush the toasted walnuts and add to the mixture, removing from the heat. Add sage, and stir in the breadcrumbs evenly throughout. Season and stir in the eggs.

Grease a dish with a little oil, and press half the roast mix firmly into the bottom. Lay the Brie and Bramley slices together over the roast mixture in the dish. Then cover with the rest of the mix, and press down firmly. Cover with foil. Bake the roast at 180° for about 50 minutes. It's difficult to tell when a roast is ready, as it doesn't turn golden: but the Brie should begin to bubble a little bit up the sides. Test with a knife poked into the middle to see if it's thoroughly hot.

SPINACH FILLED PROFITEROLES

An unusual cold main dish for lunch on a very hot day. Arrange 2 profiteroles on individual plates with a little «roast pepper relish» on one side and a small pool of warm «golden tomato sauce» or «rich tomato sauce» on the other. Garnish with fresh dill sprigs and serve with the tiniest of new potatoes and a mixture of salad leaves. These are also striking as part of a summer buffet.

1 quantity «savoury choux pastry»
1 oz (30 gm) butter
12 oz (340 gm) spinach, freshly washed
2 cloves garlic, crushed
4 oz (110 gm) Cheddar, grated
8 oz (225 gm) cream cheese
2-3 sprigs fresh dill (or 1 teaspoon dried)
salt and pepper

Spoon the pastry mix into 16 blobs on a baking tray, and cook at 225° for 15 minutes. Reduce temperature to 150° for a further 25 minutes. Cool on wire rack.

Melt butter in a pan, and add spinach and garlic. Cook until spinach is just wilted (about 1 minute). Remove and process, then mix in a bowl with the other ingredients.

When profiteroles are cool, make a hole in their sides and pipe or spoon in the spinach mixture. Alternatively, sandwich two profiteroles together with the filling.

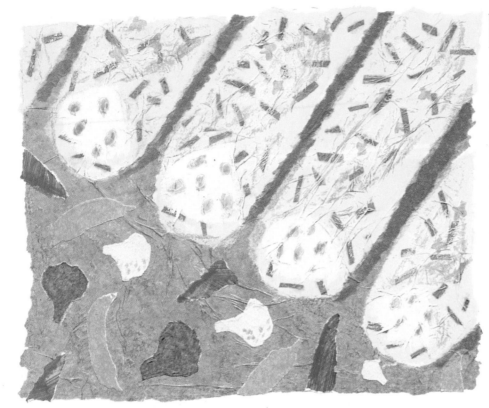

CHIVE PANCAKES WITH SUMMER VEGETABLES

1 quantity «standard pancakes»
4 tablespoons finely sliced chives

1 little cauliflower, in small florets
1 head broccoli, in small florets
12 new baby carrots, halved lengthwise
4½ oz (125 gm) mangetouts or yellow wax beans, trimmed

½ pint (300 ml) stock
½ pint (300 ml) milk
1 onion, peeled and studded with cloves
a few bay leaves

3 oz (85 gm) butter/margarine
3 oz (85 gm) wholewheat flour

zest of 2 lemons
generous handful chopped marjoram
4 tablespoons capers
1 teaspoon each salt and pepper
1 tablespoon coarse grained mustard
pinch cayenne pepper
4 fl oz (100 ml) double cream
lemon juice to taste

extra milk or stock to thin sauce
marjoram flowers for garnish

Stir the pancake batter up with the chives, and make the mixture into 8 thin pancakes.

Lightly steam all the vegetables separately and set aside.

Next, put the stock on to heat with the milk, studded onion and bay leaves. Bring to simmering point and simmer for 10 minutes.

Melt the butter or margarine and stir in the flour. Cook this roux, stirring all the time, for 1 full minute.

Still stirring, strain the milk stock infusion into the roux. Squish the onion through the strainer for maximum flavour, then discard all the solid bits. Cook gently to a thick, creamy sauce. Remove from the heat and add the lemon zest, herbs, capers and seasonings. Cook for 1 minute. Finally stir in the cream and adjust the flavour with lemon juice.

Stir half this sauce into the steamed vegetables. Fill the pancakes, rolling them up as you go, and arrange in a lightly oiled baking dish. Brush the tops with oil or melted butter. Cover the dish with foil, and cook at 180° for about 30 minutes.

Meanwhile, gently reheat the remaining sauce, thinning if necessary to pouring consistency. Serve the pancakes on individual plates with a little sauce poured over and garnished with marjoram.

FENNEL & WILD MUSHROOM FUSILI IN SAFFRON CREAM

A delectable dish for a special dinner. The colours are wonderful!

*1 lb (450 gm) fusili or other pasta shaped
to hold a sauce
olive oil*

*4 oz (110 gm) butter
3 bulbs fennel
1 onion, chopped
4 cloves garlic, crushed
1 red pepper, thinly sliced
1 lb (450 gm) button mushrooms, thinly
sliced
8 fl oz (225 ml) white wine*

*1 teaspoon (1 gm) saffron strands
5 fl oz (150 ml) hot water
8 fl oz (225 ml) single cream
8 oz (225 gm) fresh peas
1 tablespoon dried dill weed
salt and pepper*

*2 oz (55 gm) butter
12 oz (340 gm) wild mushrooms, eg
shiitake, oyster, trimmed and sliced
2 large tablespoons soured cream
handful chopped parsley*

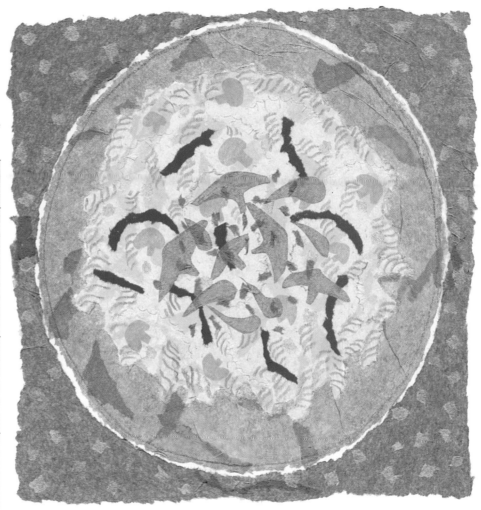

Cook fusili in boiling water with a little oil to prevent sticking. Drain and refresh under cold, running water.

Melt butter in a pan, and sauté fennel, onion, garlic and red pepper until soft. Add button mushrooms and white wine and cook for a further 2-3 minutes.

Infuse saffron in the hot water for a few minutes. When mushroom mixture is ready, add the saffron and water, cream, peas and dill and cook until thickened. Season.

Meanwhile, melt a smaller knob of butter in a flat dish in the oven at 180°. Put in wild mushrooms and cook for 3-4 minutes. Stir the pasta into the vegetables and sauce, add the soured cream and immediately place into a hot serving dish. Scatter the wild mushrooms and parsley over the top.

117

LEEK & WALNUT STUFFED ONIONS

Here, rather than stuffing the onions with their own middles, we make a magical concoction with their cousins, the leeks to provide contrasting texture and complementary flavour. Serve with onion gravy, or for a special occasion serve with «dark mushroom & cognac sauce».

8 very large red or white Spanish onions, unpeeled
4 leeks, finely sliced
2 oz (55 gm) butter
2 fl oz (50 ml) white wine
8 oz (225 gm) Cheddar, grated
8 oz (225 gm) cottage cheese
pinch of dried thyme
6 oz (170 gm) walnuts, toasted
dash of Tabasco
salt and pepper

Drop whole onions into boiling water and cook for 10-15 minutes to soften the flesh. The onions need to be soft enough to push out the middles for stuffing, but not so soft that they fall apart. When cooked, leave them to cool before peeling, and removing their hearts. Save the middles to make the sauce of your choice.

Sauté the leeks in melted butter and wine for 2-3 minutes. Then mix them with the cheese, thyme, walnuts and Tabasco, and season to taste. Stuff the prepared onions with this filling, and place in a dish with a little oil and wine in the bottom and foiled over the top. Bake at 160° for about 45 minutes, until the onions are tender but still hold their shape.

ONION GRAVY
Simply make the gravy by sautéing the chopped onion middles for a few minutes with a pinch of sugar, then simmering in stock until thoroughly tender. Thicken with arrowroot and add a dash of tamari for extra flavour.

WILD MUSHROOM, BRANDY AND STILTON PENNE

Use strongly flavoured wild mush rooms for this rather special pasta dish. Porcini or crêpes, or a mixture are best. If fresh are unavailable, reconstitute quality dried mushrooms in a little boiling water. Fresh shiitake are easy to find and are also good.

1½ lb (700 gm) penne or other tubular pasta
olive oil

4 tablespoons olive oil
6 cloves garlic, crushed
1½ lb (700 gm) button mushrooms
4 fl oz (100 ml) milk
2 tablespoons dried thyme
15 fl oz (425 ml) single cream
15 fl oz (425 ml) brandy
2 tablespoons arrowroot
12 oz (340 gm) blue Stilton, grated
salt and pepper

2 oz (55 gm) butter
1 lb (450 gm) wild mushrooms, trimmed and sliced
handful parsley, chopped

Drop penne into boiling water with a little oil. When cooked, drain and flush with cold water to prevent further cooking in the colander.

Heat olive oil in a large saucepan, sauté the garlic and button mushrooms for 1-2 minutes, then add the milk and thyme and cook until mushrooms are tender. Stir in cream and brandy. Mix the arrowroot with a little cold water in a separate dish, before adding to the pan. Keep stirring on a medium heat whilst the sauce thickens. Add the Stilton and continue cooking over a low heat. Season to taste.

Meanwhile, preheat the oven to 180º and put the butter into a baking tray to melt. Shake the wild mushrooms into the melted butter and return to the oven for 4-5 minutes to cook. Stir the pasta into the sauce, and keep over a low heat until the penne is warmed through. Serve in a hot dish with the wild mushrooms and parsley scattered over the top.

119

MUSHROOM & HARICOT CHASSEUR

Serve with «lemon-herb dumplings» or on a bed of creamy garlic tagliatelle or for an unusual treat with «potato, feta & olive gratin».

4 tablespoons olive oil
4 cloves garlic, cut into slivers
1 large onion, cut into thin strips
1 each large red and green peppers, cut into thin strips

1 lb (450 gm) mushrooms, chestnut and buttons
2 carrots, cut into half moons
1½ lb (700 gm) cooked haricot beans
4 ripe tomatoes, chopped
4 tablespoons tomato paste
2 teaspoons dried thyme
pinch cayenne pepper
1½ pints (850 ml) red wine
salt and freshly ground black pepper

Preheat the oven to 180°. Heat the olive oil and sauté the garlic, onion and peppers until just tender. Thinly slice half the mushrooms. Place both the sliced and the whole mushrooms, the onion and pepper mix, carrots and haricots into a large casserole dish. Add the tomatoes and gently mix all the ingredients together.

In a separate jug, mix the tomato paste, thyme, cayenne and red wine and a little seasoning. Pour the liquid over the ingredients in the casserole and cover with a tight fitting lid. Put into the oven and cook for about 1½ hours, stirring gently a couple of times during cooking, until carrots are soft and flavours developed. Before serving, check the seasoning and adjust if necessary. Mmmmm ...

SPINACH & NEW POTATO SHUKTA

Shuktas originate in Bengal. These vegetable stews are characterised by tender chunks of vegetable simmered slowly in a slightly bitter, aromatic broth. The flavour improves if the shukta is made the day before required and reheated to serve, but this is still a delicious dish to make on the same day if you are in more of a hurry. Accompany with a rice dish and a selection of «sambals».

2 tablespoons vegetable ghee
1 tablespoon cumin seed
1 tablespoon black mustard seed
1 teaspoon coriander seed
2 lb (900 gm) tomatoes, quartered
½ lb (225 gm) new potatoes
1 teaspoon ground cumin
2 teaspoons turmeric
1 teaspoon garam masala
1-2 teaspoons cayenne pepper
12 oz (340 gm) fresh spinach, roughly chopped
4 oz (110 gm) peas
2-4 cloves garlic, crushed
½ oz (15 gm) fresh ginger, finely chopped
salt

Heat ghee in pan. Add all the seeds. When they start to pop, add the tomatoes and cook until they form a sauce. Turn the heat down, and add the potatoes and ground spices. Cover and cook until the potatoes are almost done, adding a little water if it becomes too dry.

At this point, take the shukta off the heat and cool and refrigerate overnight. Next day, reheat gently to simmering point then add spinach to the pan with the peas. When spinach is almost cooked, stir in garlic and ginger, then season to taste. Alternatively, if you want to finish your shukta at once, continue without a break.

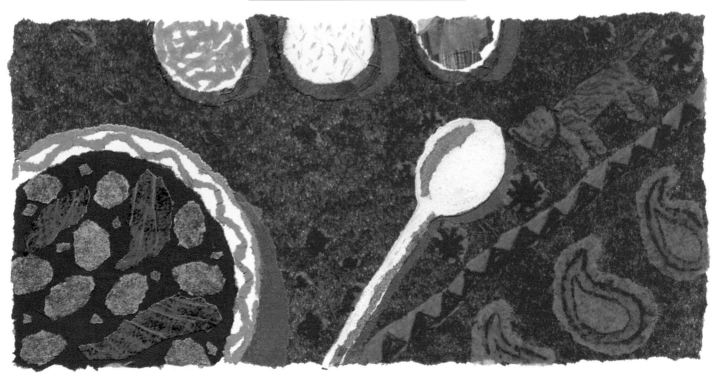

MUSHROOM & POTATO KEBABS

A summer barbecue treat! You will need 2 or 3 new potatoes and 3 or 4 button mushrooms per skewer, depending upon size. The weights given below are thus somewhat flexible, but you should have ample marinade, with plenty left over to baste. Serve 2 kebabs per person with a complementary sauce. «Orange-wine sauce», «spiced plum sauce» or «lime-ginger sauce» are all excellent! Be very careful not to over-cook the potatoes or they will fall apart when you try to skewer them.

1 whole bulb garlic, cloves separated and peeled
1½ tablespoons salt
2 tablespoons coarse grained mustard
1½ tablespoons freshly ground black pepper
4½ fl oz (125 ml) lemon juice
4½ fl oz (125 ml) white wine vinegar
9 fl oz (250 ml) olive oil
2 tablespoons tamari
2½ oz (75 gm) sugar
large handful finely chopped parsley
1½-2 lb (700-900 gm) very firm button mushrooms
2-2½ lb (900-100 gm) tiny new potatoes
bay leaves, soaked 30 minutes in boiling water

First process the garlic or crush into a large bowl, then mix or process in the rest of the marinade ingredients.

Divide the marinade between 2 large bowls and add all the mushrooms to one, turning to coat. Boil the potatoes till they can just be pierced with a fork. Immediately drain and refresh. Fork the potatoes several times and add to the second bowl of marinade, again turning to coat. Cover the bowls and let stand at least 3 hours.

Now take 16 wooden skewers and soak for 30 minutes in boiling water (this stops them burning on the barbecue). When you are ready to assemble your kebabs, thread mushrooms and potatoes alternately on the skewers, tucking a few bay leaves in between.

Either barbecue the kebabs over hot coals for 10-15 minutes, turning and basting often with leftover marinade, or bake in a 190° oven for about 20 minutes with a little marinade poured over. Save any marinade you might have left for another day!

SPANAKOPITTA

This Greek classic is generally made entirely with feta cheese. We find the texture is better if different cheeses are used, and the end result is not so salty. Good with «casseroled cannellini beans» or borlotti beans, and a salad of ripe tomatoes scattered with finely chopped red onion, black olives and fresh herbs.

1 oz (30 gm) butter
1 onion, finely chopped
4 cloves garlic, crushed
1½ lb (700 gm) fresh spinach
8 oz (225 gm) feta cheese
8 oz (225 gm) cottage cheese
8 oz (225 gm) Cheddar, grated
5 eggs, beaten
1 tablespoon dried dill weed
pepper
7 sheets filo pastry
2 oz (55 gm) butter, melted

Melt butter in a pan and lightly sauté the onion and garlic. Add the spinach and cook very lightly till just wilted. Remove from heat and chop finely or process. Place in a bowl with the cheeses, egg, dill and pepper, and mix well.

Brush the inside of a baking dish with melted butter. Line sides and base with three sheets of filo pastry, brushing each one with a little more butter, and leave the edges of the strips hanging out of the dish. Then spoon in half the spinach mix. Next lay two further sheets of filo, brushing as before. Add the rest of the spinach.

Bring in the overhanging pastry edges, put two more sheets on top, and finish with a final brush of butter.

Cook for 1 hour at 160° or until pastry is golden brown. Turn the oven off, and leave for at least 15 minutes to set.

MUSHROOM & SPINACH ROLY POLY

Serve this with «cranberrry-onion gravy» and assorted root vegetable pyramids for a lovely Sunday lunch. It contains no eggs or dairy products, so is an ideal special treat for your vegan friends.

1 lb (450 gm) wholewheat flour
2 tablespoons baking powder
2 teaspoons salt
4 oz (110 gm) vegetable suet
10-12 fl oz (300-350 ml) cold water
3 tablespoons olive oil
4 cloves garlic, crushed
1 lb (450 gm) mushrooms
5 fl oz (150 ml) white wine
1 tablespoon fresh dill
1 lb (450 gm) fresh spinach, chopped
2 oz (55 gm) wholewheat flour
2 oz (55 gm) flaked almonds
1 tablespoon lemon juice
salt and pepper

Mix together the dry ingredients for the suet pastry. Add the water a bit at a time to form a fairly firm dough.

Heat olive oil and sauté the garlic and mushrooms. Add white wine and dill, and cook until mushrooms are tender. Stir in the spinach and cook quickly. Stir in the flour and almonds, and season with lemon juice and salt and pepper. Cook until sauce thickens.

Roll out the pastry into a large rectangle. Spread the filling on it, almost to the edges, leaving ½ inch (2 cm) spare pastry all the way round. Brush the edges with cold water and roll up lengthways, squeezing in the ends to keep in the filling. Place the roly poly on a large baking sheet and bake in a preheated oven at 180° for approximately 40 minutes. The pastry should begin to turn brown and be cooked thoroughly. Rest in a warm place for 10 minutes, then cut into slices to serve.

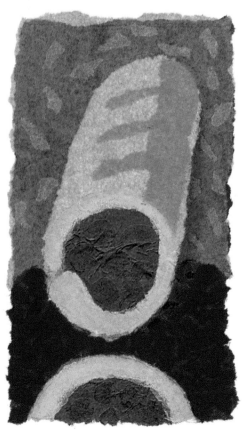

SPICY PEANUT CROQUETTES

Try these with «herbed crème fraîche» or «Italian dressing». Add a rice or potato accompaniment and a crispy salad for a complete meal.

sunflower oil
2 onions, finely chopped
2 cloves garlic, crushed
4 red peppers, finely chopped
2 teaspoons cayenne pepper
1 lb (450 gm) toasted peanuts, finely chopped
1 tablespoon peanut butter
8 oz (225 gm) breadcrumbs
2 tablespoons tomato paste
salt and pepper

Heat oil in a pan. Add onions, garlic, peppers and cayenne. Sauté gently until onion is soft. Take off heat. Stir in the rest of the ingredients. Shape into 16 croquettes. Cook on a baking sheet at 180° for 20 minutes.

MEDITERRANEAN SOUFFLÉ COTTAGE PIE

This is a sumptuous and spectacular dish, not heavy, yet robust enough to make an ideal lunch or supper for one of those cold wet days which inevitably occur during the course of a Wiltshire summer. The asparagus stalks are optional, but nice if you have them: save the tips for garnish. Make a feature of the different types of olive when decorating your soufflé topping.

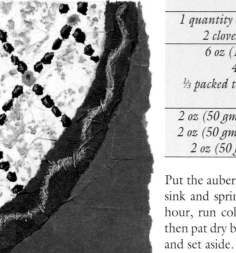

1 small aubergine, cut into ½ inch (1 cm) dice
salt
4 carrots, cut into sticks
olive oil
4 small-medium red onions, in wedges
8 cloves garlic, sliced
4 small courgettes (ideally 2 green, 2 yellow), cut in oblique slices
2 fennel bulbs, sliced
2 each red and green peppers, cut into ½ inch (1 cm) wide strips
8 asparagus stalks, in ½ inch (1 cm) lengths
2 teaspoons salt
1 tablespoon freshly ground black pepper
2 lb (1 kg) floury potatoes, roughly but evenly chopped
1 quantity «tomato garlic sauce» (use 2 cloves garlic for the finale)
6 oz (170 gm) cream cheese
4 eggs, separated
⅓ packed teacup chopped flat-leaved parsley
2 oz (50 gm) pitted black olives, sliced
2 oz (50 gm) pitted green olives, sliced
2 oz (50 gm) stuffed olives, sliced

Put the aubergine dice in a strainer in the sink and sprinkle with salt. After half an hour, run cold water over to desalinate, then pat dry between two clean tea towels and set aside. Bring a pan of water to the boil and parboil the carrot sticks for 2 minutes. Drain and refresh and pat dry with the same tea towels. Preheat the oven to 220°.

Drizzle two large baking sheets with olive oil, and distribute the aubergine, carrot, onion, garlic and the rest in a single layer. Sprinkle the salt and pepper evenly over the two trays, and drizzle with a little more oil. Pop into the hot oven and bake till just tender (10-15 minutes).

Meanwhile, bring a large pan of water to the boil and drop in the potatoes. Boil until soft enough to mash, then drain and stir in the empty hot pan to evaporate excesss moisture. Mash in the pan and set aside.

When the vegetables in the oven are perfectly roasted, tip into a bowl and mix with the tomato sauce. Check the seasoning, then put the tomatoey vegetable mix into a large, deep baking/serving dish, leaving enough headroom for the potato topping.

Return to the potatoes. Mash in the cream cheese and egg yolks. Fold in the stiffly beaten egg whites and parsley, and spoon the mixture over the vegetables, smoothing the surface. Now, drawing with the tip of a teaspoon, make a trellis pattern over the potato topping.

Arrange the sliced olives imaginatively in the trellis grooves. Return the finished soufflé to a 200° oven for 35-45 minutes, until well risen and golden brown. Meanwhile, if you have been able to include asparagus, steam the reserved tips briefly and scatter over the soufflé to serve.

MUSHROOM, DILL & WHITE WINE BREAD PUDDING

This pudding is quite moist, so can be served alone. If you would like to add a sauce, try a little «red pepper-almond sauce». «Lemon roast potatoes» and a selection of steamed garden vegetables are ideal accompaniments. This is a winter recipe, so we have to use dried dill.

3 tablespoons olive oil
1 large onion, chopped
2 lb (1 kg) button mushrooms, halved
2 heaped tablespoons dried dill weed
8 fl oz (225 ml) white wine
1½ lb (700 gm) wholewheat bread, sliced
1 lb (450 ml) Cheddar, grated
6 eggs
10 fl oz (300 ml) milk
salt and pepper

Heat oil and sauté the onion until transparent, then add the mushrooms, dill and wine and cook until the mushrooms are soft.

Grease a large, lasagne-style dish and cover the bottom and sides with sliced bread. Then cover with half the mushroom mix. Sprinkle with half the grated Cheddar. Repeat with a further layer each of bread and mushrooms, and top with a final layer of bread.

Whisk the eggs together with the milk and seasoning, and pour over. Sprinkle the remaining cheese over the top and bake at 180° for about 40 minutes. Then allow to stand in a warm place for 10 minutes before serving.

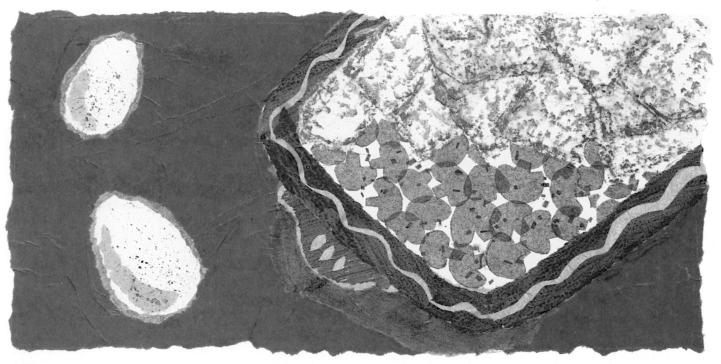

CREAMY GARLIC TAGLIATELLE

Here, peppery watercress is used as a herb together with sage to flavour this garlicky, cheesy cream. This vibrant pasta dish can also be served as a starter, adorned with a necklace of rocket leaves, corn salad and chervil or radiccio; or as a side dish to go with a tomatoey main course. Use more or less garlic according to your personal taste.

18 oz (500 gm) tagliatelle, preferably verde
dash of olive oil
1 oz (30 gm) butter
1 lb (450 gm) red onions, roughly chopped
6-8 large cloves garlic, crushed
2 tablespoons chopped fresh sage
2 cups double cream
1 large or 2 small bunches very fresh watercress with stems removed, roughly chopped
6 oz white Stilton, Wensleydale or other well flavoured white cheese, crumbled
salt and pepper
toasted chopped walnuts for garnish (optional)
extra crumbled white cheese to serve

Cook the tagliatelle in lots of boiling water with olive oil until just al dente. Drain and refresh under cold running water and set aside.

Melt the butter on low heat in a heavy pan and add the onions. Cook gently for 15-20 minutes, until soft and beginning to caramelise. Add the garlic and sage and continue to cook gently for 1 minute, stirring all the time. Stir in the cream and simmer until reduced by about a third, and beginning to thicken.

Have a large pan of rapidly boiling water ready for the pasta. Add the chopped watercress and the crumbled cheese to the sauce. Stir to mix and leave to simmer while you attend to the pasta.

Tip the cooked pasta into your pan of boiling water. Immediately the water returns to the boil, drain and turn the pasta into a large serving bowl. Season the sauce and pour over the pasta. Toss carefully just to mix. Garnish with the walnuts if you wish, and serve extra white cheese for sprinkling.

127

MUSHROOM BRIOCHE

This is a very rich dish, and makes a spectacular centrepiece for Christmas dinner or similar festive occasion. Serve with «cranberry-onion gravy» or «dark mushroom & cognac sauce». It is also very good cold. Take on a picnic with herb or fruit jelly to serve. You can double the quantity of dough and use the other half to make brioche rolls – delicious for breakfast! Bake rolls for only 10 minutes alongside the savoury mushroom brioche.

3 fl oz (85 ml) milk
½ teaspoon golden granulated sugar
1 tablespoon dried yeast
7 oz (200 gm) unbleached four
6 oz (170 gm) wholewheat flour
1 teaspoon salt
¼ teaspoon cayenne pepper
4 eggs, beaten
6 oz (170 gm) butter, melted and cooled slightly
extra flour for kneading

First start the dough. Warm milk to blood heat. Sprinkle in sugar and yeast, and prove in a warm place for 5-10 minutes till really bubbly. Put the flour in a mixer with a dough hook, or in a processor with a dough attachment. Add the salt and cayenne to the flour then pour in the yeast mixture. Beat or process 1 minute. Gradually add the beaten egg and beat to combine well. Still beating, pour the butter into the dough in a steady stream.

Your mixture will now be silky and slightly sticky. Turn out onto a lightly floured board and knead until very smooth and shiny. Put in an oiled bowl and turn to coat all sides with oil. Leave to prove in a warm place for 1½-2 hours until double in bulk. Meanwhile make the filling.

¾ oz (20 gm) butter
1 large onion, finely chopped
3 large cloves garlic, crushed
½ oz (15 gm) dried porcini or cêpes, soaked in boiling water to cover for 30 minutes
¾ lb (340 gm) chestnut or button mushrooms, chopped medium fine
4½ oz (125 gm) cream cheese
4½ oz (125 gm) cottage cheese
4 medium or 6 small spring onions, finely sliced
1 tablespoon dill weed
large pinch cayenne pepper
3 hard boiled eggs, finely chopped
large bunch parsley, finely chopped
1½-2½ oz (40-70 gm) fresh breadcrumbs
salt and lots of freshly ground pepper
egg for brushing

Melt the butter, add the onion and garlic and sauté over medium heat till the onion begins to soften. Meanwhile drain (save the water for soup) and finely slice the soaked mushrooms, then add to the pan. Add the chopped chestnut or button mushrooms and continue to cook on low heat until the mushrooms are soft. Remove from heat and stir in everything else except breadcrumbs and seasoning.

Add just enough breadcrumbs to soak up any juices. Season to taste. Preheat oven to 200°.

Knead the risen dough for 1 minute on a floured board, then roll out to a neat rectangle c 12 by 8 inches (30 by 20 cm). With the long side facing you, pile all the filling in a long sausage down the middle, leaving a ¾ inch (2 cm) border at each end. Turn in the short ends and then bring up the long edges to meet in the middle. Pinch all the seams to seal. Brush the brioche with beaten egg and bake for 20 minutes in the preheated oven. Cool slightly then serve cut into slices with a sauce of your choice.

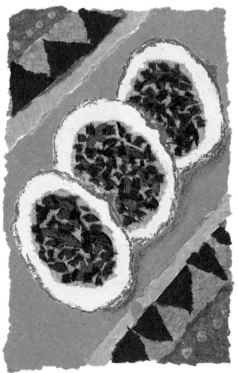

SPINACH, FETA & OLIVE FLAN

Choose one of our pasta dishes to serve with this for very hungry Italian food lovers. Or allow to cool and serve in small wedges as part of a Mediterranean buffet.

1 red onion, thinly sliced
2 cloves garlic, crushed
3 tablespoons olive oil
1 tablespoon dried thyme
1 tablespoon dried tarragon
2 oz (55 gm) wholewheat flour
¼ pint (150 ml) red wine
6 ripe tomatoes, processed
2 tablespoons tomato paste

Tabasco
salt and pepper
1 quantity «standard pastry»
1 lb (450 gm) fresh spinach
8 oz (225 gm) feta cheese, cubed
6 oz (170 gm) pitted black olives
4 eggs, beaten

Sauté onion and garlic in oil until soft, then add the thyme and tarragon. When cooked, stir in flour, then gradually add red wine to make a paste. Add the processed fresh tomatoes and tomato paste, and a dash of Tabasco and season to taste. Cook gently to a thick sauce.

Grease and flour a flan dish then line with the pastry.

Cook the spinach briefly in just the water clinging to the leaves, then chop it well. Place spinach, feta cheese and olives into the pastry lined dish. Beat the eggs into the sauce, pour it over the spinach and use your fingers to distribute it. Bake at 160° for about 1 hour, until set.

SORREL & LOVAGE FRITTATA

A frittata is basically a light and fluffy filled omelette. Here the filling and the egg mixture are cooked together in a heavy frypan, then finished under a hot grill. A frittata is never folded like an omelette, but served flat, usually cut into wedges. Serve this frittata with your choice of light, cheesy pasta accompaniments, and a crisp green salad.

1 lb 12 oz (800 gm) waxy potatoes, cut into ¼ inch (½ cm) cubes
8 eggs, separated
butter or margarine
14 oz (400 gm) leeks, finely sliced
2 teaspoons salt
½ teaspoon pepper
½ teaspoon ground mace
8 -10 sprigs lovage, finely chopped
10 large sorrel leaves, stalked and shredded

Bring a large pan of water to a rolling boil, and add the potatoes. As soon as the water returns to the boil, drain and refresh.

Beat the egg yolks in a bowl until light and foamy. Beat the egg whites in another bowl until they form stiff peaks. Fold the whites into the yolks.

Preheat your grill. Melt the butter or margarine in a 12 inch (30 cm) frypan, and when it is hot add the leeks and sea-sonings. Stir for 2 minutes then add the potato dice. Stir for 1 more minute then add the lovage and sorrel. Mix well, then pour in the egg mixture. Gently lift the vegetables several times with a slice so the egg flows underneath everything. Cook for about 5 minutes until the base is set. Pop under the preheated grill and cook the top until it is golden brown. Slide onto a heated flat serving dish, and cut into 8 wedges to serve.

BROCCOLI & RED LEICESTER TART

Serve this hot, cut into wedges, with «rich tomato sauce», a potato dish and perhaps some «marjoram braised baby carrots», or allow to go completely cold and serve with a selection of salads.

8 oz (225 gm) broccoli
1 onion, finely chopped
3 tablespoons sunflower oil
1 tablespoon dried dill
2 oz (55 gm) butter
2 oz (55 gm) wholewheat flour
½ pint (300 ml) milk
3 tablespoons soured cream
4 eggs, beaten
pinch of salt
1 quantity «standard pastry»
10 oz (280 gm) Red Leicester cheese, cut into ½ inch (1½ cm) cubes

Cook broccoli in boiling water for a couple of minutes, strain and refresh. It should still be green and crunchy to taste. Sauté the onion with the sunflower oil and add the dill.

Melt butter in a pan and stir in flour to make a roux. Cook for a couple of minutes, then gradually add milk to give a smooth sauce. Wait to cool before mixing in the soured cream, eggs and salt.

Roll out the pastry and line the bottom of a greased flan dish. Arrange the broccoli, onions and cheese in the dish, then cover with the sauce. Use your fingertips to distribute the sauce evenly and bring some of the broccoli and cheese cubes to the surface. Make it look nice! Bake at 160° until set: this takes about 1 hour.

ACCOMPANIMENTS: BREAD & PASTA

Illustrations by Pippa Sterne

CHEESE STIX

A nice change from croûtons to serve with soup. Also good for dipping into «green aïoli» or «spiced tomato sauce», or simply nibbling with a pint of beer. The recipe makes lots, but they're so moreish they'll disappear like magic!

15 oz (425 gm) wholewheat flour
½ tablespoon salt
½ teaspoon cayenne
2 teaspoons baking powder
4 oz (110 gm) hard vegetable margarine (frozen), chopped small
12 oz (340 gm) Cheddar, grated
2 eggs, beaten
cold water to mix
beaten egg for brushing

Either put the first 5 ingredients into your processor and process to crumbs, or rub the margarine into the flour mixture by hand.

Mix in the cheese, add the eggs and just enough cold water to make a firm dough. Knead lightly till smooth.

Roll out to a 2/3 inch (1 cm) thick rectangle and cut into 2/3 inch (1 cm) by 3½ inch (9 cm) long sticks. Lay on parchment covered baking sheets and brush with beaten egg. Bake in a preheated oven at 225° for 7 minutes until golden.

SMOKED CHEESE & DILL COBBLES

To use as topping for casseroles, or to serve individually as an accompaniment to salads or soups. We use smoked Caerphilly or Wedmore, which is Caerphilly with a layer of herbs in the middle. Makes 9: recipe can easily be doubled.

1 oz (30 gm) hard margarine (frozen)
½ lb (225 gm) wholewheat flour
1 tablespoon baking powder
scant ¼ teaspoon cayenne pepper
1 teaspoon salt
7 oz (200 gm) smoked cheese, grated
handful fresh dill, chopped (or 1½ tablespoons dried dill weed)
1 egg, beaten
about 2½ fl oz (60 ml) milk
egg for brushing

Chop the margarine coarsely and put in processor with the next four ingredients. Process until everything is well combined. Turn into a bowl and mix in the cheese (leaving out 2 oz/55 gm) and dill. Stir in the egg, and gradually add milk, working it in (hands are best here) until the mixture becomes a very firm dough. Turn out onto lightly floured marble or a board, and knead until smooth. Pat out to depth of 2 inch (5 cm) cutter, and cut out in about 9 rounds. Place these, the cobbles, on baking sheets leaving plenty of space for expansion. Brush with beaten egg and top each with a tight pinch of the remaining cheese. Bake in a preheated 160° oven for 15-20 minutes, until hollow sounding when tapped on the bottom. Alternatively, bake for only 10 minutes, then put on top of a bubbling, almost-ready casserole to finish cooking for a further 10-15 minutes.

MAGIC BREAD

This is the real recipe for the bread we make every day in the restaurant to serve as part of our Mason's lunch, to go with salads or with a dish of hand churned butter and our own jam, when it is still warm from the oven in the morning. Can be made by hand in a bowl, or in a mixer using a dough hook. A vegan could use maple syrup instead of honey.

3 tablespoons dried yeast
3 tablespoons clear honey
1 pint (570 ml) hand hot water
15 oz (425 gm) Malthouse flour
2 tablespoons salt
1 tablespoon carob flour
5 tablespoons sunflower oil
15-18 oz (425-500 gm) Rushall
wholewheat flour
extra oil for the bowl

Add yeast and honey to the water, and leave for about 5 minutes until frothy. Add the next five ingredients and beat for 1 minute with a dough hook or 100 times by hand. Gradually add the wholewheat flour, beating all the time, until the mixture begins to leave the side of the bowl and is just not sticky. The amount of flour required will vary according to the type used and the weather! Turn the dough out onto a lightly floured surface and knead until light and springy.

Put the dough into a large oiled bowl and turn around so the entire surface is coated with oil. Put to rise in a warm place for about 45 minutes or until double in bulk.

Preheat your oven to 160°. Punch the dough down and mould into about 15 rolls, each slightly smaller than a tennis ball. Space as widely as possible on 2 parchment covered baking sheets, and leave in a warm place for 5 minutes. Bake in the hot oven for 20 minutes, or until the rolls sound hollow when tapped on the bottom. Cool on a wire rack.

GARLIC BREAD & FRIENDS

The following foil-wrapped and baked breads are ideal accompaniments for all pasta dishes and Mediterranean style soups and casseroles. Soft in texture, they smell wonderful as you unwrap and serve them, positively oozing with strongly flavoured, fragrant butter!

JUST GARLIC BREAD

1 quantity «magic bread» dough
4 oz (110 gm) salted butter
4 fat cloves garlic, crushed
handful finely chopped parsley

Make up the bread dough, but instead of turning it into rolls, when it has risen punch it down and divide into 2. Roll

each half into a fat sausage shape, about 8 inches (20 cm) long. Keep the thickness as uniform as possible. Set the sausages on baking sheets, and bake in a preheated 160° oven for 25-30 minutes, until golden brown and hollow sounding when tapped on the bottom. Cool completely on a wire rack.

Soften the butter, and combine thoroughly with the garlic and parsley.

Now evenly slice each of your 2 loaves into 8. Spread the slices liberally with the garlic butter. Reconstruct the loaves, and wrap them both tightly with foil. Reheat at 160° for about 20 minutes. The loaves can also be baked alongside other things cooking in the oven. Just vary the time according to the temperature.

OLIVE-GARLIC BREAD

Here, and in the variations below, different ingredients are added to the actual bread dough, thus producing a more complex range of flavours and textures. Refer to «just garlic bread» for the butter recipe, and for the process of assembling the loaves and rebaking them.

4 tablespoons dried yeast
2 tablespoons clear honey
1 pint (550 ml) hand hot water
12 oz (340 gm) Malthouse flour
2 tablespoons salt
4 oz (110 gm) pitted black olives, sliced or roughly chopped in processor

6 spring onions, finely sliced
4 tablespoons olive oil
c 18 oz (500 gm) wholewheat flour
1 quantity garlic butter

To make the bread, follow the method for «magic bread» with the ingredients listed here, adding the olives and spring onions along with the olive oil. When the dough has risen, punch down and divide into 2 sausage shaped loaves. Bake in your preheated oven at 160° and cool completely.

Make the garlic butter. Cut each loaf into 8, spread the butter and bake in foil.

SUN DRIED TOMATO-OLIVE BREAD

Follow method and ingredients for «olive-garlic bread». The spring onions can be omitted or included as you prefer.

1½ oz (40 gm) sun dried tomatoes boiling water

Make a purée with just tomatoes and water, following the method in «rosemary feta & sun dried tomato crostini». Substitute this purée for an equal quantity of the hot water when you begin the dough recipe.

This bread can be spread and baked as for «just garlic bread» with a butter of your choice, but is also delicious as it is.

LEMON-OLIVE BREAD

This is a delicious and beautiful bread with nutty rye flour acting in partnership with the tangy lemon. Rye doughs will always be stickier than simple wholewheat, so be careful not to add too much flour.

3 tablespoons dried yeast
2 tablespoons clear honey
juice of 3 lemons and enough warm water
to make up 1 pint (550 ml)
6 oz (170 gm) rye flour
22-24 oz (600-750 gm) wholewheat flour
1 tablespoon salt

4 oz (110 gm) pimento stuffed olives,
sliced
zest of 3 lemons
4 tablespoons olive oil

Prove the yeast with the honey and lemon water in a large bowl till frothy. Beat in the rye flour, a heaping cupful of the wholewheat flour, and the salt. Beat for 5 minutes.

Add the olives, lemon zest and oil and beat until well incorporated. Gradually add enough of the remaining wholewheat flour until you have a firm but slightly sticky dough. Turn out onto a lightly floured board and knead till smooth and elastic. Put into a clean well oiled bowl and turn to coat all sides. Leave in a warm place to rise to double its bulk (45 minutes-1 hour). Form dough into 2 cylindrical loaves and set on lightly oiled baking sheets. Allow to rise again till almost double (about 20 minutes). Bake in a preheated 160° oven for 25-30 minutes until the loaves test done. Cool to cold on a wire rack.

Make the lemon spread. Butter, reform and bake the loaves as for «just garlic bread».

LEMON BUTTER
zest of 2 lemons and juice of 1
4 oz (110 gm) softened butter

Beat the lemon zest and juice into the softened butter.

PIZZA BREAD

An intriguing bread to serve with soup or a salad. Perfect for grilled cheese sandwiches. Makes 3 loaves.

1½ oz (40 gm) sun dried tomatoes
½ pint (300 ml) boiling water

3 tablespoons dried yeast
2 tablespoons clear honey
1¾-2 lb (800-900 gm) wholewheat flour
3 tablespoons olive oil
1 tablespoon salt
½ teaspoon freshly ground black pepper
2 tablespoons dried oregano
1-2 teaspoons crushed garlic
2 tablespoons finely chopped parsley
4 oz (110 gm) freshly grated Parmesan or
other hard cheese

Soak the tomatoes in the boiling water for 30 minutes.

Puré tomatoes with the soaking liquid, and make up to 1 pint (550 ml) with warm water. Tip into a large bowl and stir in the yeast and honey. Leave to go frothy (5-10 minutes). Add half the flour, and all the other ingredients. Beat 10 minutes. Allow to rest for 10 minutes, then beat in more flour until you have a slightly sticky dough. Turn out onto a lightly floured board and knead until smooth and bouncy, incorporating additional flour if necessary. Turn the ball of dough around in an oiled bowl and rise in a warm spot until double in size. Punch down and shape into loaves. Put the loaves into well oiled 1 lb/500 gm loaf pans and leave to rise till the dough reaches the top of the pans. Bake at 160° for 30-40 minutes until the loaves sound hollow when tapped on the base.

ROSEMARY, RED ONION & TOMATO FOCACCIA

Our focaccias are often mistaken for pizzas by our customers. Those familiar with our masterpizza or aloha pizza (see *Cooking With Stones*) could never make this error. Whilst based on the pizza principle, focaccias are thinner, the bases are not prebaked and the toppings are less complex. Focaccias are designed to accompany pasta dishes with light or creamy sauces, providing contrasting textures and complementary flavours. A squeaky fresh green and red garden salad, dressed with walnut oil, lemon juice and a little salt completes the meal. Roast your garlic cloves in their skins at 200° for 5 minutes. Plum tomatoes are best, if you have them.

½ pint (300 ml) warm water
1 tablespoon dried yeast
1 tablespoon clear honey
8 oz (225 gm) wholewheat flour
1 tablespoon salt
4 tablespoons extra virgin olive oil
1 tablespoon ground dried rosemary
(grind in spice mill)
c 8oz (225 gm) more wholewheat flour

1 tablespoon olive oil for dribbling
1 teaspoon coarse sea salt
4 tablespoons seeded, chopped tomatoes
2 small red onions, sliced

4 cloves garlic, roasted and sliced
2-4 oz (55-110 gm) Teifi or mozzarella, grated
3 medium tomatoes, sliced
2 tablespoons freshly grated Parmesan cheese
2 oz (55 gm) pitted black olives, halved
2 teaspoons chopped fresh rosemary, or
1 teaspoon dried

In a large bowl, or in the bowl of an electric mixer with a dough hook, combine the water, yeast and honey. Leave for about 5 minutes, until frothy. Add the flour, salt, oil and herbs, and beat 100 strokes by hand, or 2 minutes by machine. Gradually add more flour, beating continuously until a just not sticky dough is achieved. In an electric mixer, the dough will leave the sides of the bowl. Turn out onto a lightly floured surface and knead till smooth, silky and bouncy.

Put into a lightly oiled bowl and turn until all the surface is oily. Leave in a warm place until double in size. This can take from 20 minutes on a hot summer day to more than an hour in a winter kitchen.

Punch down the risen dough and roll out on a lightly floured surface in a round, to line a 12 inch (30 cm) diameter pizza pan or equivalent sized baking tray. Leave for 5-10 minutes until visibly risen then start the topping procedure. With your fingertips, make indentations across the surface of the dough. Drizzle with half a tablespoon of olive oil, then carefully sprinkle with the sea salt, so that it is well distributed. Next cover with the chopped tomatoes. Then the onion, then scatter with the garlic. The cheese comes next, again evenly distributed. Arrange the tomato slices over the cheese and drizzle with the remaining half tablespoon olive oil. Scatter over the Parmesan, then the olives and finally the rosemary. Bake in a preheated oven at 200° for about 20 minutes. Cut into wedges or slices to serve.

TAPENADE CROSTINI

Crostini are the perfect partners for cheesy pasta dishes. Slices of various types of bread cut from long round loaves are spread with an exciting topping and baked in a single layer until slightly crispy, or grilled. The quantities given in this and the following recipe allow for two crostini per person. Try tapenade crostini with minestrone.

---

2 cloves garlic
4 oz (110 gm) pitted black olives
2 tablespoons capers
handful parsley
zest and juice of 1 lemon
1 oz (30 gm) butter, softened
1 tablespoon olive oil
pinch salt

16 rounds day old bread (¾ inch/2 cm thick)
handful parsley, chopped

Finely process garlic. Add olives, capers, parsley, lemon zest and juice and roughly process. Add the softened butter, olive oil and salt to taste, to produce a thick buttery paste.

Spread this tapenade onto one side of the bread and lay the slices face upwards on an oiled dish. Bake at 160° for 10-15 minutes. Sprinkle with chopped parsley.

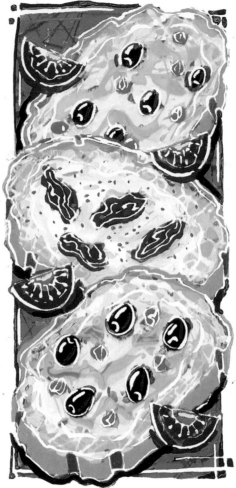

ROSEMARY, FETA & SUN DRIED TOMATO CROSTINI

These can be baked, as for «tapenade crostini», or grilled as below.

---

bread dough
1½ oz (40 gm) sun dried tomatoes
boiling water
4 oz (110 gm) feta cheese
large handful chopped parsley
2 tablespoons olive oil

Make up the dough as for «rosemary, red onion & tomato focaccia», using double the quantities. Form into 2 long sausage shaped rolls. Bake on parchment covered sheets at 160° for 20-25 minutes, till they sound hollow when tapped. Slice each into 8 rounds when completely cold.

Soak the dried tomatoes in boiling water to cover for half an hour. Turn the tomatoes with their soaking liquid into a pan and simmer gently for about 20 minutes, or until quite soft. Cool a little, then process until a slightly coarse purée is achieved. Turn into a bowl and crumble in the feta cheese. Stir in the parsley and olive oil.

Toast your bread slices lightly on one side under a hot grill (they should not brown). Now spread the tomato mixture on the other sides, and sear for 1 minute back under the grill.

QUICK CROSTINI

For simpler crostini, try just brushing your choice of bread slices with olive oil mixed with crushed garlic and a sprinkle of finely chopped fresh vegetables and/or herbs. Then bake or grill as above.

137

CHEESY CORN & PARSLEY MUFFINS

At Stones we serve these as a soup accompaniment. They're particularly nice with tomatoey soups, such as «baked tomato» or «red pepper and tomato». Try them hot from the oven, buttered, for breakfast!

4 oz (110 gm) wholewheat flour
4 oz (110 gm) fine maize meal or polenta
½ teaspoon salt
½ teaspoon mustard powder
¼ teaspoon cayenne pepper
1 tablespoon baking powder
3 oz (85 gm) Cheddar, grated
1 packed teacup finely chopped parsley
2 oz (55 gm) melted butter
1 egg
½ pint (300 ml) milk

Thoroughly mix together all the dry ingredients, including the cheese and parsley. Beat the butter, egg and milk together and combine this with the dry ingredients until just mixed: do not over beat. Two thirds fill well oiled muffin tins, and bake in a preheated oven at 200° for about 20 minutes, until well risen and golden.

LEMON-HERB DUMPLINGS

1 lb (450 gm) wholewheat flour
4 oz (110 gm) vegetable suet
1 teaspoon baking powder
zest and juice of 1 lemon
1 teaspoon salt
handful fresh herbs (eg parsley, dill, sage, marjoram), chopped
cold water

Mix together the flour, suet and baking powder. Add the lemon zest and juice, salt and herbs. Mix together thoroughly before adding enough water to form a stiff dough.

Divide the mixture into 16 golf balls. The best way to cook dumplings is to put them into a juicy casserole with adequate liquid in it (eg «mushroom & haricot chasseur»). The dumplings will swell and the tops will turn golden and crispy while the immersed part will absorb the juices and become really gooey and tasty! Dumplings should be put into a casserole 25-30 minutes before serving, with the lid left off to allow them to crisp up.

SAGE & ONION DUMPLINGS

1 onion, finely chopped
1 teaspoon freshly ground yellow mustard seed
1 teaspoon freshly ground black pepper

Make and cook as above, but omit the lemon and use all sage for the herbs. Add the onion, mustard and pepper with the sage. The perfect topping for a «marrow and chestnut hotpot»!

ONION BHAJIS

Serve these to accompany «spinach & new potato shutka» or any Indian dish.

5 oz (140 gm) chickpea flour
¼ teaspoon cayenne pepper
½ teaspoon turmeric
1 teaspoon garam masala
2 teaspoons freshly ground coriander
½ teaspoon salt
1/3 teaspoon baking powder
2 teaspoons vegetable ghee (or oil)
1 tablespoon lemon juice
6 fl oz (175 ml) cold water - or as needed
1 onion, thinly sliced
vegetable ghee (or oil) for frying

Combine the dry ingredients in a bowl.

Add the ghee or oil, lemon juice and as much water as necessary to form a thick, smooth paste. Mix in the onion slices. Heat more ghee/oil in a frying pan, and drop by spoonfuls into the hot fat. Turn each bhaji when golden brown. When both sides are done, drain and dry on kitchen paper.

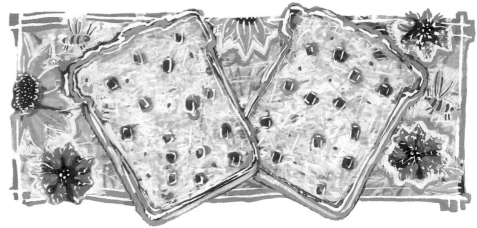

CHEESY CORNBREAD

This is really special made with blue cornmeal if you can find it! Blue corn is grown and used extensively in the Americas, particularly by indigenous peoples. We have made cornbread in Stones with Hopi cornmeal, but haven't yet traced a source in Britain. Cheesy cornbread set with green and red pepper jewels is an ideal accompaniment for any Creole or central American dish.

8 oz (225 gm) fineground cornmeal
2 oz (55 gm) wholewheat flour
1 tablespoon baking powder
1 teaspoon salt
¼ teaspoon cayenne pepper
1 egg, beaten
4 tablespoons sunflower oil
2 tablespoons pure maple syrup (or clear honey)
8½ fl oz (240 ml) milk
1 each small red and green peppers, finely diced
4 oz (110 gm) Cheddar, grated
handful parsley, chopped

Put all the dry ingredients into a large mixing bowl. Beat in, just enough to mix, the egg, sunflower oil, maple syrup (better than honey if you have it) and milk. Stir in the pepper, cheese and parsley.

Line a 2 lb (1 kg) loaf tin with baking parchment and spoon in the mixture. Bake at 190° for about 50 minutes, or until a knife poked in the middle comes out clean. Cool for 30 minutes in the tin, then turn onto a wire and cool until completely cold before slicing.

PASTA SHELLS IN BRIE & RED PEPPER SAUCE

Pencarreg, a clean, creamy Brie from a group of Welsh organic farms, is our choice for this sauce. Experiment with different, well flavoured soft cheeses.

> 1 tablespoon olive oil
> 4 red peppers, seeded and coarsely chopped
> 2 small sharp flavoured onions
> 1 tablespoon olive oil
> 2 tablespoons lemon juice
> 1 tablespoon white wine vinegar
> 1/3 pint (190 ml) stock
> 2 teaspoons chopped fresh rosemary (or 1 teaspoon dried)
>
> 18 oz (500 gm) shell pasta
> olive oil
> 4 oz (110 gm) Pencarreg, or other creamy soft cheese
> 3 fl oz (75 ml) soured cream
> 3-4 tablespoons chopped fresh chervil (or substitute parsley)
> salt, pepper and sugar to taste

Heat olive oil and gently braise the peppers, covered, for 15-20 minutes until very tender. Cool slightly, then puré and set aside.

Process together the next 6 ingredients, and simmer on medium heat for 10 minutes.

Meanwhile, start cooking the pasta in lots of boiling water with a dash of oil. Stir the pepper purée into the onion mixture and warm everything through.

Puré the Brie with the soured cream and a few tablespoons of the sauce, and add to the pan. Stir in the chervil and season with salt, pepper and a little sugar if necessary. As soon as the pasta is cooked, drain and toss with the sauce to serve. Garnish with a little extra chopped chervil if you like.

PENNE WITH RED PESTO

This can be served as a simple starter with garlic bread and some salad leaves, or as an accompaniment to casseroles or ragoûts with a Mediterranean flavour.

> 12 oz (340 gm) penne
> olive oil
> knob of margarine
> salt and freshly ground black pepper
> 1/2 quantity «red pesto»
>
> dash of red wine or cream (optional)
> 2 oz (55 gm) Parmesan cheese, preferably freshly grated
> handful chopped parsley

Drop the penne into boiling water with a splash of olive oil in it. When cooked, drain, add margarine and seasoning, then stir in the red pesto to cover evenly.

A dash of red wine and/or cream can be stirred into the pasta at this point. Serve with a sprinkling of Parmesan and fresh parsley.

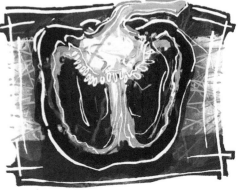

PENNE WITH LEEK & STILTON SAUCE

A very rich and flavoursome dish. An excellent accompaniment for «marinated aubergine steaks», or great as a main dish in its own right with garlic bread, crostini with a topping of finely chopped tomatoes and red onions, or «sun dried tomato olive bread». If using as a main dish, serve with a salad of mixed leaves and herbs, simply dressed with a splash of walnut or almond oil, lemon juice and a little salt.

18 oz (500 gm) penne
1 oz (30 gm) unsalted butter
1 lb (450 gm) leeks, cut into ¼ inch (½ cm) slices
4 cloves garlic, crushed
4 tablespoons good quality dry sherry
1½ oz (40 gm) wholewheat flour
1 teaspoon ground mace
12 fl oz (350 ml) stock (½ tablespoon vegetable concentrate in boiling water)
6 fl oz (175 ml) double cream
6 oz (170 gm) blue Stilton, grated or crumbled
4 oz (110 gm) Cheddar, grated
freshly ground black pepper
handful flat leaved parsley, chopped

Cook the penne according to packet directions, and refresh under a cold tap.

Melt the butter and gently sauté the leeks with the garlic for 8-10 minutes, until the leeks begin to soften. Do not allow to brown. Add sherry and increase heat. Cook for about 5 minutes until almost all the sherry has evaporated. Stir in the flour and mace, and cook, stirring for 1 minute. Gradually add the hot stock, stirring all the time, and finally the cream. Reduce the heat and cook gently until you have a thick, creamy sauce. Add the cheeses and stir until they are melted. Remove from the heat and stir the sauce up with the penne. Transfer to a hot serving dish, and sprinkle with pepper and parsley.

SPAGHETTI WITH SUN DRIED TOMATO SAUCE

Sun dried tomatoes add a distinctive Mediterranean touch to a basic tomato sauce. Here they are simmered gently in red wine then puréed with the wine and herb reduction, and added to the sauce just minutes before serving. The chunky texture of this sauce together with the relatively short cooking time ensures that the fresh flavour of the vegetables really comes through.

2 oz (55 gm) sun dried tomatoes
1 tablespoon dried oregano
1 tablespoon dried marjoram
10 fl oz (300 ml) red wine
5 fl oz (150 ml) water

4 tablespoons olive oil
4-6 bay leaves
1 extra large onion, roughly chopped
6 cloves garlic, sliced
1 each red and green peppers, cut into
½ inch (1-2 cm) cubes
3 sticks celery, cut into ¼ inch (½ cm)
slices
2 carrots, thinly sliced
3 courgettes (c 12 oz/340 gm) cut into
½ inch (1 cm) cubes
4 large ripe tomatoes, roughly chopped
salt and pepper

2 tablespoons balsamic vinegar
½ tablespoon sugar

18 oz (500 gm) wholewheat spaghetti
olive oil
freshly grated Parmesan cheese

Put the dried tomatoes in a small pan together with the herbs, wine and water.

Cover the pan and bring slowly to the boil. Lower heat, cover and simmer gently for 15 minutes. Remove lid and simmer 5 minutes more. Meanwhile prepare all the vegetables for the sauce.

Heat the olive oil in a large pan. Add the bay leaves, onion and garlic and sauté 5 minutes. Add all the other vegetables and a little seasoning. Stir, reduce heat, cover and simmer 30 minutes.

Puré the dried tomatoes with their cooking liquid and add the vinegar and sugar. Cover and simmer 10 minutes more. Adjust seasoning.

Meanwhile, cook the spaghetti in plenty of fast boiling salted water till just al dente. Drain and toss with a little olive oil. Serve topped with the sauce and lots of Parmesan.

SESAME NOODLES WITH WALNUTS

Very simple to make, yet eye appealing and very tasty. The noodles we use require only 6 minutes immersion in freshly boiled water to be cooked to perfection (or you could use whole-wheat noodles without egg). Sesame noodles and walnuts make an ideal bed on which to rest oriental kebabs.

2 250 gm packs medium egg noodles
3 fl oz (75 ml) toasted sesame oil
4 oz (110 gm) walnuts, roughly chopped
1 teaspoon salt
1 tablespoon tamari soya sauce
5 fl oz (150 ml) finely chopped parsley
4 tablespoons toasted sesame seeds

Cook the noodles according to the directions on the pack. Meanwhile, heat the sesame oil and stir fry the walnuts with the salt for 1-2 minutes. Add the tamari and toss in the cooked noodles, stirring to coat thoroughly. Stir in the parsley, and serve sprinkled with the toasted sesame seeds.

ACCOMPANIMENTS: VEGETABLE

Illustrations by Nancy Anderson

PURÉES, PYRAMIDS & SOUFFLÉS

At Stones, particularly during the spring and late autumn months, we often serve a vegetable purée as an accompaniment. Root vegetables are best for purées. The lighter, summery vegetables with their high moisture content can be featured in a purée alongside roots, particularly mild flavoured floury potatoes.

For variety, firm textured purées can be turned into pyramids and baked until crispy and golden on the outside, but still melting in the middle.

With up to 500 people coming in sporadically each day for lunch, properly made soufflés which demand precise timing and immediate serving are impractical for the Stones style. Our 'soufflés' are lightly set, richer versions of our purées. For a successful soufflé, be sure to dry your steamed vegetables thoroughly after cooking, by returning them to the cooking pan after draining, and shaking over gentle heat to remove as much moisture as possible.

Turn any of these combinations into purées, pyramids or soufflés, following the techniques described below.

Carrots cooked gently with orange zest in orange juice, and puréed with freshly ground coriander seed.

Potatoes with spinach, parsley and garlic.

Potatoes and celeriac with cinnamon and lemon zest.

Parsnips with nutmeg, and saffron infused cream, instead of butter.

Potatoes with leeks and fresh peas, seasoned with chopped thyme and summer savory.

Sweet potatoes with butter, cinnamon and a dash of rum.

Carrots cooked gently in butter, orange juice and a sprig of fresh rosemary, with a dash of Cointreau. Omit butter when mashing with additional chopped fresh rosemary.

ROOT VEGETABLE PURÉE

This is the basic purée recipe. Vary your root vegetables according to what you have available and what your main dish will be. Choose from leeks, carrots, parsnips, swede or celeriac. If making herbed vegetable purée, be careful to use herbs that complement rather than over-power the flavour of the main ingredients.

3-4 lb (1-2 kg) root vegetables, trimmed and cut into even sized pieces
a few sprigs of fresh herbs

1-2 oz (30-60 gm) butter/margarine
1-2 handfuls chopped fresh herbs (optional)
salt and pepper

Steam or boil the vegetables in a minimum of water with sprigs of herbs until tender. Remove the herbs, drain and save any liquid for soup. Return the vegetables to a dry pan and shake over the heat to remove any excess moisture.

Mash or process with the butter or margarine until smooth. Stir in the chopped herbs if using and season. Turn into an attractive warmed dish and fork the top to serve.

ROOT VEGETABLE PYRAMIDS

Make the purée as above, using only an oz (30 gm) of butter or margarine. Drop by large serving spoonfuls onto parchment covered baking sheets. Fork each mound into a pyramid shape. Drizzle the pyramids with a little melted butter/margarine, and bake alongside your main dish till golden brown.

BROCCOLI & POTATO SOUFFLÉ

This is the basic method of turning a purée into a soufflé. Here we use vegetables which require different cooking times.

---

3 lb (1⅓ kg) potatoes, chopped into even sized pieces
1 lb (450 gm) broccoli, floretted
2 cloves garlic, crushed
knob butter/margarine
salt and pepper

---

4 eggs, separated

Boil the potatoes in a large pan, and when nearly done, add the broccoli and garlic and cook 1-2 minutes, until the broccoli is crisp tender but still bright green. Drain dry and mash with butter or margarine as for a purée. Season.

Beat the egg yolks till frothy and beat into the broccoli purée. Whisk the egg whites until they form stiff peaks, and fold into the mixture. Turn the soufflé mix into a well greased baking/serving dish, and fork the top. Bake in a hot (200°) oven till risen and golden brown.

CHEESY ZAPALLO OR CHILEAN SQUASH WITH KALE

On Easter Island, this delicious squash grows at its best in late January and early February. The fruit is huge, individuals often reaching 40 lb (20 kg) in weight. Sold in the market in thick wedges, it is usually cooked with the small, sweet island tomatoes and any green vegetables that happen to be available. The flavour is similar to that of a pumpkin, but more buttery and not so sweet. Butternut squash or pumpkin (or a combination) make fine substitutes, but the nearest thing in flavour we have grown is red kuri, a rounded 4-5 inch (10-12 cm) diameter orange fleshed squash.

3 lb (1⅓ kg) whole squash
1 large onion, finely chopped
3 large cloves garlic, crushed
2 cherry or other medium hot chillis, seeded and very finely chopped
knob of butter
½ teaspoon salt
9 oz (250 gm) curly kale, ribbed and finely shredded
6 large ripe tomatoes, seeded and chopped
salt and freshly ground black pepper
Tabasco
5 oz (150 gm) mild white cheese (eg Wensleydale), crumbled

Cut unpeeled squash in half and remove any seeds. Lay cut side down on a lightly oiled baking sheet and bake until just tender (the time will vary depending on the variety of squash; red kuri takes c 30 minutes). Peel and chop the flesh into ½-1 inch (1-2 cm) chunks.

Sauté the onion, garlic and chilli in butter and a sprinkle of salt until the onion is transparent. Stir in the chopped squash, and continue to cook, stirring for 3-5 minutes, until all is completely heated through. Add the kale and stir fry until it is wilted but still bright green. Stir in the tomatoes and cook 1 minute more. Take off the heat, and add seasoning and Tabasco to taste.

Turn into a warm serving dish and top with the cheese. Sear under a hot grill until the cheese is beginning to colour. Serve immediately.

CHEESY ZAPALLO WITHOUT KALE

Try savoy cabbage or spinach instead of kale.

A FRICASSÉE OF WINTER VEGETABLES

For this rich, rooty stew, half fill a large plastic bowl (a squeaky clean rounded washing up bowl is ideal) with ice cold water and a big splash of lemon juice. Have this beside you as you chop, and drop the vegetables in. The lemony water keeps everything crisp, and stops the celeriac turning a nasty shade of grey. Use approximately equal weights of celeriac, parsnip, carrot and celery.

---

1 large celeriac, cut into ½ inch (1 cm) dice
2 parsnips, cut as celeriac
4 carrots, thickly sliced
3 sticks celery, sliced
1 very large or 2 medium onions, roughly chopped
1 small cauliflower, cut into florets
10 oz (300 gm) tiny Brussels sprouts
1½ pints (850 ml) light stock (1 teaspoon vegetable concentrate in water)
2 teaspoons each dried sage and thyme (or small handful each fresh)

---

c ¼-½ pint (150-300 ml) milk
1½ oz (40 gm) unsalted butter
1½ oz (40 gm) wholewheat flour
8 tablespoons double cream
4 tablespoons lemon juice
1 teaspoon each salt and pepper
½ packed teacup chopped fresh parsley

First prepare your vegetables. Put cut celeriac, parsnips, carrot and celery into the bowl of water. Put chopped onions in a separate small bowl, and cauliflower and sprouts in another.

Bring the stock and herbs to the boil in a large lidded pan. Add the drained root vegetables and onion, cover and simmer till just tender. Remove with a slotted spoon and set aside. Return the stock to the boil and add the cauliflower and sprouts. Cover and simmer again till just tender. Remove these vegetables from the stock and add them to the cooked roots.

Now tip the remaining stock into a measuring jug and make up to 1 pint (550 ml) with milk. In the cleaned pan, melt the butter and when it is foaming, stir in the flour. Cook this roux for 2 minutes, stirring occasionally. Now very gradually add the milk-stock, stirring all the time until you have a smooth sauce. Add the cream and lemon juice and seasoning. Return the vegetables to the pan and reheat gently, covered, till everything is warmed through. Stir in the parsley. Check the seasoning and serve.

BRAISED RED CABBAGE WITH PEARS & JUNIPER

A flavoursome accompaniment for dishes with an eastern European origin. Try this with stroganoff with noodles, or a chickpea casserole with dumplings and soured cream.

a 3lb (1⅓ kg) red cabbage, core discarded and finely sliced
1½ tablespoons juniper berries, roughly ground in a coffee mill or crushed with pestle and mortar
zest and juice of 2 oranges
8 tablespoons cider vinegar
1 tablespoon sugar
1 teaspoon each salt and pepper
1½ teaspoons mixed spice
4 pears, cored and cut into neat half moons

Put everything except the pears into a deep, lidded pan. Cook, covered, over gentle heat 30-35 minutes, or until the cabbage is tender. Carefully stir in the pears, and continue to simmer 15 minutes longer. Check the flavour and adjust with extra salt, pepper or sugar to taste. Serve hot.

BRAISED RED CABBAGE WITH PEARS & CARAWAY

Caraway seeds make a tempting alternative to juniper berries.

PEASE PUDDING

An old favourite made newly special by the addition of fresh mint. Apple mint is particularly nice.

1½ lb (700 gm) green split peas
zest of 2 lemons
1 large onion, finely chopped
2 teaspoons ground nutmeg
large handful fresh mint, chopped
2 oz (55 gm) butter
2 eggs, beaten
salt and pepper

Put peas, lemon zest and onion into a pan. Cover with water and cook gently until the peas are tender. Add more water a little at a time if necessary to prevent sticking. Process or mash and add the rest of the ingredients. Season well, and turn into an ovenproof serving dish. Cover with foil and bake at 160° for 20 minutes.

BASIL TOPPED TOMATOES

8 tomatoes
olive oil
4 cloves garlic, crushed
1 oz (30 gm) wholewheat breadcrumbs
1 tablespoon grated Parmesan cheese
2 handfuls fresh basil, chopped
salt and pepper

Cut tomatoes in half horizontally. Arrange with cut faces up in an ovenproof serving dish in a single layer. Warm the oil and garlic in a saucepan: do not let it brown. Take off the heat, and stir in breadcrumbs, cheese, basil and seasoning. Sprinkle the basil mix over the tomatoes and bake at 180° for 15 minutes.

TEQUILA GLAZED VEGETABLES WITH HOT MANGO SAUCE

Lots of tequila for a magical flavour! Serve this as it is with plain steamed rice, or leave out the kidney beans and increase the amount of courgettes and peppers, and serve with a bean based Mexican dish, such as enchiladas or «torta Mexicana».

4 or 5 large corn cobs with their husks on
3 oz (85 gm) margarine, softened
salt and pepper

3 tablespoons peanut or sunflower oil
6 fat cloves garlic, thinly sliced
3 red onions, thickly sliced
3 small courgettes, cut into batons
1 each green, yellow, red and orange
peppers, cut into ¼ inch (1 cm) dice
1 teaspoon sugar
5 oz (150 gm) red or black kidney beans,
soaked and boiled till tender
4 fl oz (100 ml) tequila

Carefully peel back the corn husks and remove as much of the green-brown tassel as you can. Spread the exposed kernels with the margarine, and sprinkle with salt and pepper. Fold the husks back and wrap each cob tightly in foil. Roast at 180° for 40 minutes. Unwrap, and when cool enough to handle, pull off the husks and scrape the kernels from the cobs. Set aside.

Heat the oil in a large frying pan or wok, and when smoky add the garlic and onion. When the garlic is beginning to brown add the rest of the vegetables and the sugar. Stir fry on very high heat for 1 minute. Add the beans and the reserved corn. Throw in the tequila and stir continuously until the liquid has almost all vanished. Serve immediately with the hot mango sauce on the side.

HOT MANGO SAUCE

2 large ripe mangos
zest and juice of 3 large limes
2 tablespoons (30 ml) maple syrup

1 tablespoon sunflower oil
2 cloves garlic, crushed
2 small red or green chillis, seeded and
very finely chopped
4 fl oz (100 ml) stock
salt and pepper
light soya sauce

Peel the mangos and cut all the flesh away from the stone. Puré the flesh with the lime zest and juice and maple syrup. Set aside.

Heat oil in a small pan and add the garlic and chillis. Cook gently until the garlic is beginning to turn golden. Add the stock and the mango mixture, and cook until heated through. Season with salt and pepper and a little soya sauce if you like.

151

COURGETTE & ROAST AUBERGINE TIAN WITH PERNOD

Some years ago a friend brought us a wide, deep earthenware dish from south America as a present. Such a dish, known in both the old and parts of the new world as a tian, is excellent for the slow baking of vegetables. This tian positively explodes with Mediterranean flavours and is made extra special by the addition of Pernod. Although we usually serve a tian as an accompaniment (very good with frittata), this dish will make a perfect light supper in its own right with a chunk of crusty bread and a bowl of freshly grated Parmesan cheese. Choose a long aubergine for lots of neat small slices.

1 long skinny aubergine (c 12 oz/340 gm), sliced ½ inch (1 cm) thick
salt
2 tablespoons olive oil
6 tablespoons Pernod

2 onions, sliced
5 or 6 cloves garlic, crushed
4 tablespoons olive oil
2 teaspoons fennel seed, freshly ground
2 teaspoons dried rosemary
salt and pepper
4 courgettes (c 1½ lb/700 gm), sliced ¼ inch (½ cm) thick

6 tomatoes, quartered
3 oz (85 gm) pitted black olives

2 tablespoons olive oil
generous pinch black pepper

Put aubergine into a strainer and sprinkle with salt. Leave for half hour then rinse and pat dry. Lightly olive oil a baking sheet and lay the slices out in a single layer. Drizzle with oil and half the Pernod. Bake at 200° for 7-10 minutes until just tender. Set aside.

Sauté onion and garlic in half the oil for 5 minutes, with half the fennel and rosemary and a large pinch each of salt and pepper. Set aside. Sauté the courgettes with the remaining oil, fennel and rosemary, and more salt and pepper, stirring continuously for 3 minutes. Set this aside too.

Now assemble the tian. Tip the onion mixture into the bottom of the dish. Lay the aubergine slices on top, overlapping slightly if necessary. Cover the aubergine with the courgettes and pack down. Arrange the tomato quarters on top and sprinkle with the olives. Drizzle with olive oil and the rest of the Pernod. Sprinkle with pepper and cover tightly with foil. Bake at 150° for 1 hour. Serve straight from the dish.

SUCCOTASH

In the southern United States, this dish is made with fresh lima beans, which look like a small, bright green seeded version of the British broad bean. We have tried twice to grow them, but have been defeated on both attempts by unexpected early frosts. The flageolet is a close relative of the lima bean, and dried flageolets make an acceptable substitute.

---

1 oz (30 gm) butter
2 red onions, finely chopped
2 teaspoons sugar
3 tablespoons tequila
1 each green and red pepper, diced
corn scraped from 6 large cobs
(c 1 lb/450 gm)
½ teaspoon salt
1 teaspoon pepper
½ teaspoon cayenne pepper
4 fl oz (100 ml) stock
5½ oz (150 gm) dried flageolets, soaked and boiled till just tender (or if you can find them, 12-14 oz/350-400 gm fresh lima beans)
4 fl oz (100 ml) double cream
fresh coriander (or parsley) to serve, chopped

Melt the butter in a deep pan. Add onion and sugar and cook gently, uncovered, until the onion is tender and beginning to brown. Increase the heat to high and add the tequila. Stir for 30 seconds, then tip in the peppers, corn and seasonings. Stir for 30 seconds more, then add the stock and reserved flageolets. Cook, stirring occasionally, for 10-15 minutes, until everything is very hot and all the vegetables are tender.

Stir in the cream and serve immediately, garnished with the chopped herbs.

SESAME BROCCOLI

---

2 lb (900 gm) broccoli (or enough for 8 people)
4 tablespoons sesame oil
3 tablespoons sesame seed
salt and pepper

Break broccoli into large florets and steam until just tender. In another pan, warm the oil over a low heat. Add the seeds and toast until golden. Toss the broccoli in the oil with the seeds, and season.

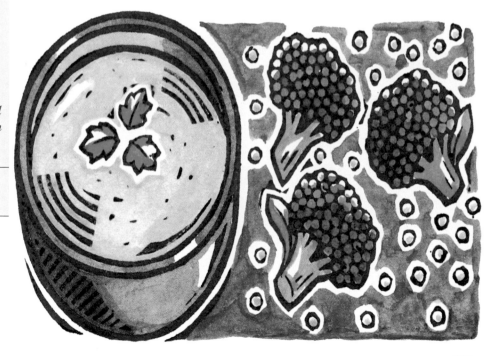

SPICED GREEN BEANS

Serve these hot as an accompaniment to curries and casseroles.

5 tablespoons vegetable ghee
2 tablespoons black mustard seed
1 tablespoon cumin seed
1½ lb (700 gm) green beans
½ pint (300 ml) water
1 tablespoon ground coriander
1 teaspoon salt
1 teaspoon sugar

Heat ghee in a thick based pan. When hot add the mustard and cumin seeds, and cook until cumin turns dark and mustard pops. Add the beans and stir fry for 2-3 minutes, before adding the water. Cover with a tight fitting lid and cook gently for 10-12 minutes, until the beans are tender but still crunchy.

Uncover the beans and turn up the heat. Stir in the coriander, salt and sugar, and cook rapidly for a few minutes to evaporate most of the liquid.

BROCCOLI IN BROCCOLI SAUCE

1 onion, finely chopped
½ teaspoon ground mace
1 lb (450 gm) broccoli
8 oz (225 gm) cream cheese
2 tablespoons lemon juice
2 tablespoons white wine
1 tablespoon arrowroot
½ teaspoon ground cardamom
pinch cayenne pepper
salt and pepper
2 hard boiled eggs, chopped
1½ lb (700 gm) broccoli in large florets
4 oz (110 gm) Cheddar or blue Stilton, grated

Cook onion with the mace in a tiny bit of water until soft. Add broccoli and cook until tender.

Puré onion and broccoli with any remaining cooking liquid and the cream cheese, lemon juice, wine, arrowroot and spices, and season. Warm the sauce over a very low heat until thickened, and stir in the chopped eggs.

Steam the rest of the broccoli until just tender and bright green. Place in a serving dish, cover with the sauce and sprinkle with a well flavoured cheese. Bake at 180° for a few minutes until the cheese melts and turns golden.

LEEKS BRAISED IN MUSTARD-LIME SAUCE

*7 good sized leeks, trimmed, halved
lengthways and washed
½ oz (15 gm) butter/margarine
zest of 2 large limes
8 tablespoons (120 ml) medium sherry
juice of 1 large lime
8½ fl oz (250 ml) stock
2 tablespoons coarse grained mustard
sugar to season (optional)*

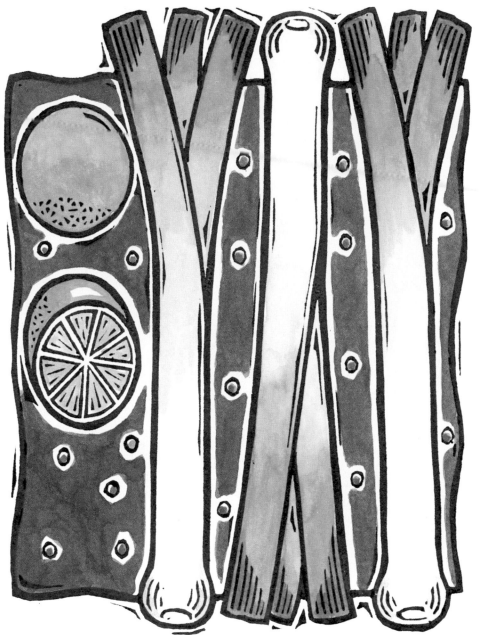

Select the 2 largest leek halves, chop very finely, and set aside. Cut the remaining leek halves in half again, and steam for about 10 minutes until crisp-tender. Lay the steamed leeks attractively in a lidded, shallow casserole to await the sauce.

Sauté the finely chopped leek in the melted butter or margarine with the lime zest on low heat. When the leek is softish, turn the heat up to medium high and add the sherry. Cook until the liquid has virtually evaporated, then add the lime juice, stock and mustard. Turn the heat down again and simmer about 15 minutes until the sauce has thickened a little. Taste, and add a little sugar if you feel the sauce is too sharp. Pour the sauce over the steamed leeks, and bake, covered, in a preheated 190° oven until the sauce is bubbling and everything is heated through.

CAPONATA

A Sicilian inspired variation on the ratatouille theme. A nice alternative as part of a Mediterranean meal.

olive oil
1 onion, chopped
6 sticks celery, sliced
3 cloves garlic, crushed
1 aubergine, chopped
3 red peppers, diced
8 tomatoes, chopped
2 tablespoons red wine vinegar
2 teaspoons sugar
2 oz (55 gm) capers
2 oz (55 gm) pitted green olives, chopped
2 oz (55 gm) currants or raisins
1 oz (30 gm) pine nuts, toasted
2 teaspoons dried basil
pinch chopped parsley
salt and pepper

Heat oil in a pan and sauté onion, celery and garlic for 2-3 minutes. Add aubergine and peppers and cook 1 minute more. Next add tomatoes, vinegar and sugar, cover and cook 5 minutes. Add the rest of the ingredients and continue cooking, covered, on a very low heat till all vegetables are tender. Season to taste.

PUMPKIN GRATIN

1½ lb (700 gm) pumpkin, deseeded, peeled and cut into pieces ¼ inch (½ cm) thick
1 onion, sliced
sunflower oil
4 oz (110 gm) Cheddar, grated
salt and pepper
handful fresh parsley, chopped
¼ pint (150 ml) cream
4 oz (110 gm) wholewheat breadcrumbs

Arrange half the pumpkin slices, then half the onion, over the bottom of an oiled dish. Next add half the cheese, a sprinkle of salt and pepper and half the parsley. Repeat the layers, and pour the cream over. Top with the breadcrumbs, and bake at 160° for about 30 minutes.

MARJORAM BRAISED BABY CARROTS

2 oz (55 gm) butter
1 lb (450 gm) baby new carrots, washed and trimmed
3 fl oz (75 ml) orange juice
handful fresh marjoram
salt and pepper

Melt the butter in a pan over a low heat. Add the carrots and pour in the orange juice. Cover and simmer, stirring occasionally until the liquid has reduced just to glaze the carrots, taking care towards the end that they don't burn: add a little more juice if necessary. Take off the heat and toss in the chopped marjoram and seasoning.

MARINATED AUBERGINE STEAKS

2 large aubergines, thickly sliced
2 tablespoons olive oil
8½ fl oz (250 ml) red wine
pinch dried oregano
pinch dried thyme
½ teaspoon each salt and pepper
olive oil for greasing and frying

Lay the aubergine slices in a single layer in a dish. Mix the oil and wine together and stir in the herbs and seasonings. Beat so everything is well combined, then pour evenly over the aubergines. Cover and put in a cool place for 30 minutes. Turn over the slices and leave covered for another 30 minutes. Transfer the marinated aubergines to a shallow oiled baking tray, again in a single layer. Drizzle with any remaining marinade.

Bake at 160° for 10 minutes, then turn each piece over and bake for a further 10 minutes, or until the steaks are tender and all the wine absorbed.

To serve, heat a little oil in a frypan and shallow fry the steaks for 1-2 minutes each side.

MORE AUBERGINE STEAKS

Before finally panfrying the steaks, dip each one into beaten egg, and coat with breadcrumbs.

For a special occasion, make a thick cheese sauce with blue Stilton. Beat a couple of eggs into the sauce, and spread it thickly over the baked steaks. Instead of panfrying, sear under a hot grill for 2-3 minutes.

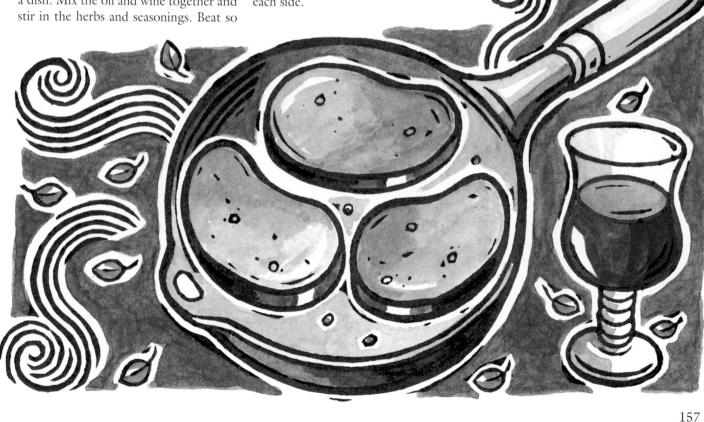

COLCANNON

Colcannon is an Irish dish traditionally made with potatoes and cabbage, and eaten with buttered oatcakes, cheese and pickle. Here we use celeriac instead of potato, add broccoli to the mixture for variety of texture, flavour and colour, and incorporate cubes of hand made cheese. This light textured celeriac colcannon is an ideal accompaniment to robust winter casseroles with lots of small potatoes, and perhaps, dumplings! Use margarine instead of butter and omit the cheese for a vegan dish. Experiment with different green vegetables.

2-2½ lb (900-1100 gm) peeled and trimmed celeriac
lemon juice
knob of butter

2 oz (55 gm) butter
¾ lb (340 gm) trimmed leeks, thinly sliced
¼ white cabbage with core removed
(c 8 oz/225 gm), thinly sliced
2 teaspoons freshly grated nutmeg
1 teaspoon each salt and pepper
4 oz (110 gm) broccoli, in small florets
3 oz (85 gm) Red Leicester cheese, in ½ inch (1 cm) cubes

Roughly chop the celeriac and boil in water with a heavy splash of lemon juice, until soft. Drain and shake in dry hot pan to help evaporate any excess moisture. Mash with butter until a smooth purée. Set aside.

Melt butter in a heavy pan and add the leeks and cabbage and all the seasonings. Cook 5 minutes on low-medium heat, stirring frequently. Add the broccoli and continue cooking for a further 3 minutes. Remove from heat and stir into the mashed celeriac, and adjust the seasoning.

Lightly butter a shallow ovenproof serving dish (a 10 inch/25 cm quiche dish is ideal) and spoon in the celeriac mixture, spreading it evenly. Push the cheese cubes into the surface and bake in a hot (200°) oven for 25-30 minutes until nicely golden and bubbly.

SPICED LEEKS WITH APPLES & HAZELS

4 large leeks, cut into thick chunks
3 tablespoons sunflower oil
1 teaspoon cinnamon
1 teaspoon ground mace
1 tablespoon dried rosemary
4 oz (110 gm) toasted hazelnuts
3 red eating apples, cut into moons
3 fl oz (75 ml) lemon juice
salt and pepper

Sauté leeks gently in oil for about 5 minutes, or until they are beginning to soften. Add spices, rosemary, nuts, apple and lemon juice. Cook until the leeks are tender, and the apples just soft. Season to serve.

SPINACH WITH PINE NUTS & APRICOTS

This is a good way to serve end of season spinach when the leaves are sometimes slightly bitter.

4 oz (110 gm) dried whole apricots,
snipped into little pieces
3 tablespoons olive oil
2 bunches spring onions, sliced (white &
green parts)
3 cloves garlic, crushed
2 lb (900 gm) spinach, stalks and tough
midribs removed
1 teaspoon freshly ground nutmeg
3½ oz (100 gm) pine nuts, toasted

Soak the apricots for 10 minutes in just enough boiling water to cover. Drain and set aside.

Heat the olive oil in a large pan or wok, and sauté the onion and garlic gently for 3-5 minutes, until the onion is softening. Do not brown. Increase the heat to high and stir in the spinach. Stir vigorously until just wilted, then toss with the nutmeg and reserved apricots. Turn immediately into an attractive warm serving dish and scatter with the pine nuts.

SPINACH WITH APRICOTS & CREAM

For a special treat, stir in 3-4 tablespoons double cream along with the apricots! The cream also helps to counteract any bitterness in the leaves.

LEEK BLANQUETTE

A nice accompaniment to firm textured pastry topped dishes or tarts.

8 potatoes, thinly sliced
4 oz (110 gm) butter
4 leeks, thickly sliced
4 oz (110 gm) wholewheat flour
2 pints (1150 ml) milk, warmed
4 bay leaves
pinch grated nutmeg
1 tablespoon coarse grained mustard
salt and freshly ground black pepper

Bring a large pan of water to the boil. Add the potatoes and boil 1 minute. Remove from the heat and drain.

In another pan, melt butter, add leeks and cover to cook gently until tender. Then sprinkle in the flour and stir into a roux. Gradually add the milk, a little at a time to form a smooth sauce. Add the potatoes, bay leaves, nutmeg and mustard, and cook covered on a very low heat until the potatoes are done. Remove the bay leaves and season to serve.

CORN FRITTERS

This makes enough for 16 fritters – 2 for each person – ideal to accompany chillis and casseroles. Your pan must be very hot when you start, but you may need to turn the heat down a little once you get going.

10 oz (280 gm) fine maize meal or polenta
4 oz (110 gm) wholewheat flour
2 teaspoons baking powder
½ teaspoon cayenne pepper
2 teaspoons salt
1 red pepper, very finely chopped
8 oz (225 gm) fresh sweetcorn kernels, blanched
4 tablespoons lemon juice
4 eggs, beaten
milk to mix
sunflower oil

Mix together the dry ingredients. Add the red pepper and sweetcorn. Mix in lemon juice and eggs, then add enough milk for a soft dropping consistency.

Heat a thick based frying pan and a little oil. When the oil begins to smoke, drop dessertspoonfuls of mixture into the pan. Cook for 1-2 minutes each side, flattening gently with a frying spatula.

ACCOMPANIMENTS: BEANS, RICE & GRAINS

Illustrations by Celia Whitchard

BUTTERBEAN HUMMUS

This is a quick and easy creamier alternative to the traditional chickpea hummus. Dark tahini is a naturally unhulled roasted sesame paste, and has a richer flavour than light tahini – but either is good for this recipe.

8 cloves garlic, crushed
2 lb (900 gm) cooked butterbeans (drain and save the water)
4½ fl oz (120 ml) lemon juice
4 tablespoons dark tahini
4½ fl oz (120 ml) olive oil
6 fl oz (180 ml) water from cooking beans
salt and pepper

Place ingredients into a processor, and blend to give a smooth purée. Season.

Serve as a dip with crudités and toasted pitta, or as part of a Greek mezze with tzatziki and «dolmades». Or again, as a hot side dish with «spanakopitta» or «ratatouille filo pie». To heat, put in an ovenproof dish, sprinkle with a little extra olive oil and paprika, and bake at 180° for 25-30 minutes.

GINGERED MILLET PILAFF

Millet pilaffs are particularly appropriate for dishes with a north African flavour, and also go well with rissoles (eg «celery & pecan cakes») with a yogurty sauce. If you find walnut oil difficult to obtain, sunflower oil can be substituted but walnut best complements the nutty flavour of the roast millet. Stem ginger in syrup is available in good supermarkets. You need a large, heavy based frypan with a tight fitting lid for this recipe.

1 lb (450 gm) millet
8 oz (225 gm) red onions, chopped
2 large leeks, thinly sliced
1 large carrot, thinly sliced
4 fat cloves garlic, crushed
3 tablespoons walnut oil
2 teaspoons ground ginger
1 teaspoon salt
1 pint (550 ml) miso stock (1 tablespoon miso in boiling water)
4 oz (110 gm) stem ginger in syrup, cut into matchsticks
1 large red pepper cut into ¼ inch (½ cm) dice
4 oz (110 gm) green beans, finely sliced
juice of ½ lemon
3 oz (85 gm) roast sunflower seeds

Roast the millet in a dry pan on high heat until it smells toasty and starts to pop. Remove from pan and reserve.

In the same pan, sauté the onions, leeks, carrot and garlic in the walnut oil. When the carrot slices are beginning to soften, stir in the ground ginger, salt, reserved millet and stock. Reduce the heat, cover and simmer for exactly 10 minutes.

When the cooking time is up, remove the pan lid and scatter the ginger sticks, pepper and beans over the millet. Do not stir. Replace the lid and cook undisturbed exactly 10 minutes more.

Remove from heat, remove lid, stir up and sprinkle with lemon juice. Adjust the seasoning and serve from the pan or from a serving dish scattered with the sunflower seeds.

HOPPIN' JOHN

This oddly named bean and rice concoction is popular throughout the southern United States. Spices vary from area to area, and from cook to cook. Hoppin' John can be made with or without cheese, and can include all sorts of different vegetables. Corn and okra, for example, are particularly popular in Louisiana and Georgia. For best flavour use fresh red chillis, but cayenne can be substituted.

This is great as part of a Creole or Mexican inspired dinner, or serve it as the centre piece of a late supper, surrounded by bowls of crisp fried tortillas, grated cheese, crisp lettuce and guacamole or soured cream. Our version of Hoppin' John is a symphony of flavours compiled from the notes of various regional cuisines.

---

12 oz (350 gm) red kidney beans, soaked and cooked
9 oz (250 gm) long grain rice, cooked
3 onions, chopped
3 tablespoons sunflower oil
1 tablespoon freshly ground allspice
2 small red chillis, seeded and minced (or 1 teaspoon cayenne)
3 tablespoons chopped fresh basil, or 1 tablespoon dried
3 fl oz (80 ml) orange juice
3 tablespoons tamari
a few bay leaves
2 each red and green peppers, seeded and cubed
5 oz (150 gm) baby corn, halved lengthwise
salt and pepper
9 oz (250 gm) smoked cheese, cubed
6 firm tomatoes, cut into wedges
chopped fresh coriander or parsley to garnish

Sauté the onion with the oil, spices and basil until the onion is softening. Add the orange juice, tamari and bay leaves. Cover and simmer for 5 minutes. Add the peppers, corn, cooked beans and rice. Cover and simmer very gently for about 45 minutes until everything is tender. Season generously with salt and pepper. Cool quickly and refrigerate for several hours or overnight to allow the flavours to develop.

Reheat gently, covered, until everything is piping hot. Check the seasoning. Stir in the cheese cubes and cook for just a few minutes until the cheese begins to melt. Stir in the tomato wedges and serve garnished with the herbs.

163

KASHA WITH WILD MUSHROOMS

Kasha, or roasted buckwheat as it is otherwise known, is used extensively in Jewish cooking. We use kasha in salads, usually in combination with puy lentils, chopped apricots and lots of fresh parsley. We also make roast buckwheat 'pilaffs', adding a wide range of finely chopped vegetables. Kasha with wild mushrooms, the most elegant kasha dish we have yet devised, may be served as an accompaniment to «blinis» or with goulash or stroganoff in place of the more usual noodles. Topped with a lattice of slow cooked omelette strips, snipped olives and chopped cherry tomatoes, it stands as a main course in its own right.

1 oz (30 gm) dried shiitake mushrooms
1 pint stock (2 tablespoons barley miso in boiling water)
4-5 inch (10-12 cm) piece of kombu (optional)

2 tablespoons toasted sesame oil
2 tablespoons sunflower oil
12 oz (340 gm) onion, finely chopped
4 cloves garlic, crushed
1 inch (2-3 cm) knob fresh ginger, peeled and grated
3 eggs
1 teaspoon salt
12 oz (340 gm) roast buckwheat (kasha)

8 oz (225 gm) button mushrooms, quartered
knob margarine
lemon juice
1 teacup finely chopped parsley
salt and black pepper

Soak the shiitake mushrooms in the boiling water with the miso and kombu (if using) for 15 minutes. Remove the mushrooms and slice thinly, discarding any hard bits of stem. Save the miso stock.

Heat the oils in a large heavy based pan with a lid. Gently sauté the onion, garlic and ginger until the onion is transparent. In a bowl, beat the eggs with the salt. Stir the kasha into the egg mix to coat all the grains. Turn the heat under the onion pan to high, and add the eggy kasha. Stir vigorously until the egg is dry and the grains are separated.

Remove the kombu (if used) from the miso stock and discard. Stir the stock all at once into the pan. Lower heat, cover and simmer 8-10 minutes. By this time, all of the liquid should have been absorbed. If any remains, cook with lid off until the kasha is dry. Take off heat and fluff with a fork.

While the kasha is cooking, sauté the button mushrooms with margarine and a splash of lemon juice. Add all the mushrooms to the cooked kasha. Stir in the parsley and add lemon juice and seasoning to taste.

164

REFRITOS

These are refried beans made exciting with the addition of spices and orange. Refritos freeze extremely well, so it makes sense and saves fuel to cook enough for several meals at once. For «torta Mexicana» you will need a quarter of this recipe. So freeze the rest in 3 separate containers for future use to make another torta (they're very moreish!), to fill enchiladas, make nachos, or serve as an accompaniment to any bean-free Mexican meal.

1½ lb (700 gm) red kidney beans, soaked and cooked till just tender
4 large onions, finely chopped
6-8 cloves garlic, crushed
3 small red or green chillis, seeded and minced
3 tablespoons sunflower or peanut oil
2 tablespoons freshly ground coriander seed
1 tablespoon ground cinnamon
1 tablespoon cumin seed
5 sticks celery, trimmed and finely sliced
1 yellow and 2 red large peppers, seeded and small cubed
zest of 4 large oranges
2 400 gm cans plum tomatoes in juice salt and pepper

Briefly sauté the onion with the garlic and chillis in the oil. Stir in the spices and continue to sauté 1 minute more. Add the celery, peppers and orange rind.

Liquidise the tomatoes with their juice, and add to the pan. Add the cooked beans and stir well. Cover and simmer on low heat 50-60 minutes, until everything is very soft. Season generously with salt and pepper. Roughly process half the mixture and stir everything back together. Use immediately or cool quickly and freeze.

RICE, PILAFFS & RISOTTOS

Plain boiled rice is served everywhere with dishes with Asian and central-southern American influences. To turn boiled rice into a pilaff or rice 'dish' is easy, and to us makes for a much more interesting accompaniment. Cooked rice is drained, and just stirred up with other prepared ingredients. Rice dishes can be as simple or as complex in flavour as you like, depending on what other delights are being served. The examples here are just to get your imagination going! Use long grain brown rice, Surinam or basmati rice, or long grain brown with a little wild rice.

HERBED RICE

This is the easiest of all rice creations. Think about the flavours of your other dishes when choosing the oil and herb or herb combination. Use, for example, olive oil and fresh basil, marjoram and/or oregano for a Mediterranean meal; groundnut oil with lots of chopped coriander to go with a magic Mexican feast; or sunflower or walnut oil with fresh dill or sage and thyme for a meal with a more temperate accent.

14-16 oz (400-450 gm) rice
2-3 fl oz (60-80 ml) oil
packed teacupful chopped fresh herbs
1 tablespoon salt
½ tablespoon pepper

Drain the rice thoroughly after cooking and tip into a bowl. Stir in the oil (just enough to coat the rice) and herbs and seasoning. Turn into an attractive warmed dish, and serve immediately.

SPICED RICE

Use the same quantity of rice as you would for «herbed rice», but instead of herbs, add 2-3 tablespoons of freshly ground spices. Always try to stir in some freshly chopped parsley to make the dish attractive. These spice mixtures make more than is necessary for 1 quantity of spiced rice, but the remains can be stored for several weeks in an airtight container in a dark place. Use freshly ground spices for the best flavour.

CARIBBEAN SPICE

1½ tablespoons allspice berries
2 tablespoons black peppercorns
1 tablespoon cloves
1-2 teaspoons cayenne pepper
1 teaspoon salt

Grind the seeds, and mix with cayenne and salt to taste.

CHILLI SPICE

2 tablespoons mustard seed
6 tablespoons coriander seed
3-4 dried chillis
1 teaspoon cayenne pepper
4 tablespoons paprika
1½ tablespoons garlic powder
1½ tablespoons ground cinnamon
1½ tablespoons ground turmeric
1 tablespoon black pepper

Grind the mustard, coriander seeds and chillis, and mix everything together.

ORIENTAL SPICE

2 tablespoons star anise
3 tablespoons coriander seed
2 teaspoons allspice berries
4 tablespoons cardamom pods
1 tablespoon dried ginger
1 tablespoon ground cloves
1 tablespoon ground mace
zest of 4 large oranges, dried in a slow oven

Grind the first 4 ingredients and mix in the rest.

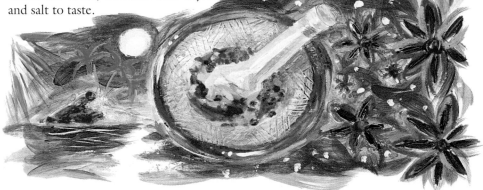

SOUTH INDIAN SPICE

2 tablespoons coriander seed
2 tablespoons cumin seed
1 teaspoon fennel seed
1 teaspoon fenugreek seed
1 teaspoon black mustard seed
2 teaspoons green cardamom pods
½ teaspoon ground cloves
½ teaspoon cayenne pepper
1 teaspoon ground cinnamon

Roast the first 6 ingredients in a dry frypan until the mustard seeds are popping and everything is beginning to brown. Grind all the toasted seeds and stir in the cloves, cayenne and cinnamon.

DILLED MUSHROOM PILAFF

Perfect with goulash or other eastern European inspired dishes.

11 oz (300 gm) rice
3 oz (85 gm) butter
1 large onion, medium-finely chopped
4 large cloves garlic, crushed
1 lb (450 gm) button mushrooms
juice of large lemon
splash of tamari
pinch of chilli powder
1½ teaspoons dill seed
4½ fl oz (120 ml) double cream
salt and pepper
½ packed teacup chopped fresh dill

While the rice is cooking, melt the butter and sauté the onion and garlic until the onion is transparent. Add the mushrooms and stir fry for 1 minute. Add the lemon juice, tamari, chilli powder and dill seed, and cook gently 7-10 minutes or until the mushrooms are just tender. Stir the drained rice into the mushroom mixture and stir in the cream. Season to taste, and finally mix in the fresh dill. Serve immediately.

167

LEMON-PEPPER PILAFF

This is nice with spicy Mexican type dishes. Serve soured cream on the side.

12-14 oz (350-400 gm) rice
4 large cloves garlic, crushed
zest and juice of 3 lemons
1 tablespoon coriander seeds, ground
2 teaspoons ground turmeric
¼ pint (150 ml) water
1 each red, green and yellow peppers, cut into small dice
4 tablespoons groundnut oil
salt and pepper
Tabasco
handful chopped fresh coriander
lemon slices

Whilst the rice is cooking, simmer the garlic, lemon and spices in the water, following the instructions for the same process given for «citrus rice». Add the peppers to the lemon mixture when the rice is almost cooked, and continue to simmer, covered, for 5 minutes.

Drain the rice and mix with the lemony peppers, and the oil. Season to taste. Stir in the coriander and decorate with lemon.

CITRUS RICE

Good with salty oriental dishes such as stir fried vegetables, «oriental spring rolls» or anything containing marinated tofu or tempeh. Citrus rice can also be chilled and served as a salad, with added roast nuts and diced red peppers. Check the seasoning when quite cold and add a little white wine vinegar if necessary.

14 oz (400 gm) rice (preferably 1 part wild rice to 3 parts long grain brown rice)
3 large cloves garlic, crushed
zest of 4 oranges
zest and juice of 3 lemons
1 tablespoon paprika
2 teaspoons coriander seed, ground
½ teaspoon cayenne pepper
1 teaspoon ground ginger
¼ pint (150 ml) water
flesh of 2 oranges, chopped
4 tablespoons almond or sunflower oil
handful chopped parsley
salt and pepper
lemon slices
cinnamon

When you put the water on to boil for the rice, put all the next group of ingredients in another pan. Bring to the boil, then cover and simmer gently all the time the rice is cooking. Check occasionally, and if the mixture seems to be evaporating, add a little more water.

Drain the rice and tip into a bowl. Stir in the spiced orange and lemon mixture, the orange flesh, oil and parsley. Season and turn into a warmed serving dish. Decorate with lemon slices, and sprinkle lightly with cinnamon to serve.

PINEAPPLE-CASHEW RICE

Serve this in the hollowed pineapple shells for a spectacular accompaniment to any oriental meal. It is important to use light soya sauce for this dish: tamari has too powerful a flavour and should not be substituted.

14 oz (400 gm) brown basmati or Surinam rice
7 oz (200 gm) cashew nuts
2 teaspoons toasted sesame oil
salt
2 small ripe pineapples with attractive green crowns
1 tablespoon sunflower oil
1 tablespoon toasted sesame oil
1 large onion, finely chopped
4 cloves garlic, crushed
1 inch (3 cm) knob of fresh ginger, grated
4 fl oz (100 ml) light soya sauce
1 teaspoon sugar
1 teaspoon freshly ground white pepper
2 red peppers, finely diced
small bunch (c 12 sprigs) fresh basil, roughly chopped
4 spring onions, finely sliced

Cook the rice in lots of boiling water and drain and set aside.

Toast the cashews with the sesame oil drizzled over in a 200° oven for about 7 minutes, or until golden brown (you can do this anytime you have the oven at this temperature for another dish), then sprinkle with a generous pinch of salt. Turn the nuts into a bowl and set aside.

Cut both pineapples in half lengthways, right through the bright green crown. Carefully run a sharp pointed knife between the flesh and the shell of all four halves, going as deep as you can without damaging the shell. Then make a series of oblique cuts into the flesh, as deep as your first cuts. Ease out the slices, and cut those from the first pineapple into triangles. Set aside. If you're creating this for a special dinner party and have a little help, the innards of the second pineapple will probably vanish; otherwise save for another purpose (perhaps breakfast with pancakes, butter and maple syrup?). Arrange the pineapple shells like boats on a serving platter.

Heat the oils in a large frypan or wok until beginning to smoke. Toss in the onion, garlic and ginger and stir fry for 1 minute. Add the soya sauce, sugar and ground pepper and stir until the soya has reduced by half. Toss in the reserved rice and nuts, pineapple, red peppers, and basil and stir vigorously until everything is heated through. Pile the mixture into the waiting pineapple shells, scatter the spring onions over and serve with a flourish.

169

RISOTTO MILANESE

The risotto is the most complicated of our rice accompaniments, because here, instead of simply being boiled in lots of water, the rice is cooked slowly in a measured amount of liquid containing some of the flavouring ingredients. This is our version of this northern Italian classic. It is essential to use only freshly grated Parmesan (preferably Reggiano) for this wonderful creation. Serve with a platter of artfully arranged roasted or grilled Mediterranean vegetables and a crisp green salad.

2½ oz (70 gm) butter
1 onion finely chopped
5 cloves garlic, crushed
4-5 nice inner celery stalks, finely sliced
18 oz (500 gm) long grain brown rice
14 fl oz (400 ml) dry white wine
22 fl oz (600 ml) stock
1 teaspoon (1 gm) saffron strands, infused
in 4 fl oz (100ml) boiling water
6 oz (175 gm) frozen petits pois, thawed
3½ oz (100 gm) freshly grated Parmesan cheese
3 tablespoons double cream
salt and freshly ground black pepper
flat leaved parsley, chopped
extra Parmesan to serve

Melt the butter in a deep pan, and sauté the onion, garlic and celery, until the onion is transparent. Add the rice, wine, stock and saffron infusion. Lower the heat, cover the pan and gently simmer for 45-50 minutes until the rice is perfectly cooked and all the liquid absorbed. Check frequently towards the end of the cooking time, and if the rice seems to be drying out but is not yet done, add a little water.

As soon as the rice is perfect, stir in the peas, Parmesan and cream. Season to taste. Serve immediately, garnished with the parsley if desired. Have extra Parmesan available at the table.

WARM CHAPEL CORNER BEAN SALAD

From our Chapel Corner garden during August, every day come mountains of assorted beans. In addition to the usual green runners, we might have yellow wax beans, climbing yellow and white skinned runners, or green and lush dark purple French beans (these last, like purple peppers, sadly turn green on cooking: it is, however, a sumptuous dark green and contrasts well with the paler shade of the more conventional French bean). As a change from serving them steamed with butter, salt and lemon or herb butter, we sometimes make hot bean salad to accompany one of our main dishes.

1½ lb (700 gm) freshly picked beans of varied colours
4½ fl oz (120 ml) olive oil
4 tablespoons white wine vinegar
2 tablespoons each chopped flat leaved parsley and sage
1 teaspoon salt
½ teaspoon freshly ground black pepper
pinch cayenne pepper
6 oz (170 gm) red kidney beans, soaked and cooked

Destring and diagonally slice runner bean varieties. Top and halve French and yellow wax beans. Steam separately until just tender and refresh under a cold tap.

Mix the oil and the vinegar with the herbs and seasonings in a small saucepan and heat gently till not quite boiling. Add the red kidney beans and heat through. Pour the dressing and red kidneys over the cooked garden beans and stir to mix thoroughly. Serve immediately as a side dish, or cool completely, refrigerate and serve as part of a salad platter.

171

QUINOA & PISTACHIO PILAFF

6 oz (170 gm) shelled pistachios
splash of sunflower oil
sprinkle of salt

1 lb (450 gm) quinoa
¾ pint (425 ml) stock
½ pint (300 ml) orange juice
1 tablespoon freshly ground coriander seed
2 teaspoons salt

4 tablespoons sunflower oil
1 tablespoon freshly ground green cardamom
1 tablespoon freshly ground green peppercorns
8 oz (225 gm) carrots, cut into matchsticks
8 oz (225 gm) celery, finely sliced diagonally
8 oz (225 gm) onion, finely chopped
1 oz (30 gm) butter/margarine, melted
½ packed teacup chopped parsley
orange slices

First roast the nuts on a baking sheet with oil and salt at 200° for 7 minutes. Reserve.

Put quinoa in a fine sieve and wash under cold tap for at least 1 minute. Bring stock, orange juice and coriander to a boil in a covered pan. Add salt and quinoa. Lower heat and simmer, covered, for 20 minutes. Remove from heat and let stand, covered, for 10 minutes.

While the quinoa is cooking, heat the oil in a large frypan or wok, and when it is beginning to smoke, throw in the cardamom and ground green pepper. Stir and add the carrots. After 1 minute, add the celery and onion and stir fry until everything is crisp-tender.

Fluff the quinoa with a fork and stir in the vegetables and reserved pistachios. Turn into a warm serving dish and drizzle with the butter or margarine. Scatter the parsley over all and garnish with orange slices.

CASEROLED CANNELLINI BEANS

This slow-cooked herby bean 'stew' goes well with most eastern and western Mediterranean dishes. As always, fresh herbs are better, but if you have to use dried, halve the quantities given. If you have no fresh rosemary add a teaspoon of dried along with the sage and thyme.

1 lb (450 gm) cannellini beans, soaked overnight and drained
3 sticks celery, finely sliced
2 carrots, finely sliced
1 large onion, chopped
a few bay leaves
1 or 2 sprigs fresh rosemary
½ pint (300 ml) dry white wine
2 pints (1200 ml) light stock (2 tablespoons vegetable concentrate in boiling water)
1 teaspoon each salt and freshly ground black pepper

4 tablespoons olive oil
5 fat cloves garlic, crushed
1 tablespoon chopped fresh sage
1 tablespoon chopped fresh thyme
extra olive oil to serve
freshly grated Parmesan cheese (optional)

Put the beans with the vegetables, bay leaves and rosemary into a large, deep pan with a tight fitting lid. Cover with the wine and stock and add the seasoning. Bring to the boil and skim off any froth. Reduce the heat to very low and cover and simmer for 1-1½ hours until the beans are tender. Remove the herbs and drain the beans, reserving the liquid.

Heat the olive oil in the cleaned pan, and sauté the garlic gently for 2-3 minutes. Do not brown. Add the reserved cooking liquid and simmer, uncovered, for 5 minutes. Add the beans and the sage and thyme and simmer 5-10 minutes more till everything is heated through.

Check seasoning and serve drizzled with a little extra olive oil and a dish of Parmesan on the side if you wish.

ACCOMPANIMENTS: POTATO

Illustrations by Nadine Wickenden

LEMON CASSEROLED POTATOES

Very small new potatoes are best for this dish. Cut them in half or fork them a little so that they really take up the citrus flavour. Serve as a casserole with the cooking liquid.

2 onions, finely chopped
3 cloves garlic, thinly sliced
3 tablespoons olive oil
zest and juice of 2 lemons
24-32 small new potatoes
1½ pints (850 ml) stock
salt and pepper
3-4 sprigs fresh parsley

Sauté onion and garlic in oil until soft, add lemon zest and juice and reduce the liquid to half.

Add potatoes and stock and bring to the boil. Cover with a tight fitting lid and allow to simmer, stirring every now and then until the potatoes are just tender. Season and garnish with parsley sprigs.

ORANGE CASSEROLED POTATOES

Use oranges instead of lemons, and add 4 tablespoons white wine vinegar and 1 tablespoon freshly ground coriander seed along with the stock.

FENNEL & NEW POTATO GRATIN

2 bulbs fennel, thinly sliced (reserve feathery tops for garnish)
5 fl oz (150 ml) water
2 cloves garlic, crushed
zest and juice of 1 lemon
salt and pepper
4 potatoes, thinly sliced
sunflower oil
2 heaped tablespoons fromage frais/crème fraîche
1 tablespoon fresh marjoram
3 fl oz (75 ml) double cream
4 oz (110 gm) wholewheat breadcrumbs
3 oz (85 gm) freshly grated Parmesan cheese

Braise fennel in the water with the garlic and lemon zest and juice until soft. Season.

Boil potato slices about 3 minutes or until nearly cooked. Oil a serving dish and arrange half the potatoes in the dish. Cover with half the fromage frais and half the fennel. Sprinkle over with half the marjoram and repeat with the rest of the potato, fromage frais, fennel and herbs.

Pour the cream over the top and cover with breadcrumbs and Parmesan. Bake at 160° for 35 minutes, until the breadcrumbs are crispy. Serve garnished with the feathery parts of the fennel.

JAPANESE STYLE ROAST POTATOES

Umeboshi plums are salty pickled plums from Japan. Potatoes roasted with an umeboshi plum paste make an unusual alternative to rice to serve with stir fried vegetables and nuts with added fruit (pineapple and firm mango are always nice) or with sweet and sour sauce. As optional garnishes, you could prepare a handful of arame strands soaked for 15 minutes in boiling water, then strained; and radish roses and spring onion flowers, soaked for 30 minutes in iced water.

2 lb (900 gm) small new potatoes
2 tablespoons hazelnut oil
3 tablespoons lemon juice
2 tablespoons umeboshi plum paste
1 tablespoon tamari
2 tablespoons wholewheat flour

Wash the potatoes and put in a pan with cold water to cover. Bring to the boil and boil for 2 minutes. Drain. Meanwhile, preheat oven to 190°, with a baking dish with the hazelnut oil inside.

Mix the lemon juice, plum paste and tamari thoroughly together in a large bowl and sprinkle the flour onto a plate. Add the potatoes to the bowl and stir round to coat completely. Next roll the coated potatoes in the flour and put in the oiled, preheated baking dish. Drizzle with any remaining plum paste mixture and bake for 30-40 minutes, until the potatoes are tender and golden brown. Remove to a heated serving dish and scrape any remaining bits from the baking sheet over the top. Garnish if you like with the arame, onion flowers and radish roses.

GRATIN SAVOYARD POTATOES

This wonderfully rich potato dish is traditionally made with Swiss Gruyère or Emmenthal. We use Teifi, which has the same melting properties and an equally interesting flavour. Use Swiss cheese or Cheddar if you like. The result will be different, but very good. Serve to accompany light, summery casseroles.

6 potatoes, thinly sliced
1 large onion, thinly sliced
1 tablespoon olive oil
1 tablespoon butter

2 oz (55 gm) butter
thyme
salt and pepper
8 oz (225 gm) Teifi, Swiss cheese or Cheddar, grated
18 fl oz (500 ml) single cream

Drop the potatoes for 1 minute into rapidly boiling water. Drain and refresh. Sauté the onion in olive oil and butter until soft.

Grease the sides of a casserole dish with a little extra butter or oil. Layer up the potato and onion with small knobs of butter, thyme, seasoning and cheese. Keep back a little cheese, and pour cream over everything. Sprinkle the top with the remaining cheese and cover with a tight fitting lid: be careful to choose a large enough dish for the lid not to touch the cheese.

Bake in a preheated oven at 160° for 35 minutes with the lid on. Remove the lid for a further 15-20 minutes, to allow the gratin to crisp and turn golden.

BAKED POTATO WITH CHEESY VEGETABLES

Here, baked potatoes are topped, rather than filled, with vegetables in a strong cheese sauce. Try broccoli and cauliflower with blue Stilton; carrots and leeks with Cheddar; peppers, baby corn and olives with mozzarella and Parmesan. This recipe is a good way of using up leftover cooked vegetables. Just select a complementary cheese.

8 large baking potatoes
3 oz (85 gm) butter
3 oz (85 gm) wholewheat flour
1 heaped teaspoon strong English mustard
1 pint (550 ml) milk
8 oz (225 gm) cheese, grated
salt and pepper
2-3 lb (900-1300 gm) vegetables, cut small

Bake potatoes as for «apple & Derby jackets».

Melt the butter, stir in the flour and cook for a couple of minutes. Add the mustard and milk a little at a time to give a thick sauce. Stir in the cheese and season to taste.

Steam the vegetables so they are tender but crisp and retain their colours, and stir into the sauce. Cut a big cross into the top of the potatoes. Spoon the cheesy vegetable mix over.

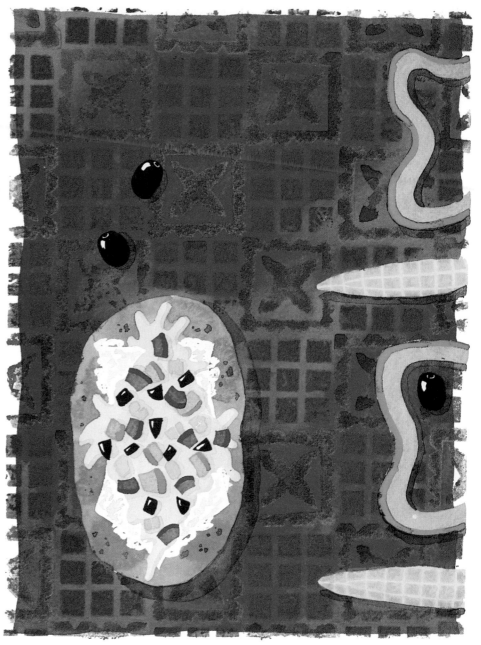

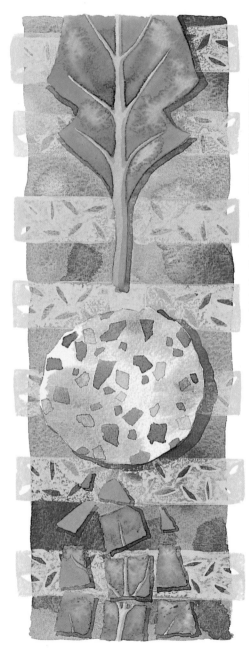

SPINACH & POTATO CAKES

2½ lb (1 kg) potatoes
4 tablespoons olive oil
salt and pepper
1 onion, finely chopped
8 oz (225 gm) fresh spinach, roughly chopped
1 egg, beaten

Cover the potatoes with water in a pan and cook till soft. Drain and mash together with 3 tablespoons of the oil and season. Meanwhile, lightly fry the onion in the rest of the oil, then add to mashed potato along with the raw spinach. Mix well. Shape into 16 small cakes, and dip each one in the egg. Arrange on a well oiled or parchment covered baking sheet and cook in the oven at 180° for about 20 minutes, until golden.

CHEESY POTATO CAKES

You can bake these and «spinach & potato cakes» together. We often serve one of each with a light vegetable gratin or crumble.

4 lb (2 kg) potatoes
3 tablespoons olive oil
salt and pepper
12 oz (340 gm) Cheddar, grated
1 tablespoon mustard
4 oz (110 gm) wholewheat breadcrumbs
4 oz (110 gm) mixed nuts, finely chopped
olive oil
1 egg, beaten

Boil the potatoes until well cooked. Mash with the oil and salt and pepper. Leave to cool. Add the cheese and mustard and mix well. Shape into round cakes about 2 ½ inches (6 cm) diameter and ¾ inch (2 cm) thick.

Mix the breadcrumbs and nuts together with a dash of olive oil. Dip the cakes in the egg and roll in the crumb mix. Cook on a baking sheet at 180° for 20-30 minutes.

MAGIC MASH

It is rare to find someone who doesn't adore potato simply mashed with butter and milk. Whenever we serve it at Stones, it's greatly appreciated and we never have any left over ... everyone in the kitchen sees to that! Here are a few variations on this well-loved theme. Choose floury potatoes for mashing: we like Maris Piper best.

OLIVE & HERBED MASHED POTATOES

8-12 potatoes
salt and pepper
olive oil
handful fresh mixed herbs (eg sage, parsley, basil, chives)

Boil potatoes until soft. Strain and return to pan, and shake over heat to evaporate off any excess moisture. Mash with salt and pepper, and some olive oil for a smooth texture. Mix in the herbs and serve immediately, or pour a little more oil over and bake to give a crispy topping for a few minutes. You could also sprinkle the potato with cheese to make a more sumptuous baked top.

PESTO MASHED POTATOES

Follow above method, but omit herbs and olive oil and instead mash potatoes with 4-5 tablespoons «pesto» or «red pesto» to taste.

MASHED POTATO WITH GOAT CHEESE & OLIVES

Follow method above. Along with the herbs, mix in 9 oz (250 gm) goat cheese cut into ½ inch (1 cm) cubes, and 4-8 oz (100-200 gm) mixed pitted green and black olives, whole or sliced.

POTATO & ONION PANCAKES

One for the processor! Serve these light, tasty pancakes with main dishes (good with hearty mushroomy things) or on their own with «spiced tomato sauce» or «apple sauce». Great for breakfast with fried eggs and maple syrup. Makes about 20 3-4 inch (8-10 cm) pancakes.

3 large cloves garlic, peeled
8 oz (225 gm) onion, cut into rough chunks
1 lb (450 gm) potatoes, cut into rough chunks

4 oz (110 gm) wholewheat flour
1 teaspoon baking powder
2 teaspoons salt
1 teaspoon freshly ground black pepper
2 eggs, beaten with 4 fl oz (100 ml) milk
sunflower oil

Process the garlic, then add the onion and potatoes and process until finely chopped, but not puréed. If you have a litre capacity processor bowl, you will have to do this in 2 batches.

In a large bowl, mix the flour, baking powder and seasonings. Add the chopped potato mixture, then the egg-milk mix. Stir everything together just to combine.

Pour a little oil into a hot heavy based frypan, and swirl to coat the bottom. When the oil is just beginning to smoke, drop the potato mixture in by the tablespoonful, spacing 3-4 inches (8-10cm) apart. When the underside of each is golden brown (2-3 minutes), turn over, flatten with a frying slice and cook the other side. Take out of pan and drain on kitchen paper. Keep warm whilst cooking the rest of the mixture.

POTATO & APPLE PANCAKES

Omit garlic, and substitute 4 oz (110 gm) grated tart eating apple for the same amount of onion. Add 1 teaspoon of cinnamon.

LEMON ROAST POTATOES

8 medium potatoes or 16 small new
potatoes
4 tablespoons olive oil
juice 2 lemons
3 tablespoons fresh thyme, or 1½
tablespoons dried
salt and pepper
zest 2 lemons

Parboil the potatoes for 5 minutes. If using new potatoes, these are better cooked whole: otherwise, cut potatoes into large chunks.

Heat the oil in a large roasting dish in the oven at 200°. When the oil begins to smoke, add the partly cooked potatoes, lemon juice, thyme and a little seasoning. Salt sprinkled on the potatoes will help them crisp up. Bake for about 40 minutes to 1 hour, giving the potatoes a shake after 20 minutes, to coat them with oil and ensure even cooking. Just before serving (the potatoes should be crisp and golden), sprinkle with the lemon zest.

GARLIC-ROSEMARY ROAST POTATOES

Omit the lemon and thyme, and add 4 crushed cloves of garlic and 2 tablespoons fresh or 1 tablespoon dried rosemary to the pan along with the potatoes.

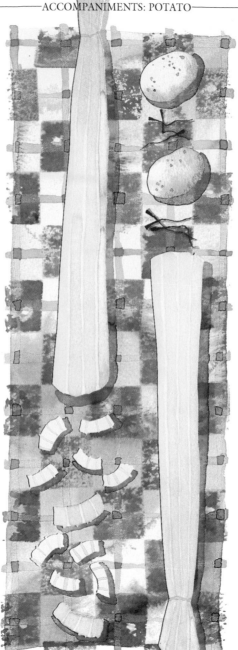

SAFFRON & WINE CASSEROLED NEW POTATOES

Sumptuous potatoes for special occasions!

1 teaspoon (1 gm) saffron strands
2 onions, chopped
4 cloves garlic, crushed
3 sticks celery, chopped
olive oil
3 lb (1½ kg) baby new potatoes
1 pint (550 ml) stock
8½ fl oz (250 ml) dry white wine
handful fresh parsley, chopped
salt and pepper

First, cover the saffron with about 2 tablespoons of boiling water and leave to stand. Sauté onion, garlic and celery in oil. Add potatoes and cook 2-3 minutes. Pour over the stock and wine, and cook a further 5 minutes. Add the saffron infusion to the pan and cook for another 10 minutes uncovered, or until potatoes are tender. Add parsley and season to taste.

POTATO, FETA & OLIVE GRATIN

Serve this as part of a Greek or Italian inspired lunch or dinner, or by itself with a crisp green salad and chunks of freshly baked bread to soak up the delicious juices!

2½ lb (1½ kg) potatoes
8 oz (225 gm) feta cheese, cubed
2 oz (50 gm) butter, chopped
4 oz (110 gm) pitted black olives
2 tablespoons fresh thyme, or 1 tablespoon dried
olive oil to coat dish
4 fl oz (100 ml) dry white wine
4 fl oz (100 ml) single cream
freshly ground black pepper
4 oz (110 gm) Parmesan or mozzarella, grated

Cut potatoes into small mouth-sized pieces, and boil until just done. Mix the potatoes together with the feta, butter, olives and thyme. Coat ovenproof dish with oil and put in potato-feta mix. Pour over the wine and cream and sprinkle with a little pepper. Scatter with Parmesan or mozzarella and bake in a preheated oven at 180° for about 45 minutes, until cheese is brown or bubbling.

MEXICAN OVEN BAKED POTATOES

Serve this with a bowl of freshly grated cheese and a salad for a quick and easy supper. A good dish to include in a Mexican buffet. Increase the chilli content if you really like it hot!

2½ lb (1100 gm) small potatoes, or larger ones cut into even sized chunks
1 oz (30 gm) margarine
1 very large or 2 good sized medium onions, finely chopped
4 cloves garlic, crushed
½ teaspoon freshly ground black pepper
½ teaspoon freshly ground hot chilli
2 teaspoons freshly ground cumin
4 green peppers, seeded an cut into ½ inch (1 cm) squares
2 tablespoons wholewheat flour
330 ml bottle good quality flavoursome lager (Mexican if possible)

1½ teaspoons vegetable stock concentrate dissolved in 8 tablespoons (120 ml) boiling water
2 tablespoons tomato paste
½ teaspoon sugar
3 large ripe tomatoes, roughly chopped
1 teacupful finely chopped fresh coriander
handful chopped fresh parsley
salt, pepper, Tabasco and sugar to season
2 tablespoons sunflower oil
salt

Parboil the potatoes till half cooked, and set aside.

Melt the margarine, and sauté the onion and garlic with the spices for 7 or 10 minutes, on medium heat, until the onion is softening.

Add the green peppers and continue to sauté for 5 minutes more. Sprinkle in the flour and cook, stirring, for a further 2 minutes. Turn up the heat and gradually add the lager, stirring and pausing after each addition, keeping the sauce really thick (be patient, this takes a few minutes ...). When all the lager has been incorporated and the sauce is of a double cream-like consistency, add the dissolved stock concentrate, the tomato paste, sugar and tomatoes. Cook until the sauce has thickened to a thick pouring consistency. Stir in the coriander and parsley, reserving a little for garnish. Season as required, according to taste.

Heat 2 tablespoons sunflower oil in a shallow lidded (but leave the lid off at this point) casserole in a hot (200°) oven. When the oil begins to smoke, add the potatoes in a single layer, and sprinkle with a little salt. Roast, uncovered, for about 20 minutes, shaking occasionally, until beginning to brown.

Stir half of the sauce up with the potatoes. Cover the casserole and continue to bake 10 minutes longer. Sprinkle with the remaining herbs to serve, and offer a bowl of soured cream and the rest of the reheated sauce in a jug on the side.

SCALLOPED POTATOES WITH MUSHROOMS & DILL

Mushroom, dill and paprika has long been a favourite combination of ours. Here these ingredients re-emerge alongside potatoes. This dish is slow cooked, as tightly sealed as possible, then finished uncovered to brown to perfection. Serve as an accompaniment to a light main course, or enjoy by itself for a late supper. Cooking for a longer time at a lower temperature is fine. Just turn the oven up to 160° for the final browning. You can substitute some or all the Paris mushrooms with buttons, but Paris have the better flavour and texture.

3 tablespoons wholewheat flour
2 teaspoons salt
1 teaspoon pepper
2 tablespoons paprika

2 tablespoons dried dill weed
1 tablespoon dill seed

butter for the dish
2 lb (900 gm) new potatoes sliced as thinly as possible
2 onions, thinly sliced
1 lb (450 gm) Paris mushrooms, sliced lengthways
2 oz (55 gm) butter
pepper
6 fl oz (175 ml) milk
6 fl oz (175 ml) stock

Combine the ingredients for the paprika flour and the dill mixes in separate bowls.

Lightly butter a deep lidded casserole dish. Lay a third of the potatoes in the base of the dish, overlapping the slices. Sprinkle with a little of the seasoned flour and a little of the dill mixture. Arrange half the sliced onion and half the sliced mushrooms over the potatoes, and sprinkle with a little more of the flour and herb mixtures. Dot with a third of the butter, cut into small pieces. Lay the next third of the potatoes in the dish, again overlapping the slices. Repeat the herb seasoning, onion and mushroom, herb seasoning and buttering. Layer the final third of the potatoes on top. Dot with the last of the butter and sprinkle with a little extra pepper.

Mix the milk and stock together and pour this over everything. Cover the casserole tightly with foil and put the lid on. Bake at 160° for 1¼ hours. Remove the lid and foil and bake 20-30 minutes longer, until the top is nicely browned. If the casserole seems a little dry when its lid comes off, add a little more stock.

SESAME ROAST POTATOES WITH MUSHROOMS

When we made this in the restaurant, the leftovers at the end of lunch instantly and mysteriously vanished in the kitchen ... If in the unlikely event you do have any left, slice the potatoes, keep the mushrooms whole and add everything to an oriental salad. Ideally the potatoes and mushrooms you use should echo each other in size.

2 tablespoons sunflower oil
3 tablespoons toasted sesame oil
1½ lb (750 gm) small new potatoes steamed until just tender and refreshed
2 teaspoons salt

2 tablespoons sunflower oil
3 tablespoons toasted sesame oil
3 cloves garlic, crushed
zest and juice of 1 large lemon
4 fl oz (100 ml) tamari
2 lb (1 kg) tiny button mushrooms
2 tablespoons toasted sesame seeds

2 tablespoons toasted sesame seeds
1 large lemon cut into 8 wedges
chopped parsley

Heat the first group of oils together in a 200° oven in a shallow (1 inch/2 cm) baking tray, large enough to fit in all the cooked potatoes in a single layer. When the oil begins to smoke, add the potatoes and sprinkle with the salt. Give the tray a quick shake, and return to the oven for 20-30 minutes or until the potatoes are golden brown. Put a similar but empty baking tray in the oven to preheat after the first 10 minutes of cooking time.

Meanwhile, beat the second group of oils together with the garlic, lemon zest and juice and the tamari in a large bowl. Add the mushrooms and sesame seeds and stir to coat all surfaces. When the potatoes have turned to gold, remove from the tray with a slotted spoon and keep warm in an attractive serving dish. Divide the coated mushrooms evenly between the now empty potato tray and the freshly heated tray. Return both trays to the oven and bake for 15 minutes, shaking occasionally.

Stir up the mushrooms with the potatoes, scraping any residual sesame-tamari mix over all. Sprinkle with more sesame seeds and garnish with the lemon wedges and a little chopped parsley.

ROSTI

This crispy potato cake smells wonderful as it cooks, filling the kitchen with the fragrance of fresh garden herbs. Use half curly or flat leaved parsley and half oregano, marjoram, basil or lemon balm. Or increase the parsley and add just a couple of tablespoons of finely chopped rosemary, lovage or hyssop. Equal quantities of parsley, sage and thyme make another excellent combination. Experiment with whatever you have growing! Rosti is good with almost any main dish which does not contain potatoes, or try it for breakfast with fried eggs and grilled tomatoes and mushrooms.

2 lb (1 kg) potatoes (choose 6 even sized ones)
1 large or 2 medium onions (c 10 oz/300 gm), very finely chopped
2 teaspoons salt
1 scant teaspoon pepper
3 tablespoons olive oil
½-¾ packed teacup finely chopped herbs
1½ tablespoons olive oil for frying

Bring a large pan of water to a rolling boil. Drop in the potatoes, bring the water back to the boil, and boil for exactly 4 minutes. Immediately remove the potatoes from the water and cool. When cold enough to handle, grate them on the coarse side of your grater into a bowl. Add all the rest of the ingredients except the frying oil and mix thoroughly.

Heat the remaining oil in a 12 inch (30 cm) diameter frying pan until it is just beginning to smoke. Add all the potato mix and press down firmly with the palm of your hand. Cook 5 minutes. Meanwhile, preheat your grill. Remove the pan from the stove and pop under the grill, 3 inches (7-8 cm) from the heat source for 7-8 minutes, or until golden brown on top. Leave in the pan for 2 minutes, then either gently slide onto a preheated serving plate, or cut into wedges in the pan to serve.

SOLO ROSTI

To make individual rosti, put 4 egg poaching rings into your oiled frying pan and fill them with the mixture when the oil is hot enough. After 5 minutes, turn the rings over in the pan to cook the other side for 5 minutes more, or until golden brown. Carefully remove the rings and keep the four rosti warm whilst you repeat the process with the rest of the mixture, using a little more oil.

POTATOES IN LYONNAISE STYLE WITH GREEN BEANS & LOVAGE

You need a very large frypan with a lid for this recipe. As an alternative to the butter and lovage with the beans, you could choose one of the «herb butters».

2 lb (1 kg) tasty new potatoes, cut into bite-sized chunks
2½ oz (70 gm) butter/margarine
2 large onions, roughly chopped
5 cloves garlic, crushed
2 teaspoons sugar
1 teaspoon salt
1 oz (30 gm) butter/margarine
2 tablespoons cognac
2 tablespoons tamari
18 oz (500 gm) French or runner beans, sliced
2 oz (50 gm) butter/margarine
salt and pepper
handful chopped lovage

Bring a pan of water to a rolling boil and drop in the potato chunks. Bring back to the boil and after 4-5 minutes, when the potatoes are still slightly under-done, drain and set aside.

Melt the butter in a very large frypan on low heat. Add the onion and garlic, sprinkle with the sugar, and cook gently, covered, for about 20 minutes, until the onions begin to caramelise.

Uncover the pan and turn up the heat. When the onion is really sizzling, toss in the cooked potatoes and the salt. Add the butter and stir rapidly until the potato begins to brown all over. Drizzle in the cognac and tamari and stir for a further 1-2 minutes, until everything is well blended and the potatoes are done. Cover and keep warm.

Quickly steam the beans until they are crisp and tender. Toss with the butter and season. Stir in the chopped lovage. Pile the potato-onion mixture into the centre of a warmed platter, and surround with the beans to serve.

APPLE & DERBY JACKETS

---
8 baking potatoes
14 oz (400 gm) Sage Derby cheese, in ½ inch (1 cm) cubes
4 large eating apples, cored and diced
½ teacup chopped parsley
1/3-½ pint (200-300 ml) «mayonnaise» (or to taste)
salt

Prick the potatoes with a fork and bake in a hot oven for about 50 minutes, or until tender.

When the potatoes are cool enough to handle, cut a lengthways ½ inch (1 cm) slice off the top of each and set aside to serve as a hat. Scoop the centre out of all the potatoes, leaving a ½-1 inch (1-2 cm) thick shell. A melon baller works well for this. Put all the middles into a bowl and mash with a potato masher or fork. Stir the cheese, apples and parsley into the potatoes and mix in the mayonnaise until the taste is perfect! Pile the mixture into the reserved shells and sprinkle each with a scant pinch of salt. Put the hats back on without pushing the filling down, and place in a baking dish. Cover with foil and bake at 180° for about 20 minutes until the cheese is melting and everything is heated through.

PINEAPPLE POTATOES

These are nice served with steamed, buttered baby sweetcorn (with lots of pepper!) and a green salad of oriental leaves. Save any pineapple not used for fruit salad.

---
8 baking potatoes
6 oz (170 gm) cream cheese
1 tablespoon light soya sauce
1 teaspoon Chinese 5 spice
½ a small pineapple, finely cubed
8 radishes, sliced
1 can water chestnuts, roughly chopped
1 bunch watercress, stalked and roughly chopped
pepper

Bake and scoop the potatoes as for «apple & Derby jackets», again reserving the hats. Mash the middles with the cream cheese, soya sauce and spice. Stir in the vegetables and fruit and season with a little freshly ground white pepper. Fill and reheat as for «apple & Derby jackets».

MORE PINEAPPLE POTATOES

Add different vegetables, such as lightly steamed broccoli and/or sautéed whole button mushrooms. For a vegan version, omit the cheese and mash the potato middles with a little soya margarine or sesame oil. Increase the quantity of light soya sauce and perhaps stir in some baked marinated tofu, or smoked tofu. Toasted cashew nuts are another nice addition.

DESSERTS

Illustrations by Richard Eckford

ICED MANGO SOUFFLÉ

A little more complex, but with the right equipment and perfect mangos you can produce this truly magical dessert for a special day. You will need a sugar thermometer (available at any well stocked hardware shop) and 8 ramekin moulds. These look like miniature soufflé dishes and can be bought quite cheaply (try your nearest 'seconds' china shop).

| 6-7 perfectly ripe mangos |
| 6 egg whites |
| 11 oz (300 gm) demerara sugar |
| 1 pint (500 ml) crème fraîche |

Peel the mangos, and remove the flesh from the stones. Process to make about 18 oz (500 gm) of mango purée.

Whisk the egg whites till they form stiff peaks. Put the sugar in a heavy bottomed pan, and add just enough water to cover. Put the sugar thermometer into the pan (or follow instructions). When the thermometer reads 121°F (49.5°C) remove immediately from the heat. Cool slightly then gradually beat the syrup into the egg whites.

Mix half the mango purée with the crème fraîche, and the other half with the raw meringue. Fold together.

Cut out 8 strips of greaseproof paper about 4 by 12 inches (10 by 30 cm). Roll a strip around the outside of each of your ramekins, and attach tightly with an elastic band. The paper should stick up above the rim to form an extended cup for the soufflé. Pour the mix into the lined moulds and freeze. Remove the papers to serve, garnished with sliced fresh mango, strawberry halves and fresh mint leaves.

HONEY BRULÉ

This is our version of the classic French dessert Crème renversée en caramel. You will need those 8 ramekin moulds again.

2 eggs
3 egg yolks
1 tablespoon whisky
2 tablespoons honey
2 oz (50 gm) sugar
1 pint (½ l) milk or single cream
½ oz (15 gm) butter
4 tablespoons demerara sugar

POPPY SEED PARFAIT

A rich dessert with an unusual flavour. Make this in your ramekins, 8-10 depending on their size (see «iced mango soufflé») or in a fluted jelly mould. Wet the mould before putting the mixture in to freeze. Stand the ramekins or mould briefly in a container of hot water (only up the sides!) to turn out easily.

8½ fl oz (250 ml) milk
3½ oz (100 gm) poppy seed
1 vanilla pod, split
4 egg yolks
3½ oz (100 gm) golden granulated sugar
1 tablespoon clear honey
¾ pint (400 ml) double cream
poppy seeds for garnish

Bring half the milk to the boil with the poppy seeds added, then remove from the heat. Add the vanilla pod, and simmer for a further 8 minutes. Remove the pod and pass through a fine strainer. Discard the seeds.

Beat the egg yolks with half the sugar and honey, until light and creamy. Bring the rest of the milk to the boil, cool slightly then whisk into the egg mix. Pour into a clean saucepan over a low heat, and stir until it thickens slightly. Remove from heat and cool. Stir in poppy-vanilla milk. Cool completely then refrigerate.

Whip the cream as stiffly as possible with the remaining sugar and honey. Fold together the poppy-vanilla flavoured mixture and the cream. Spoon into ramekins or mould and freeze. Remove from the freezer a few minutes before serving. Turn out and garnish with a sprinkle of poppy seeds and perhaps a creative touch of your own!

Beat together the eggs and egg yolks, and add the whisky, honey and sugar. Put the milk or cream in a pan with the butter, and bring gently to the boil. Cool slightly, whisk gradually into the egg mix and strain to catch any bits of cooked egg. Pour into ramekins.

Put the filled moulds into a deep baking dish and pour in enough hot water to come half way up their sides. Bake at 160° for 20-30 minutes. Watch the water level! The custards are done when a knife comes out clean. Remove from the baking dish and chill.

Before serving, take from the fridge and sprinkle sugar over the tops. Hold under a hot grill until the sugar is crisp and bubbly, and serve at once before it sets.

BLACK & WHITE TERRINE

An irresistible treat for chocolate lovers! Use a terrine mould if you have one, but a 2 lb (1 kg) loaf tin or soufflé dish works equally well for this recipe. Look for white chocolate in your delicatessen or in a good supermarket, and buy a little more than you need to make shavings for garnish.

2½ oz (75 gm) plain unsweetened chocolate
2½ oz (75 gm) white chocolate
4 tablespoons dark rum
2 oz (55 gm) agar agar powder hot water
3½ oz (100 gm) golden granulated sugar
6 eggs, separated
16 fl oz (450 ml) double cream, lightly whipped (keep in fridge)

Wet your chosen mould and line with cling film. Put to one side. Break up the chocolates and put separately into bowls sitting on top of pans of simmering water (resist the temptation to pop them into the microwave: you won't get such an even melt). When the chocolates are liquid, beat half the rum into each and remove from the heat. Leave the bowls over the pans to prevent the chocolates hardening while you prepare the rest of the ingredients.

Put the agar agar into a pan and add just enough hot water to cover. Warm on stove and stir till granules are dissolved.

Beat half the sugar with the egg yolks till frothy. Beat the other half of the sugar with the egg whites till stiff.

Now take the dark chocolate bowl, and fold in half the agar agar, half the whipped cream, half the yolk mix and half the egg white mix. Fold the other half of the ingredients into the white chocolate bowl. Pour all the dark mixture into the mould and carefully level off. Pour the white mix over the top, and level this too with a clean palette knife. Cover the top with cling film and freeze until solid.

Remove from the freezer half an hour before serving, and put in the fridge, just to loosen the sides slightly. Remove the top cling film and invert onto a plate. Remove the rest of the film and serve in slices garnished with shaved chocolate.

TANGERINE & LYCHEE ICE CREAM

Winter wonderland! Tangerines which we always associate with Christmas, and rarely available lychees freeze together in this superlative dessert for the festive season.

8 fresh lychees (or use canned if fresh not available)
6 firm skinned tangerines
4 oz (110 gm) demerara sugar
1 pint (550 ml) double cream

Peel the lychees, remove the flesh from the stones and chop (if using canned fruit, drain them well). Zest 4 of the tangerines and rub the zest into the sugar, or process sugar and zest until thoroughly mixed. Now juice all the tangerines and stir the juice up with the chopped lychees.

Mix the tangerine flavoured sugar with half the cream in a heatproof bowl. Perch the bowl over a pan of simmering water and stir until the sugar is completely dissolved. Remove from heat and cool. Blend with the tangerine-lychee juice. Whip the remaining cream to stiff peaks, and fold into the mixture. Pour into containers (well washed ice cream tubs are good for this), and freeze. Remove from the freezer to stir every 30 minutes or so until the mix is semi-frozen. Then leave 2-3 hours to freeze completely.

STONED FLUMMERY

A flamboyant celebration of the magical season of the fruits of summer, still young and vibrant when its short life ends. Cape gooseberries or physalis make the perfect garnish. They are really easy to grow: one packet of seeds would fill at least 10 greenhouses! They are also readily available in good supermarkets. To garnish, just spread out their little hats for an umbrella effect, and pop them on the top of your flummery. Toast oats on a baking sheet at 200° for 3-5 minutes until golden and crisp, and cool before using.

½ pint (300 ml) double or whipping cream
3 tablespoons Drambuie
2 tablespoons clear honey
4 oz (110 gm) toasted jumbo oats
4 oz (110 gm) fresh raspberries
4 oz (110 gm) fresh redcurrants
8 Cape gooseberries
mint sprigs (2 joined leaves if possible)

Whip the cream until it is just beginning to form soft peaks. Add the Drambuie and honey, and continue to whip to stiff peaks.

With a metal spoon, fold in the oats, raspberries and redcurrants. Spoon into tall wine glasses and chill until ready to serve.

At serving time, top each glass with a Cape gooseberry (umbrella side up) and a mint sprig.

CARAMEL APPLE PIE

This gorgeous toffee-glazed upside down pie makes a pleasant change from the usual double crusted version. You need a large, heavy based sauté pan. This looks like a frying pan without the long handle. Attractive enamelled cast iron sauté pans are easily found. Ask for one for your birthday! You can vary the pie by sprinkling a little ground cloves, cinnamon and ginger over the fruit. Buy puff pastry as required – just like filo.

4 oz (110 gm) unsalted butter
6 oz (170 gm) demerara sugar
2 lb (900 gm) Bramleys, weighed after coring and slicing
1 sheet puff pastry large enough to cover the pan when rolled out

Melt butter in the sauté pan on top of the stove. Stir in the sugar and continue cooking till it has all dissolved. Turn down the heat and layer in the apple slices. Continue cooking gently for 4-5 minutes. Meanwhile, preheat your oven to 220°.

Remove the sauté pan from the heat and lay a disc of puff pastry on the top to cover all the apple. Pop the pan into the hot oven, and bake for 10 minutes.

Remove the 'pie' from the oven (the pastry will be well risen, crispy and light gold), and carefully turn the whole thing upside down onto a baking sheet. Remove the sauté pan. Finish baking for 20 minutes or until the apple is crispy and toffee gold. Slide onto a hot plate, and serve with cream.

CHOCOLATE & DRAMBUIE SOUFFLÉ

Hot soufflés are not at all difficult to make. You just have to serve them as soon as they are cooked, otherwise they will collapse; they still taste good but you loose the effect. This richly flavoured, feather-light soufflé makes a fitting finale for an elegant meal. However, once you have ceased to fear the soufflé goblins you'll make this to celebrate every trip to the duty free!

4 oz (110 gm) plain chocolate
8 oz (225 gm) butter
8 oz (225 gm) demerara sugar
6 oz (170 gm) wholewheat flour
1 pint (550 ml) hot milk
8 egg yolks
4 tablespoons Drambuie
10 egg whites, whipped to stiff peaks
butter for greasing dish

Melt the chocolate in a bowl sitting on top of a pan of simmering water and beat till smooth. Be very careful not to boil.

Melt the butter in a pan and add sugar and flour to form a roux. Cook 2-3 minutes. Meanwhile, gradually beat the hot milk into the melted chocolate. Now slowly add this chocolate milk to the roux, stirring all the time. Still stirring, bring the mixture to the boil, till just bubbling. Remove from heat, and cool slightly.

Beat the egg yolks and add a little of the chocolate mix. Then pour the eggs into the rest of the chocolate, mix in the Drambuie and return to low heat, stirring constantly until the mixture thickens. Remove from heat and cool. When cold, fold in stiff egg whites. Pour into a lightly buttered soufflé dish. Place dish in a deep baking tray two thirds full of hot water, and bake at 100° for about 45 minutes. Serve immediately.

197

STEAMED GINGER PUDDING

A reassuring dessert for a cold winter night. Not at all what you remember from school dinners (unless you went to a school very different from any of ours)!

4 oz (110 gm) vegetable suet
4 oz (110 gm) wholewheat flour
1 level teaspoon ground ginger
½ teaspoon ground cinnamon
1 level teaspoon baking powder
8 fl oz (250 ml) molasses
1 egg, beaten
8 fl oz (250 ml) milk
unsalted butter for greasing

In a bowl, mix together the suet, flour, ginger, cinnamon and baking powder. Make a well in the centre and add the molasses and egg, folding the dry ingredients in as you pour. Slowly stir in the milk, and beat till everything is well blended.

Pour into a buttered 2 pint (1 l) pudding basin. Cover with greaseproof paper (also buttered) and aluminium foil, folded over the rim of the basin and tied around with string. Cook in a steamer, or stand in a covered pan half full of boiling water, for about 2 ½ hours. Turn out and serve with a rich vanilla custard.

LEMON & ROSEMARY SORBET

Make this light, refreshing dessert in early summer when the rosemary bush is burgeoning! Spears from older growth are much too woody to use. This is so delicious, yet so easy to make. Just remember to give it an occasional stir while it freezes.

1¾ pints (1 l) water
juice and zest of 6 lemons
12 oz (350 gm) sugar
2 oz (50 gm) green rosemary tips

Gently bring everything to a boil in a heavy pan, stirring frequently to make sure all the sugar has melted. Simmer for 2 minutes, then remove from the heat. Leave to stand for 15 minutes, then strain and discard the fruit zest and rosemary. Cool the lemon-rosemary syrup and pour into a suitable container (with stirring room!) for freezing. Freeze, stirring every 30 minutes or so. The result will be a mass of flavoursome crystals which you spoon into dessert glasses to serve, each garnished with a sprig of fresh rosemary.

APPLE DUMPLINGS

Baked apples in evening dress!

8 Bramleys
1 quantity «standard pastry»
milk for brushing
1 lb (150 gm) mixed dried fruit,
marinaded overnight in 4 fl oz (100 ml)
brandy, or to taste
4 oz (110 gm) demerara sugar
sugar to sprinkle

Peel and core the apples. Roll out the pastry and cut 8 circles, each large enough to completely cover an apple (save pastry leftovers for decoration). Brush each circle with milk, and place an apple in the centre. Mix marinaded fruit with the sugar and pack the holes left by the apple cores. Fold the pastry round to encase the fruit, and turn upside down so the joint is hidden on the bottom. Roll out the pastry remains and cut 16 leaves. Attach 2 to the top of each parcel with a little milk. Brush all over with milk again and sprinkle with sugar. Spike a small hole near the leaves to allow steam to escape. Place in a baking dish and cook at 180° for 30 minutes.

SAFFRON & VANILLA BABA

We all know rum baba: rich buttery dough redolent of dark rum and bursting with dried and crystalised fruits. This is a lighter version wonderfully flavoured with precious saffron. Perfect for one of those strange but typically English July or August days when summer seems to have deserted us ...

8 egg yolks
4 oz (110 gm) light muscovado sugar
6 oz (170 gm) wholewheat flour
1 oz (30 gm) dried yeast
¼ pint (150 ml) lukewarm milk
few drops of vanilla essence
pinch saffron
4 oz (110 gm) melted butter

Whisk together the egg yolks and sugar over hot water (place the bowl over a gently simmering pan), until thick and creamy, and your whisk will trail a complete letter M on the surface of the mixture. Fold in the flour.

Dissolve yeast in the milk and leave to bubble for about 5 minutes.

Blend the yeast, vanilla and saffron into the egg mixture. Add butter and mix well. Fill a greased round tin to about a third of its depth. Cover and prove in a warm place, until well risen. Bake at 180° for about an hour, until a knife comes out cleanly. Cool slightly and turn out onto an attractive dish. Serve with double cream whipped with cinnamon.

199

MELON MONBAZILLAC

This is a simple fruit dessert. Three different varieties of melon are bathed in a honey-rich wine (inextricably linked, for one of us, with memories of the Dordogne and the archaeologist Glyn Daniel). A dash of ginger wine brings out all the flavours and imparts a mysterious afterglow. Do try to find these melon varieties. Different flesh and subtly different degrees of sweetness make for a wonderful combination.

1 galia melon
1 charentais melon
1 ogen melon
zest and juice of 1 lemon
zest and juice of 1 lime
zest and juice of 1 orange
bottle Monbazillac
splash Stone's ginger wine

Halve and seed the melons and extract the flesh with a melon baller, or simply peel and seed the fruit and chop into small cubes. Place in a large bowl.

Blanch the citrus zest in a small pan of simmering water for 30 seconds, then drain. Add the blanched zest to the melon bowl, and stir up with the citrus juice. Pour the wines over. Chill for at least an hour or until ready to serve. At serving time, spoon the fruit into tall wine glasses and garnish with a sprig of mint.

PORT POACHED PEARS

Good pears are available during the latter months of the year. Make this as a light, alternative dessert for festive feasts such as Thanksgiving or Christmas. Choose only the very best unblemished pears, and treat them with reverence throughout the recipe.

8 very fine, perfectly ripe pears
8 oz (225 gm) demerara sugar
port to taste
bottle of red wine
seasonal berries and chervil or fennel for garnish

Gently peel and core the pears, leaving the stalks intact. Place them vertically into a saucepan, sprinkle over the sugar and cover with port and red wine (if necessary, top up with water so the pears are submerged). To keep the pears moist, seal with a disc of greaseproof paper resting inside the pan. Simmer for 15 minutes or until pears are soft and just tender. Remove from heat, and allow to cool in the liquid. Using a slotted spoon, carefully fish out the pears and stand, still blossom end down, on a plate in the fridge. Reserve the poaching liquid.

To serve, cut the pears in half lengthways. Slice into each half from the blossom end, keeping the slices attached below the stalk (or top end). Carefully fan out the slices on an individual plate. Garnish with berries and a herb frond. Gently pour on a little swirl of the cooking liquor around the outside of the fan.

LEMON & LIME TART

In a 10 inch (25cm) flan mould, this recipe will serve 8-12 people.

1 quantity «sweet pastry»
6 eggs
6 oz (170 gm) golden granulated sugar
zest and juice of 4 limes
zest and juice of 4 lemons
7 fl oz (200 ml) whipping cream

Line the dish with the pastry. Cover pastry with greaseproof paper, and hold it down closely with dried beans. Bake blind in a preheated oven at 180° for 15 minutes. Remove the paper and beans, and return to the oven for a minute or 2 to dry. Turn the oven down to 150°.

Whisk together the eggs and sugar until light and fluffy. Beat in the zests and juices. Whip the cream until it forms soft peaks, then fold into the mixture. Pour into the lined pastry case. Bake for about 30 minutes until the filling is set. Cool and refrigerate. Serve chilled, cut into wedges, garnished creatively with lemon and lime twists or a little zest.

CAKES & BISCUITS

Illustrations by Tania Lomas

BANANA LOAF

Makes 1 loaf. Will keep in fridge for 2-3 days. Freezes well, and will mature in flavour and texture.

4 oz (110 gm) soft margarine
8 oz (225 gm) light muscovado sugar
2 eggs
8 oz (225 gm) wholemeal flour
2 teaspoons baking powder
3 fl oz (75 ml) natural yogurt
2 bananas, chopped into small chunks
6 fl oz (175 ml) sunflower seeds

Cream together margarine and sugar. Add eggs with flour and baking powder. Mix thoroughly.

Add yogurt and mix. Add chopped bananas and seeds and mix. Pour into a loaf tin lined with baking parchment.

Bake at 160° for 1¼ to 1½ hours. After 30 minutes, cover top with foil to avoid burning. Test with knife, until it comes out clean.

CHOCOLATE, BRANDY & ORANGE BROWNIES

Makes 24. Keep in fridge in sealed container 3-4 days. Will freeze well after syruping, before cutting up (wrap well in cling film).

CAKE
1 lb (450 gm) soft margarine
1 lb (450 gm) light muscovado sugar
8 eggs
12 oz (340 gm) wholewheat flour
4 oz (110 gm) cocoa powder
1 tablespoon baking powder
2 oz (55 gm) plain chocolate, chopped

SYRUP
juice of 3 oranges
2½ fl oz (60 ml) brandy
2-3 oz (55-85 gm) light muscovado sugar

Cream margarine and sugar together. Add eggs slowly with a little of the flour. Add rest of dry ingredients, and mix well. Pour into a parchment lined baking tray 10 by 14 in (25 by 36 cm). Bake at 160° for 30 minutes. Cool in tin.

To make the syrup, mix juice, brandy and sugar together in a pan on low heat until sugar dissolves, and cool. Leave the cake in the tin, and prick the cooled cake all over with a fork. Pour the syrup over. Leave in fridge for an hour to allow the cake to absorb the liquid. Remove from tin, using the baking parchment to carry it to a chopping board. Cut into 24 squares.

APRICOT MUESLI SNOWBALLS

Makes about 20. Keep 4-5 days in fridge.

2½ lb (1150 gm) chopped apricots
¼ pint (150 ml) apple juice concentrate
½ pint (300 ml) water
2 oz (55 gm) sesame seeds
4 oz (110 gm) rice puffs
8 oz (225 gm) sunflower seeds
4oz (110 gm) desiccated coconut
10 oz (280 gm) porridge oats
12 oz (340 gm) oatmeal
½ pint (300 ml) sunflower oil
½ pint (300 ml) Golden Syrup
apricot jam and desiccated coconut for coating

Simmer apricots in concentrate and water until liquid is absorbed, but mix is still sludgy.

Add other ingredients while apricots are still hot, and shape mix into balls. If you use your measuring jug for the oil first, the coated jug will release the syrup easily. Place on a parchment covered tray and bake at 160° for 20 minutes.

When cold, cover balls in apricot jam and roll in coconut.

203

CHOCOLATE & CRANBERRY COOKIES

Makes about 10. Keep for 4-5 days in sealed container (although in Avebury they're unlikely to remain uneaten for 4-5 hours).

8 oz (225 gm) soft margarine
7 oz (200 gm) demerara sugar
9 oz (250 gm) wholewheat flour
1 teaspoon baking powder
½ teaspoon salt
1 teaspoon vanilla essence
1 large or 2 small eggs
10 oz (280 gm) porridge oats
5 oz (140 gm) quality white chocolate, chopped
5 oz (140 gm) dried cranberries

Beat marg and sugar together. Add flour, baking powder, salt, vanilla essence and egg, and mix in.

Combine remaining ingredients in a bowl, and add to mix to make a stiff dough. Roll into about 10 balls, and flatten each slightly onto a parchment covered baking tray. Bake at 160° for 15-20 minutes, until golden brown.

BANANA MUFFINS

Makes 6-8. Best served with fine unsalted butter on the day of baking, preferably when still warm.

12 fl oz (350 ml) wholewheat flour
8½ fl oz (250 ml) light muscovado sugar
½ teaspoon salt
½ teaspoon bicarbonate of soda
¼ teaspoon baking powder
4 egg whites, whisked to light peaks
8 tablespoons sunflower oil
1½ teaspoons vanilla essence
2 very ripe bananas, mashed
8 tablespoons sultanas
4 tablespoons natural yogurt

Mix dry ingredients together.

Add egg whites, oil and vanilla essence, and stir.

Stir in fruit and yogurt until just combined. Divide batter into greased muffin tins, or paper cases, and bake at 160° for 20-25 minutes.

CARROT CAKE

Makes one sponge cake. The sponge will freeze well by itself, but is best consumed on the day of filling.

just under a pint (550 ml) wholewheat flour
1 tablespoon baking powder
1 teaspoon salt
¾ tablespoon ground ginger
¾ tablespoon freshly ground coriander
1 teaspoon ground cinnamon
½ teaspoon freshly ground allspice
8 tablespoons (120 ml) (packed) desiccated coconut

6 fl oz (175 ml) sunflower oil
8½ fl oz (250 ml) light muscovado sugar
3 eggs, beaten till frothy
4 finely chopped carrots (chop in batches in the processor for best results)
8 oz (225 gm) cream cheese or fromage frais
fruit such as black or green grapes or strawberries for decoration

Combine the flour, baking powder, salt, spices and coconut in a large bowl, stirring well.

In a separate large bowl beat together the oil and sugar until smooth. Add half of the beaten egg together with a heaped wooden spoonful of the flour mix, and beat vigorously again till smooth. Repeat with the other half of the beaten egg. Stir in the fine chopped carrot and gently fold in the remaining flour mix till everything is just combined. Do not over beat.

Pour the batter into a well greased cake tin (9½ in/24 cm), and bake at 180° for 45 minutes. Test with knife until it comes out completely clean. Cool in the tin for 15 minutes then turn onto a wire rack to finish cooling.

When cold, cut horizontally and fill and top with cream cheese/fromage frais. Cut into slices and decorate.

BAKEWELL TART

Makes 1 tart. Will freeze. Keeps 3-4 days in sealed container in fridge.

½ quantity «standard pastry»
2 tablespoons homemade jam (strawberry or raspberry)
6 oz (170 gm) softened unsalted butter
3 oz (85 gm) light muscovado sugar
3 eggs
6 fl oz (175 ml) wholewheat flour
4 oz (110 gm) ground almonds
1 teaspoon baking powder
½ teaspoon almond essence
few drops vanilla essence
flaked almonds for topping

Roll out pastry and line a parchment covered shallow round tin (8½ in/22 cm), bringing the pastry up the edges. Spread bottom of pastry with jam (keeping the sides clear).

Cream butter and sugar in bowl. Add eggs slowly one at a time, each with a little flour to prevent curdling. Mix thoroughly after each egg. Add rest of flour, ground almonds, baking powder and essences. Spoon the mix into the pastry base, making sure it seals to the pastry, so that jam does not rise up the sides whilst cooking (or the pastry edge will break off). Sprinkle with flaked almonds.

Bake at 160° for 25-30 minutes, until firm and golden brown or until a knife comes out clean. Cool, remove from tin and cut into 8 portions.

FRUIT & NUT BARS

Makes 20 bars. Keep up to 2 weeks in fridge.

3½ lb (1 ½ kg) mix of chopped apricots, chopped dates and chopped prunes
½ pint (300 ml) apple juice concentrate
1 pint (550 ml) water
1 pint (550 ml) mixed chopped nuts (eg walnuts, pecans, hazels, brazils)
½ pint (300 ml) peanuts
½ pint (300 ml) desiccated coconut
½ pint (300 ml) rice flakes
¾ pint (425 ml) soya flour
8 tablespoons sunflower oil
sesame seeds for decoration

Simmer fruit, concentrate and water on very low heat until all fluid is absorbed.

Add other ingredients (except sesame seeds) and mix well. Spoon mix into deep baking tray lined with parchment (we make our bars 1-1½ in/2-4 cm thick).

Sprinkle with sesame seeds. Bake at 160° for 30 minutes. Cool and place on wooden board for cutting. With a very sharp serrated knife, trim off hard edges of whole bake and cut rest into bars.

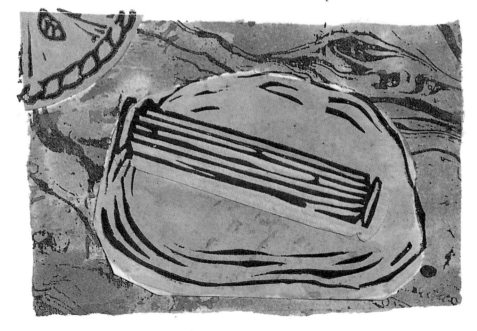

SPICY FRUIT CAKE

Makes 24 squares. Will keep 2 days in sealed container in fridge, but be careful - it dries out quickly.

1 lb (450 gm) soft margarine
½ lb (225 gm) light muscovado sugar
1 lb (450 gm) Golden Syrup
4 eggs
2 lb (900 gm) wholewheat flour
½ lb (225 gm) sultanas
½ lb (225 gm) currants
6 oz (170 gm) glace cherries
6 oz (170 gm) ground almonds
1 oz (30 gm) mixed spice
1 oz (30 gm) ground ginger
pinch ground cloves
2 teaspoons bicarbonate of soda
1 pint (550 ml) dark ale (not *light ale*)

Cream margarine and sugar in mixer. Warm syrup in a plastic bowl in microwave, and add. Beat in eggs.

Add flour, fruit, almonds and spices and mix in.

Dissolve soda in ale, and add.

Pour into deep parchment lined tray (10 by 14 in/25 by 36 cm). Bake at 140° for 1½ hours. Check with knife, which will come out clean when cake is cooked. Remove from tray and cool on wire rack. Cut into squares.

CHEDDAR CRACKERS

Makes about 20 biscuits. Keep 4-5 days in airtight container. Do not freeze.

6 fl oz (175 ml) wholewheat flour
4 tablespoons cornmeal
1 tablespoon poppy seeds
¼ teaspoon salt
¼ teaspoon baking powder
2 oz (55 gm) hard salted butter, chopped into small pieces
8½ fl oz (250 ml) grated cheddar
4-5 tablespoons cold water
egg and salt for finishing

Process all dry ingredients together.

Add butter to processor, until all has been mixed in. Add cheese and water and mix to a stiff dough. Roll out fairly thin, and cut into biscuits with a cutter. Brush with beaten egg and sprinkle with coarse salt. Bake at 160° for 20 minutes.

ROCK BUNS

Makes about 12 buns. Keep 4-5 days in sealed container.

1 lb (450 gm) soft margarine
2 lb (900 gm) wholewheat flour
4 tablespoons baking powder
4 teaspoons mixed spice
12 oz (340 gm) demerara sugar
12 oz (340 gm) currants
zest of 4 lemons
3 eggs
splash of milk

Process margarine, flour, baking powder and spice, and transfer to a bowl.

Mix in sugar, currants and lemon zest. Add eggs and milk, and combine. The mix should be of quite a stiff consistency; add more milk if it is too dry and crumbly. Make into balls, then scrunch them up into alpine shapes on a parchment lined baking tray.

Bake at 170° for 15-20 minutes. They will come out very slightly wet, but will carry on cooking and will set as they cool.

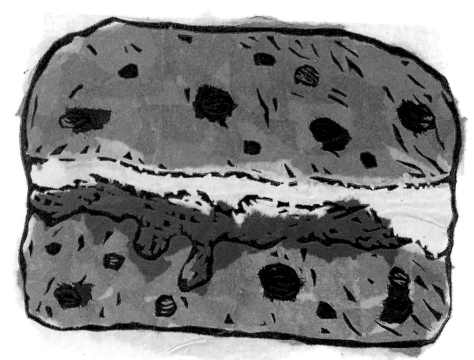

LEMON CAKE

Makes one sponge cake. Will keep in fridge 3-4 days. Sponge, topping and curd can all be frozen separately.

CAKE

8 oz (225 gm) soft margarine
8 oz 225 gm) light muscovado sugar
4 eggs
8 oz (225 gm) wholewheat flour
½ teaspoon baking powder
zest of 1 lemon
juice of ½ lemon

TOPPING

2oz (55 gm) light muscovado sugar
2 oz (55 gm) softened unsalted butter
zest of 1 lemon
juice of ½ - 1 lemon
lemon slices to decorate
«lemon curd» for filling

Cream margarine and sugar together in bowl until smooth. Add eggs, one at a time, each with a little of the flour. Add the rest of the flour and baking powder. Add lemon zest and mix in. Slowly add the lemon juice, mixing well after each addition to prevent curdling. Pour into greased cake tin (8 in/20 cm).

Bake at 160° for 30-45 minutes, until knife comes out clean.

To make the topping, cream together sugar and softened butter in a bowl. Stir in lemon zest. Add juice very, very slowly or it will curdle, mixing thoroughly until required taste is achieved.

Half sponge crosswise, and fill with lemon curd. Top with icing. Cut into 10 and decorate with lemon slices.

LEMON CURD

Makes 3 pints (1 ¾ litres), which can be frozen in small pots. The whole process (excluding final cooling) should take about 45 minutes or so. When you take a pot from the freezer to use, defrost and keep in the fridge.

juice of 10 lemons
12 eggs
1 lb (450 gm) light muscovado sugar
1 lb (450 gm) unsalted butter, chopped into small cubes

Put a saucepan (chosen to hold a plastic bowl in its rim) one third full of water on to boil. Pour lemon juice into a plastic jug, and microwave for 1-2 minutes. Whisk eggs till foamy, and pour into another jug.

When water is boiling, pop plastic bowl over top of saucepan so that it fits snugly without touching the water. Add juice and sugar to the bowl. Stir constantly until sugar dissolves. When the lemon syrup is hot, slowly add whisked eggs, stirring constantly to make sure they do not cook independently (or you'll get scrambled egg). Make sure everything is well blended, and stir frequently. In time the mix will begin to thicken around the edges. When it is quite thick all through, slowly add butter cubes, a few at a time, stirring constantly. When all butter is dissolved, transfer into plastic pots.

Once cool, put lids on pots, label and transfer to freezer .

LEMON FINGERS

Makes 20. Keep in fridge in sealed container 3-4 days. Freezes well as a whole cake, with the syrup added.

CAKE

1 lb (450 gm) soft margarine
1 lb (450 gm) light muscovado sugar
8 eggs
1 lb (450 gm) wholewheat flour
1 level tablespoon baking powder

SYRUP

4 oz (110 gm) light muscovado sugar
juice of 5 lemons

Cream margarine and sugar together. Add eggs one by one, each with a little flour to prevent curdling. Fold in the remaining flour with the baking powder. Bake in parchment lined tray 10 by 14 in (25 by 36 cm), at 160° for about 30 minutes or until golden and knife comes out clean.

When cold, leave in tin and prick all over with fork. Melt sugar in lemon juice, and pour over cake. Leave to soak in fridge for an hour. Lift from tin by the baking parchment, trim off edges and cut into fingers.

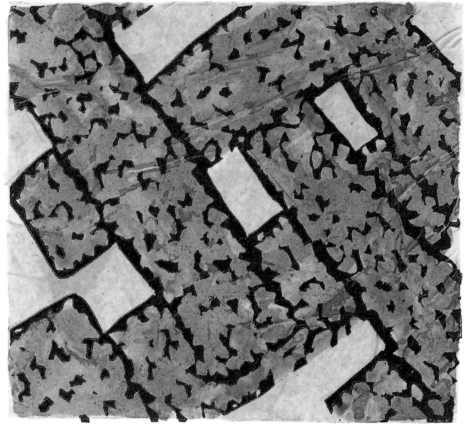

FLAPJACKS

Makes 20. Keep well fridged in airtight container 5-7 days.

18 oz (500 gm) soft margarine
13 oz (370 gm) light muscovado sugar
6 oz (170 gm) Golden Syrup
2¼ lb (1 kg) porridge oats
1 teaspoon salt

Melt margarine, sugar and syrup in a pan. Stir in oats and salt. Press mix into parchment lined tray 10 by 14 in (25 by 36 cm).

Bake at 170° for 15-25 minutes, until golden brown, and just crispy to touch. Remove from tin and cut while hot, after removing the very ends of the whole bake.

COFFEE CAKE

Makes one sponge cake. Filled cake will keep in fridge 3-4 days. Sponge and filling will freeze separately.

CAKE

8 oz (225 gm) soft margarine
8 oz (225 gm) light muscovado sugar
4 eggs
4½ oz (125 gm) wholewheat flour
½ tablespoon baking powder
¾ teaspoon coffee powder or coffee essence
2½ oz (70gm) finely chopped walnuts

CREAM

4 oz (110 gm) softened unsalted butter
4oz (10 gm) light muscovado sugar
¾ teaspoon coffee powder or coffee essence
½ teaspoon brandy
walnuts to decorate

Cream margarine and sugar till smooth. Add eggs gradually, each with a little of the flour. Add rest of the flour, and baking powder. Mix in coffee and walnuts. Pour into greased cake tin (8 in/20 cm) and bake at 160° for 30-40 minutes, until knife comes out clean.

For filling, cream butter and sugar until smooth. Add coffee and brandy. Slice cake in half horizontally and fill with half the mix. Top with rest of the icing. Cut into 10, and decorate with walnuts.

DATE & BANANA BROWNIES

Makes 24. Keep in fridge in sealed container 3-4 days. Whole cake can be frozen without the topping.

1½ lb (700 gm) chopped dates
½ lb (225 gm) margarine
6 eggs
9 oz (250 gm) soya flour
6 bananas, roughly mashed
1 teaspoon vanilla essence
6 oz (170 gm) lexia raisins
1 tablespoon baking powder
14 oz (400 gm) carob chips

Cook dates in pan on very low heat in enough water to cover, until all liquid is absorbed, and the mix has a sticky consistency. Be careful not to stick the dates to the pan.

Beat margarine, eggs and flour in mixer. Add mashed bananas, essence, raisins and baking powder. Stir in cooked dates. Bake at 160° for 30-35 minutes in parchment lined tray 10 by 14 in (25 by 36 cm). Cool on wire rack.

Melt carob chips in a pan on very low heat, and spread evenly over the cake. Leave to set partly, then score into square portions. When set, cut through scored lines with a hot knife (stand knife in jug of hot water).

GINGER PEOPLE

Makes 15. Keep in fridge up to 3 days. Will not freeze (cryogenics remains an untested risk).

12 oz (340 gm) wholewheat flour
2 teaspoons ground ginger
1½ tablespoons baking powder
4 oz (110 gm) soft margarine
6 oz (170 gm) light muscovado sugar
4 tablespoons molasses
1 egg
chocolate or carob chips or currants to decorate

Mix flour, ginger and baking powder in bowl. Rub in margarine until the mix has a crumbly texture. Stir in sugar and mix thoroughly. Add molasses (if you dip the spoon in sunflower oil first, the molasses runs off easily) and egg and mix to a soft dough.

Knead, roll and cut people out with shaped cutters. Decorate. If using currants, pop into water before placing on the people: it helps them to stay on after cooking.

Bake on parchment lined trays at 160° for 10-25 minutes. Remove from oven and allow to cool and harden.

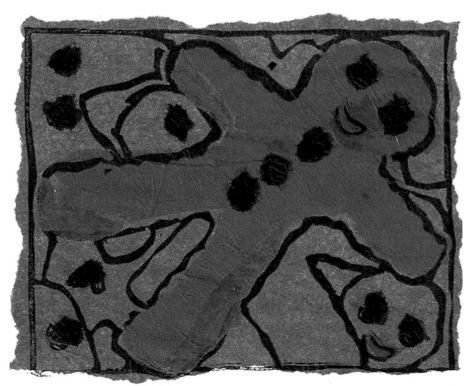

SHORTBREAD

Makes 1 round of 6 portions. Keeps fridged in airtight container 4-5 days. Does not freeze.

5 oz (140 gm) fairly soft unsalted butter
3 oz (85 gm) light muscovado sugar
6½ oz (180 gm) wholemeal flour
1 oz (30 gm) white rice flour

Mix butter and sugar in processor. Add flours, and process until firm. Scoop out into circular tin (7 in/18 cm diameter) with a disk of baking parchment on the bottom. Press down until smooth, and mark with a fork around the rim.

Bake at 150° for about 45 minutes, until just golden brown. Remove from oven and cut into 6 in tin while hot.

DATE SLICES

Makes 24 squares. Keep 5 days in sealed container in fridge.

1 lb 10 oz (750 gm) dried dates
8 tablespoons wholewheat flour
1¼ pint (700 ml) water
1 teaspoon vanilla essence
1¼ lb (550 gm) carob chips
1½ lb (700 gm) soft margarine
12 oz (340 gm) light muscovado sugar
1 lb 10 oz (750 gm) wholewheat flour
1 lb (450 gm) porridge oats
4 oz (110 gml) jumbo oats
1 tablespoon baking powder

To make the filling, melt all the first group of ingredients in a saucepan over a very low heat, until the mix begins to thicken. Stir frequently to prevent sticking and burning. Remove from heat.

Begin the crumble by melting the margarine in a pan. Remove from heat, and add the other ingredients.

Spread half the crumble mix in a deep parchment lined tray (10 by 14 in/25 by 36 cm). Pour on filling, and spread flat and even. Cover with rest of crumble, and press down gently with fingers.

Bake at 150-160° for 25-30 minutes. When cool, remove from tray, trim edges with a sharp knife and cut into squares.

CHOCOLATE CAKE

Makes one sponge cake. Keeps 3-4 days in sealed container in fridge (make sure you use good, fresh cream). Sponge will freeze, but not fillings.

CAKE

4 oz (110 gm) melted plain chocolate
6 oz (170 gm) melted salted butter
4 eggs
zest of 1 orange
5 oz (140 gm) light muscovado sugar
2 oz (55 gm) plain flour
2 oz (55 gm) ground almonds
1 heaped teaspoon baking powder
2 oz (55 gm) plain chocolate chips
2 oz (55 gm) white chocolate chips

First make the sponge. Melt the chocolate and butter and leave to cool.

Mix eggs, orange zest and sugar until slightly frothy. Add chocolate butter mix. Add flour, almonds and baking powder. Mix in chocolate chips. Put into greased cake tin (8 in/20 cm) and bake at 160° for 30-45 minutes. Remove from tin and cool on wire rack.

FILLING

2 oz (55 gm) plain chocolate
1 dessert spoon light muscovado sugar
1 dessert spoon natural yogurt
drop vanilla essence
2 dessertspoons freshly whipped cream

Melt the chocolate, and allowing to cool a little. Stir in sugar, yogurt and essence. Slowly fold in the cream. Cut the sponge in half crosswise, and spread filling on each piece (this way the cake slices will hold together better).

TOPPING

4 oz (110 gm) unsalted butter
6 oz (170 gm) dark chocolate
almonds for decoration

Slowly melt butter and chocolate together in a saucepan. Once spread, leave to set slightly. Cut cake into 10 before the topping has hardened, and decorate with almonds.

INDEX

Illustration by Jerry Hoare

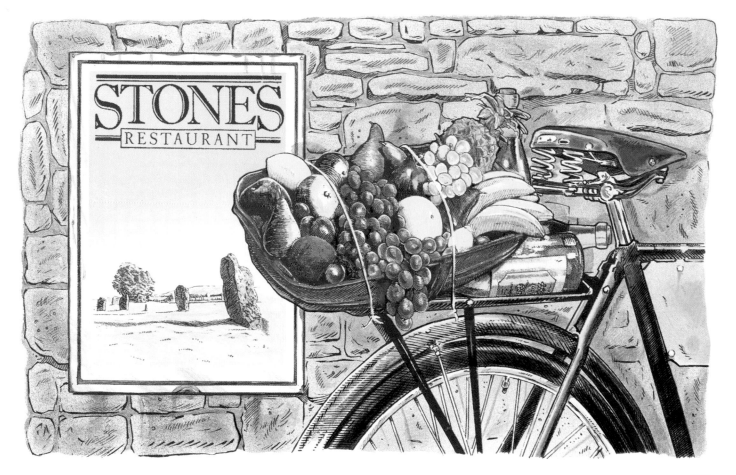

Carrots
- cake 205; Casseroled cannellini beans 173; Chive pancakes 116; Gingered millet pilaff 162; Golden temple curry 107; A fricassée of winter vegetables 149; Purées, pyramids & soufflés 146; Marjoram braised baby - 156; Marrow & chestnut hotpot 114; Mediterranean soufflé cottage pie 125; Mushroom & haricot chasseur 120; Oriental spring rolls 86; Pencarreg & walnut roast 115; Quinoa & pistachio pilaff 172

Cashews
More pineapple potatoes 190; Pineapple - rice 169

Cauliflower
- & cumin soup 77; Broccoli & - with smoked Caerphilly 57; - broccoli & potato pies 90; Chive pancakes 116; A fricassée of winter vegetables 149; Golden temple curry 107; Paté tricolore 74

Celeriac (Celery root)
Colcannon 158; A fricassée of winter vegetables 149; Matchstick slaw with Red Leicester 57; Purées, pyramids & soufflés 146

Celery
Caponata 156; Casseroled cannellini beans 173; - & pecan cakes 89; - & Stilton sauce 47; Corn, potato & parsley chowder 80; A fricassée of winter vegetables 149; Marrow & chestnut hotpot 114; Quinoa & pistachio pilaff 172; Refritos 165; Risotto Milanese 170; Roast sweet potato - & apple soup 73; Saffron & wine casseroled new potatoes 183; Spinach & Stilton boulangère 112

Chard
Cream of sorrel soup 69

Cheese
general 19; Baked potato with cheesy vegetables 179; Cauliflower, broccoli & potato pies 90; Celery & pecan cakes 89; Herbed polenta 91; Standard - sauce 48; blue Caesar salad 61; potato & - gnocchi 68; Brie - & cranberry filo parcels 111; Pasta shells in - & red pepper sauce 140; Pencarreg & walnut roast 115; Caerphilly Corn circles 108; Salade niçoise 64; cheddar Aubergine & spinach pasticcio 101; Broccoli & mushroom gougère 104; Broccoli in broccoli sauce 154; Caesar salad 61; - crackers 208; Cheese stix 132; Cheesy corn & parsley muffins 138; Cheesy cornbread 139; Cheesy potato cakes 180; Glamorgan sausages 93; Gratin savoyard potatoes 178; Leek & walnut stuffed onions 118; Millet & - wedge 79; Mushroom dill & white wine bread pudding 126; Paté tricolore 74; Penne with leek & Stilton sauce 141; Pumpkin gratin 156; Spanakopitta 123; Spinach filled profiteroles 115; Tomato, mushroom & courgette shoo pie 102; Torta Mexicana 113; Cloisters Herbed polenta with eggs florentine 91; cottage Aubergine & spinach pasticcio 101; Broccoli & - roly poly 98; Cream of sorrel soup 69; Leek & walnut stuffed onions 118; Mushroom & spinach romanoff 88; Mushroom brioche 128; Red pepper & French bean romanoff 88; Spanakopitta 123; cream Asparagus & fresh herb tart 96; Bavarian galette 97; Broccoli in broccoli sauce 154; Duet of stuffed mushrooms 92; Herbed polenta with eggs florentine 91; Mediterranean soufflé cottage pie 125; Mushroom brioche 128; Paté tricolore 74; Pineapple potatoes 190; Spinach filled profiteroles 115; Tomato, apple & - soup 72; feta Duet of stuffed mushrooms 92; Greek salad 56; Potato - & olive gratin 184; Rosemary - & sun dried tomato crostini 137; Spanakopitta 123; Spinach - & olive flan 129; goat Mashed potatoes with - & olives 181; herbed Tomato, fresh basil & - salad 65; mozzarella Aubergine & spinach pasticcio 101; Tomato, fresh basil & herbed cheese salad 65; Potato, feta & olive gratin 184; Parmesan general 19; Aubergine & smoked cheese ravioli 100; Basil topped tomatoes 150; Duet of stuffed mushrooms 92; Fennel & new potato gratin 176; French bean, walnut & Stilton lasagne 99; Herbed polenta with eggs florentine 91; Mediterranean butter 36; Mediterranean pasta with Parmesan 60; Minestra 95; Pan bagna 76; Penne with red pesto 140; Pesto 39; Pizza bread 135; Potato, feta & olive gratin 184; Risotto Milanese 170; Rosemary focaccia 136; Sun dried tomato & walnut tagliatelle 111; Red Leicester Broccoli & - tart 130; Colcannon 158; Matchstick slaw with - 57; Sage Derby Apple & - jackets 190; - sausages 93; smoked Aubergine & - ravioli 100; Broccoli & cauliflower with - Caerphilly 57; Cheesy surprise sausages 93; Corn circles 108; Hoppin' John 163; - & dill cobbles 132; - blinis 78; Stilton Broccoli & - soup 81; Broccoli in broccoli sauce 154; Celery & - sauce 47; French bean, walnut & - lasagne 99; More aubergine steaks 158; Pear, chicory & - salad 66; Penne with leek & - sauce 141; Post-cambrian sausages 93; Spinach & - boulangère 112; Wild mushroom, brandy & - penne 119; Swiss Gratin savoyard potatoes 178; Teifi Bavarian galette 97; Gratin savoyard potatoes 178; Rosemary focaccia 136; white, crumbly Cheesy zapallo with kale 148; Creamy garlic tagliatelle 126

Chervil, fresh
Pasta shells in Brie & red pepper sauce 140

Chestnuts
- & orange filo purses 89; Marrow & - hotpot 114

Chicory (Belgian endive)
Pear, - & Stilton salad 66; - grapefruit & walnut salad 65

Chickpea flour (Gram flour)
general 14; Gram pancakes 33; Onion bhajis 139

Peppers, chilli (Chile peppers)
Cheesy zapallo 148; Corn chowder 80; Golden temple curry 107; Hoppin' John 163; Hot mango sauce 151; Mango chutney 46; Refritos 165

Chives
Chicory, grapefruit & walnut salad 65; - pancakes with summer vegetables 116; Lovage butter 36

Chocolate
Black & white terrine 194; - & cranberry cookies 204; - & Drambuie soufflé 197; -, brandy & orange brownies 202; - cake 214

Cider (Strong cider)
Apple & - sauce 37; West country hotpot 98

Coconut, creamed
general 26; Banana & - raita 45; Curried golden courgette soup 71; Golden temple curry 107; Pumpkin & - soup 79

Cointreau
Orange wine sauce 50